ESSENTIALS OF
CROSS-CULTURAL
COUNSELING

ESSENTIALS OF
CROSS-CULTURAL
COUNSELING

Lawrence H. Gerstein
Ball State University

P. Paul Heppner
University of Missouri, Columbia

Stefanía Ægisdóttir
Ball State University

Seung-Ming A. Leung
The Chinese University of Hong Kong

Kathryn L. Norsworthy
Rollins College

Los Angeles | London | New Delhi
Singapore | Washington DC

Los Angeles | London | New Delhi
Singapore | Washington DC

FOR INFORMATION:

SAGE Publications, Inc.
2455 Teller Road
Thousand Oaks, California 91320
E-mail: order@sagepub.com

SAGE Publications Ltd.
1 Oliver's Yard
55 City Road
London, EC1Y 1SP
United Kingdom

SAGE Publications India Pvt. Ltd.
B 1/I 1 Mohan Cooperative Industrial Area
Mathura Road, New Delhi 110 044
India

SAGE Publications Asia-Pacific Pte. Ltd.
33 Pekin Street #02-01
Far East Square
Singapore 048763

Acquisitions Editor: Kassie Graves
Editorial Assistant: Courtney Munz
Production Editor: Eric Garner
Typesetter: Hurix Systems Pvt. Ltd.
Proofreader: Susan Schon
Indexer: Rick Hurd
Cover Designer: Bryan Fishman
Marketing Manager: Katharine Winter
Permissions Editor: Adele Hutchinson

Copyright © 2012 by SAGE Publications, Inc.

Printed in the United States of America.

Library of Congress Cataloging-in-Publication Data

Essentials of cross-cultural counseling / editors, Lawrence H. Gerstein ... [et al.].
   p. cm.
Includes bibliographical references and index.

ISBN 978-1-4129-9950-2 (pbk. : acid-free paper)

1. Cross-cultural counseling.

I. Gerstein, Lawrence H.

BF636.7.C76E87 2012

361'.06--dc23   2011025832

This book is printed on acid-free paper.

11 12 13 14 15 10 9 8 7 6 5 4 3 2 1

Contents

Acknowledgments

W e are extremely grateful to our spouses and partners (Annie, Dawa Lhamo, Deena, Dennis Lee, Mary), children (Guðný, Arnbergur, Lilja, Ellen, Eric, Erica, Timothy, and Grace), grandchildren (Tenzin Choedon, Mikael, Haidyn, and Kane), and other family members for the great support and understanding we received throughout the process of completing this book. We also want to deeply thank our Acquisitions Editor, Kassie Graves, at Sage Publications for encouraging us to write this book. Once again, you provided us with excellent direction, wisdom, support, and resources to make this project possible. Additionally, we want to express our appreciation to all the other staff at Sage Publications especially Courtney Munz and Eric Garner that were involved in the production of this book. Finally, we are grateful to Dennis Lee for the creation of the magnificent artwork that appears on the cover of this book.

Acknowledgments

Chapter One

Cross-Cultural Counseling

History, Challenges, and Rationale

Lawrence H. Gerstein, P. Paul Heppner, Stefanía Ægisdóttir,
Seung-Ming Alvin Leung, and Kathryn L. Norsworthy

Global economics, foreign and domestic policies, and technological advances have contributed to the emergence of a worldwide system of countries and cultures all mutually affecting one another. Larger, more powerful nations have significant influence on the daily lives of citizens of smaller ones (Friedman, 2000), while smaller, less powerful nations have the potential for global influence through advanced communication and computer technologies (Friedman, 2005). From another perspective, modern physics has demonstrated that we are all interconnected (Bohm, 1980), leading some scholars to suggest that this perspective is even relevant to counseling (Bozarth, 1985; Gerstein & Bennett, 1999; Lucas, 1985). When electrons move in one area of space, others change position, even though the links are not readily visible. Furthermore, events happening in one location can simultaneously occur in another location.

While the world gets smaller and we become more aware of our interconnectedness, the global population continues to exponentially increase. Issues such as poverty, substandard living conditions, malnutrition, human rights abuses, illiteracy, and environmental pollution have risen dramatically (United Nations Population Division, 2007). Human migration and immigration connected to political oppression, economics, poverty, and the need for employment bring challenges for everyone involved. Obviously, ethno-political conflict, war, natural and human disasters, and situations

1

of mass trauma, such as the 9/11 attacks on the United States, the 2005 tsunami in Southeast Asia, the 2008 terrorist attacks in Mumbai (India), and the 2011 earthquake and tsunami in Japan reverberate globally and require responses beyond the borders of the countries in which the events took place. The same can be said for the global economic crisis that began in 2008, affecting all nations around the world.

Counseling and counseling psychology are embedded in this worldwide system of interconnectedness, with the United States having taken the historical lead in the development of the counseling profession, which is now expanding rapidly to other parts of the globe (Heppner, Leong, & Gerstein, 2008; Leong & Ponterotto, 2003; Pedersen & Leong, 1997). It is rather apparent, therefore, that U.S.-based models of psychology and counseling have greatly influenced both positively and negatively the science and practice of the mental health professions worldwide. The entire counseling field, however, needs to be responsive to 21st-century human, environmental, and technological concerns, with particular awareness and sensitivity of, and respect for, the cultural contexts from which they arise. With an ethic of care, compassion, responsibility, and non-harm at its foundation, the counseling profession relies on culturally appropriate and effective strategies to help guide our efforts to meet such challenges.

As will become apparent in this and the following chapters, while there is a growing worldwide recognition of interconnectedness among the counseling professions and a strong interest in expanding the scope of counseling to include international issues, currently there is only one book and very few published journal articles on these topics. This book, *Essentials of Cross-Cultural Counseling*, therefore, is rather unique and addresses a critical gap in the scholarly literature. It is structured to provide a comprehensive resource with a strong theoretical, research, and practical focus.

This particular chapter focuses on the importance of the counseling professions embracing an interconnected philosophy of understanding the human experience, the history of the U.S. counseling profession and international issues, and the international work of non-U.S. professionals. It also provides definitions of important concepts and terms found throughout the book and an overview of the rationale and vision for the book.

Interconnectedness, the Global Environment, and Need for Psychological Assistance

Martin Luther King Jr. (U.S. civil rights leader), Paulo Freire (Brazilian liberation activist), Thich Nhat Hanh (Vietnamese Monk and peace worker), His Holiness The Dalai Lama (Tibetan Monk, leader of the Tibetan people, and Nobel Peace Prize Laureate), Aung San Suu Kyi (Myanmar [Burma] Nobel Peace Prize Laureate and pro-democracy leader), and many other revered world leaders have all pointed out that our humanity, liberation, and futures are inextricably woven together. In other words, when individuals or groups of people suffer, experience oppression, discrimination, or exploitation, or are thwarted in their growth and development, we all suffer and are harmed. Our humanity is damaged. Stated another way, the well-being and freedom of others support and contribute to our own well-being and vice versa.

One of the historic strengths of counseling and counseling psychology is its emphasis on human growth and development, an ethic of care, compassion, and more recently, its focus on firmly centering context and culture in understanding human functioning, and conceptualizing and implementing intervention and research strategies. The professional care ethic grounding counseling professionals' work requires knowledge of individuals' psychological concerns or problems as well as an understanding of their cultural, ethnic, racial, and national identities, and their social locations, group associations, and places of residence. The more we as counseling professionals know about people around the world, the greater empathy, warmth, respect, and connection we feel toward those who were previously not known. When one has direct knowledge and contact with individuals who have experienced human suffering, the more compelled one may become to take action to support people in reaching their potential and to change or eliminate any conditions that create and maintain their suffering. Thus, an increased awareness and knowledge of others and their circumstances beyond the confines of one's own communities, cultural groups, and countries sets the stage for our becoming socially responsible and action-oriented global citizens and mental health helping professionals who are actively engaged in contributing to a world that supports human potential, freedom, and liberation. Pawlik (1992) offered a similar observation when speaking of some functions of the internationality of psychology. He reported that one function is facilitating cross-national understanding and goodwill among individuals. In part, the International Council of Psychologists (ICP) was established in 1941 to achieve this goal (Pawlik & d'Ydewalle, 1996) in addition to advancing the science and practice of psychology worldwide.

Due to the rapid process of globalization, where cultures and countries influence one another, with the most profound effects coming from larger global economies such as the United States, there is a disturbing trend toward cultural homogenization (Bochner, 1999). Before discussing the implications of this trend, it is important to define the term *globalization* as it has been applied in many different ways in the literature, including the counseling literature. In this book, globalization refers to increased contact between countries affecting, for instance, economic, social, cultural, and political features of life. Interdependence among nations is thought to be an essential component of globalization (see Figure 1.1).

Figure 1.1   Key Terms and Definitions

Term	Definition	Usage
Internation-alization of counseling	An ongoing process of integrating knowledge from research and practice derived from different cultures and employing this knowledge to solve problems in local and global communities. Involves collaboration and equal partnerships where cultural sensitivity and respect are necessary for success. Efforts to indigenize the field of counseling in various regions in order that theories, practice, and systems are established and anchored in the local culture (Leung et al., Chapter 6).	Inconsistent
Globalization	Varies with the context of analysis. In general, means an increasing interaction across national boundaries that influence many aspects of life (e.g., economic, social, cultural, and political). For instance, globalization frequently refers to the growing economic interdependence of nations worldwide (United Nations Economic and Social Survey of Asia and the Pacific [UNESSAP], 1999).	Inconsistent
Psychologist	In the United States, persons with a doctoral degree in psychology from an organized, sequential program in a regionally accredited university or professional school (see http://www.apa.org/about).	Inconsistent
Counseling	A focus on using a broad array of psychological strategies and activities aimed at the process of helping others to reach individual, group, organizational, and systems goals.	Inconsistent

Figure 1.1

Term	Definition	Usage
Counseling psychology	In the United States, a psychological specialty that integrates theory, research, and practice with a sensitivity to cultural and diversity issues to facilitate through a variety of strategies (e.g., individual, family, group, community, systems, organizational) personal and interpersonal functioning across the life span with a focus on emotional, social, vocational, educational, health-related, developmental, and organizational concerns (see http://www.div17 .org/students_defining.html).	Inconsistent
Culture	A socially transmitted phenomenon learned through enculturation and socialization that is passed on from one generation to the next and one individual to another. Information sharing of knowledge allows people to behave in ways found to be acceptable, understandable, and meaningful to one another in that culture. As such, there is a shared collective experience of a specific group of people. That is, the individuals recognize themselves and their cultural traditions as unique as compared with other people and other cultural traditions. Variability and complexity in behavior is expected, but there are also regularities or common patterns in behavior (Gerstein et al., 2007; Peoples & Bailey, 1994; Schultz & Lavenda, 2001).	Inconsistent
Cultural psychology (Volkerpsychologie)	Enhancing the understanding of people in a historical and sociocultural context using concepts meaningful within that culture (Adamopoulos & Lonner, 2001).	Inconsistent
Indigenous psychology	Psychological knowledge that is native, not transported from another location, and constructed for its people (Kim, 1990) by scholars from the culture under consideration (Adamopoulos & Lonner, 2001).	Consistent

(*Continued*)

Figure 1.1 (*Continued*)

Term	Definition	Usage
Transcultural psychology	The entire discipline of psychology focused on ensuring that theories and findings have transcultural application, and not the naive transference of one culture to another without the recognition of the specific context (Hiles, 1996).	Inconsistent
Multicultural counseling	Both a helping role and process employing strategies and goals congruent with individuals' experiences and cultural values. Recognizes persons' identities in individual, group, and universal dimensions. Advocates using universal and culture-specific techniques and roles in the healing process (Sue & Torino, 1994).	Inconsistent
Multicultural psychology	Investigates the effect of race, racism, ethnic culture, and/or xenophobia on psychological constructs such as attitudes, cognitions, psychological processes, and behaviors (APA, 2003).	Inconsistent
Cross-cultural counseling	The pursuit and application of universal and indigenous theories, strategies (e.g., direct service, consultation, training, education, prevention), and research paradigms of counseling and mental health help seeking grounded in an in-depth examination, understanding, and appreciation of the cultural and epistemological underpinnings of countries located worldwide.	New definition (Inconsistent in the literature)
Cross-cultural psychology	A discipline of psychology primarily focused on how culture affects behavior with an aim of developing an inclusive universal psychology (Adamopoulos & Lonner, 2001) and research that is frequently comparative in nature.	Inconsistent
Cross-national counseling	Collaborative professional activities (e.g., program development and implementation, training, teaching, consultation) jointly pursued by mental health professionals residing in at least two countries.	New definition

Figure 1.1

Term	Definition	Usage
Transnational	Focus on the worldwide intersections of nationhood, race, gender, sexuality, and economic status, in the context of an emergent global capitalism that reinforces colonialism and oppression. In transnational discourses, there is an emphasis on the elimination of global north/south hierarchies by embracing and valuing the multiplicity of cultures, languages, experiences, voices, and so on (Mohanty, 2003).	Consistent

Rapid globalization and the attendant pressures toward cultural homogenization can disrupt cultures and identities in smaller, more vulnerable countries (Arnett, 2002), including the "globalization" of the counseling profession. Counselors and counseling psychologists in the West, particularly in the United States, are members of professions that have significant influence on the development of similar fields outside the West (Heppner, Leong, & Chiao, 2008; Leong & Blustein, 2000; Leung, 2003). In fact, the U.S. counseling profession is currently engaged in a systematic internationalization process. Thus, it is highly probable that the counseling and counseling psychology professions originating in the United States and grounded in U.S. worldviews, values, principles, and practices are greatly impacting the evolution of counseling in other countries. This assumption was confirmed in the chapters on the counseling profession around the world in Part II of the *International Handbook of Cross-Cultural Counseling: Cultural Assumptions and Practices Worldwide* (Gerstein, Heppner, Ægisdóttir, Leung, & Norsworthy, 2009). Yet, it was also evident that professionals outside the United States are engaged in numerous efforts to "indigenize" the counseling profession in their home countries based on the specific cultural contexts (Leung, 2003; Tanaka-Matsumi, 2004); thus resisting hegemonic globalization. Moreover, the work of professionals in countries other than the United States has broadened the worldview of individuals in the entire counseling profession (e.g., see Chapters 7 and 8).

As reported in many chapters of the *International Handbook of Cross-Cultural Counseling: Cultural Assumptions and Practices Worldwide* (Gerstein et al., 2009), individuals throughout the world, particularly those who live in rural areas or have little income, continue to seek the assistance of indigenous healers when experiencing a host of problems, including ones of a psychological nature. Obviously, indigenous approaches to counseling based on unique cultural contexts have the potential to greatly enrich the entire counseling profession. In fact, this impact is already occurring as the internationalization of the profession continues to evolve and affect the activities of mental health professionals worldwide. The cultural context not only affects cultural expressions of psychological distress based on local norms and worldviews but also constructions of cultural systems of healing and helping, clinical assessment, and the type of counseling interventions developed and employed (see Cheung, 2000).

It should be noted that the term internationalization is often either not defined or inconsistently defined in the literature, resulting in confusion and an inability to clearly and accurately discuss pertinent issues and challenges. For the purpose of consistency in this book, therefore, it is important to highlight that we have generated a definition of internationalization that is relevant to counseling within a global context. As shown in Figure 1.1, our definition stresses a collaborative process of acquiring information through counseling research and practice from various cultures in a sensitive manner and using the results to solve issues at home and abroad. Furthermore, our definition focuses on the indigenization of counseling in different countries whereby the profession itself and all its features are tied to the local culture (see also Chapter 7).

Depending on how the field of counseling in the United States further develops, it can either support the unique circumstances of mental health professionals in other countries or it can become a part of the larger process of global homogenization, thereby disrupting cultures, identities, and ways of life (Arnett, 2002; Marsella, 1998; Pedersen, 2003). Therefore, in the internationalization process, it is crucial to avoid the colonizing effect of the unconscious exportation of Western U.S.-based counseling models and their implicit worldviews, values, and counseling and research strategies. Mental health professionals worldwide who are engaged in the internationalization of counseling must be keenly aware of the importance of critically examining and evaluating the validity and applicability of Western models of counseling and psychology, particularly ones derived in the United States, as they are transported to countries outside the West. Embracing such a perspective can enhance the probability that when models and strategies are constructed and employed from culture to culture, or country to country, they indeed support the development and well-being of the members of the communities to be served. Clearly, colleagues "across the world have developed tremendous knowledge bases through their research and practice spanning hundreds and thousands of years" (Heppner, Leong, & Chiao, 2008, p. 79). Stated another way, counseling and counseling psychology must be reconstituted and indigenized country by country, and culture by culture, to affirm and effectively respond to local needs and concerns (Pedersen, 2003). This can only be done successfully through meaningful engagement, collaboration, and learning among colleagues globally.

Related to the importance of establishing and maintaining worldwide professional relationships, diversity is the key to the survival, enhancement, and prosperity of all living organisms and systems (Wheatley, 2006). Creativity, complexity, and reinvention based on local context and changing circumstances all contribute to organisms, including human beings, surviving and reaching their full potential as they face new challenges. This concept is quite applicable not only for humans but also for the profession of counseling itself. In rising to the occasion of making counseling and counseling psychology relevant and applicable within a wide range of contexts and cultures, a broader range of knowledge and skills will emerge. By sharing these diverse ways of responding to the needs and concerns of local people, our repertoire as a global profession for healing, helping, and problem solving increases and becomes more complex. Thus, our relevance is enhanced in the contexts of our own cultures and countries and also when we cross cultural and national borders to work, teach, practice, or conduct research in settings other than our own. In the end, culturally related knowledge from around the world will bring tremendous advantages to help conceptualize intervention strategies to address old problems with new solutions (Heppner, Leong, & Chiao, 2008).

We also view counseling as peace work (Norsworthy & Gerstein, 2003). In the face of escalating global violence, conflict, and misunderstanding, the knowledge and skills brought to the table by counselors and counseling psychologists has never had more relevance. At the end of the day, counseling professionals graduate from training programs that equip them to do much more than work in individual offices. They have gained specialized knowledge and skills in advocacy, social justice, nonviolent communication, conflict resolution, problem solving, negotiation, and other elements of peace building and social change. Furthermore, counseling professionals learn to understand group process, to facilitate group dialogue, and to design and implement group interventions aimed at supporting and fostering deeper respect, appreciation, and understanding of self and others. The old adage, "with knowledge comes responsibility," calls on all of us to use our knowledge and skills to engage in what is called in the Jewish tradition, *Tikkun olam,* repairing or changing the world (Brown, 1997). Given the magnitude of the current global problems we are all facing, never has the need been greater to reach beyond our own borders for understanding and to join hands with our global brothers and sisters, particularly those in our counseling profession, to create a more peaceful, just, compassionate, and loving world.

History of U.S. Psychology Profession and International Issues

The first International Congress of Psychology took place in 1889 in Paris, France (Evans & Scott, 1978). According to Brehm (2008), from the very inception of the field of psychology in the 19th century, there was a tie between professionals in the United States and Europe. At this time, psychology was a collaborative project pursued by William James in Massachusetts, Ivan Pavlov in St. Petersburg, and Wilhelm Wundt in Leipzig. The first International Congress of Psychology to be held in the United States was scheduled to occur in 1913, but it failed to transpire because of a power struggle among the U.S. psychologists (Evans & Scott, 1978). Eventually, the Congress was convened in 1929 at Yale University with J. McKeen Cattell serving as the president (Evans & Scott, 1978).

At the time of World War I and for years to follow, however, U.S. psychologists were focused on the United States (Sexton & Misiak, 1984), and they tended "to ignore or neglect psychology abroad" (Rosenzweig, 1984, p. 877). Interestingly though, psychology in the United States flourished because European psychologists fleeing fascism rooted in Germany immigrated to North America.

The European influence on U.S. psychology is truly remarkable (as well as psychology from other countries such as China). For example, common theories and strategies such as gestalt psychology, psychoanalysis, psychological statistics, the Rorschach test, Pavlovian classical conditioning, and intelligence testing emanate from Europe (Sexton & Misiak, 1984).

In the early 1940s, the American Psychological Association (APA) formed the Committee on International Planning (CIP). An early goal of this group was to communicate with psychologists abroad and determine their needs. One conclusion from this effort was the assumption that non-U.S. psychologists needed "American literature from 1940 on" (Hunter, Miles, Yerkes, & Langfeld, 1946, p. 123). Another was the need to develop a list of psychologists living abroad.

In 1944, the Committee on International Relations in Psychology (CIRP) replaced the CIP. The main mission of CIRP continues to be developing contact between psychologists in the United States and psychologists living elsewhere. In 1996, the CIRP introduced an important new feature in the APA journal the *American Psychologist*—a special section on international psychology. It should be mentioned that 20 years earlier, in 1977, a special issue of the *American Psychologist* was published featuring research and conceptual articles written by psychologists living outside the United States, including Israel, Iran, Costa Rica, the former Soviet Union, Mexico, India, and Japan (Cole, 1977). The APA International Affairs Committee generated the idea for this special issue.

In 1979, the APA Office of International Affairs (OIA) was established and a full-time staff person was hired (S. Leverty, personal communication, March 4, 2009). OIA serves as APA's central clearinghouse for international information, activities, and initiatives within APA's central offices and across the association. This office also leads outreach and interaction with APA's international members and affiliates, coordinates APA's participation and representation in international venues, and facilitates exchange with national psychology associations and global policy bodies (http://www.apa .org/international/contactus.html).

APA also has a separate Division (52) of International Psychology whose members are U.S. psychologists and psychologists from other countries. As stated on the Division 52 Web site, the Division "represents the interest of all psychologists who foster international connections among psychologists, engage in multicultural research or practice, apply psychological principles to the development of public policy, or are otherwise concerned with individual and group consequences of global events" (see http://www.internationalpsychology.net/about).

According to the APA Office of International Affairs, as of March 2011, there were 4,094 international affiliate members of APA and these psychologists were also members of their own national psychology associations. Additionally, the Office of International Affairs reported there were 1,568 APA members and student affiliates living outside the United States as of March 2011 (M. Bullock, personal communication, March 17, 2011). As Fleishman (1999) remarked, "Psychology is now a global discipline" (p. 1009).

Clearly, the discipline of psychology in the United States has a long history of engaging in international activities. As reported by Kelman and Hollander (1964) in the early 1960s, the most common international activity pursued by U.S. psychologists was collaborative research. Later on in this chapter and in the remainder of this book, it will become apparent that U.S. psychologists are now engaged in many more diverse and rich international activities. Perhaps, this is because in the 1980s, U.S. psychologists became more interested in psychology elsewhere (Rosenzweig, 1984; Sexton & Misiak, 1984).

While U.S. psychologists may have become more interested in international work in the 1980s and the years to follow, it appears that, in general, they were not fully equipped to employ culturally appropriate and effective theories, methods, and strategies. Some scholars believed that U.S. psychologists had very limited information about the international literature (Kennedy, Scheirer, & Rogers, 1984; Rosenzweig, 1999; Sexton & Misiak, 1984), especially if it was not published in English (Ardila, 1993; Brandt, 1970; David, 1960; Rosenzweig, 1984) or by leading figures in psychology outside the United States (Denmark, 1998). These observations and more current observations have led many scholars to claim that U.S. psychology is ethnocentric (Berry, Poortinga, Segall, & Dasen, 1992; Leung, 2003; Marsella, 1998; Pedersen & Leong, 1997; Takooshian, 2003), U.S.-centric (Leong & Ponterotto, 2003), or Anglocentric (Cheung, 2000; Trimble, 2001). Indeed, in a recent analysis of a sample of psychology journals, Arnett (2008) argued that American psychology has focused on 5% of the world's population and neglected the other 95%. Within this context, many scholars have claimed that one of the biggest challenges facing U.S. psychologists is now overcoming their ethnocentrism (e.g., Gerstein, 2006; Heppner, 2006; Heppner, Leong, & Chiao, 2008; Leong & Blustein, 2000; Marsella, 1998).

Interestingly, some authors have argued that the U.S. psychology literature is read by persons around the world (Ardila, 1982; Rosenzweig, 1984), while individuals in the psychology and counseling professions in the United States rarely read publications in other languages (Leung, 2003; Ægisdóttir, Gerstein, & Çinarbas, 2008). English also has been viewed as the language of psychology (Russell, 1984), with the U.S. journals the most preferred outlet for publication (David & Swartley, 1961). While some have concluded that psychologists publishing in non-English-language journals are isolated (Ardila, 1982) because their publications are not read by English-reading professionals, others have argued just the opposite. For instance, Smith (1983) stated that the professional who reads only English is isolated. Psychologists in non-English-language countries usually "have access to a wide literature because of the common multilingualism" (p. 123). Smith went on to claim that to increase English language professionals' knowledge base, it is important for doctoral programs in these countries to reinstate the foreign language requirement. In the early 1960s, there was an effort led by the Council of Editors of the APA to include a greater number of non-English-language abstracts in *Psychological Abstracts* and *Contemporary Psychology* (David & Swartley, 1961). This practice, however, has been discontinued. *Psychological Abstracts* no longer covers publications not written in the English language (Draguns, 2001).

Offering a somewhat different analysis about the influence of U.S. psychology on other countries, Ardila (1982) claimed that psychologists tend to know the research and issues of their own countries best and that "the implicit *Weltanschauung* (worldview) of psychology today is the worldview of a specific culture in a specific moment of history" (p. 328). Consistent with this perspective, Moghaddam (1987) argued that there are three worlds of research and practice in psychology. The first is knowledge and application tied solely to the United States, while the second is psychological knowledge and application established by other industrialized nations. Finally, the third world of psychology has evolved from developing countries. Commenting on the impact of American psychology from around 1893 to 1968, Berlyne (1968) indicated, "American psychologists have earned the abundant gratitude of the rest of the world. But like all parents of ambitious children . . . they had better not expect much in the way of thanks" (p. 452). Of course, this is a paternalistic perspective that infantilizes professionals outside the West and renders invisible the colonial elements of the internationalization process.

Psychology grew dramatically around the globe following World War II (Brehm, 2008) and in the past few decades of the 20th century (Draguns, 2001). As of 2008, there were national psychological associations in more than 90 countries. Seventy-one of these associations were members of the International Union of Psychological Science (IUPsyS) representing countries in every continent. The IUPsyS consists of no more than one national member association per country and also accepts affiliated organizations. In 2008, there were approximately 12 of these groups. This organization was founded in Stockholm in 1951 with 11 charter organizations. The Assembly of the Union last met in Melbourne, Australia in July of 2010 in conjunction with the XXVII International Congress of Applied Psychology. Five years earlier, the union president, Bruce Overmier stated that, "the Union remains focused on fulfilling its mission to advance psychology as an applied and basic science by serving as the voice for psychology on an international level" (Ritchie, 2008, p. 930). The next meeting of the General Assembly will be held during the XXX International Congress of Psychology in Cape Town, South Africa, in 2012.

History of U.S. Counseling Profession and International Issues

The history of the counseling professions' involvement in international activities also dates back many years beginning in the 1940s (for details on developments from 1940 to 1969, see Heppner, Leong, & Chiao, 2008; Savickas,

2007; Chapter 2, this volume). For this chapter, we will begin with a discussion of internationalization efforts that began in the 1980s. During this time, U.S. counseling psychologists and counselor educators began to secure Fulbright positions. Since then, at least 112 individuals have secured awards in 45 countries, such as the former Soviet Union, Turkey, England, Sweden, Iran, Norway, Australia, Iceland, Peru, Malaysia, and Zambia (McWhirter & McWhirter, 2009).

Another major development in the internationalization of the U.S. counseling psychology profession also occurred in the 1980s (Heppner, Leong, & Chiao, 2008). In 1988, Bruce Fretz, incoming editor of The Counseling Psychologist (*TCP*)—the flagship journal of APA Division 17 (Society of Counseling Psychology)—launched the International Forum (*IF*). Fretz (1999) claimed that this forum "was as much a hope for something to develop as it was a reflection of a body of knowledge ready to be disseminated" (p. 40). The mission of *IF* was (and still is) to offer "a venue where psychologists learn to cross borders, whether physical or psychological, to be enriched and to enrich others" (Kwan & Gerstein, 2008, p. 182). At first, however, this section of *TCP* featured articles almost entirely written by U.S. counseling professionals who shared their international experiences. This trend began to change when P. Paul Heppner became the editor of *TCP* in 1997. As a result of some modifications in how *TCP* functioned (e.g., appointment of leaders in the international movement in counseling psychology as *IF* coeditors, instituting a more culturally sensitive review process, and selecting the first international scholar, S. A. Leung from Hong Kong, to serve as associate editor), a greater number of international counseling professionals began to publish in *TCP* (Heppner, Leong, & Chiao, 2008). In short, through the efforts of the former (Paul Pedersen, Frederick Leong, Joseph Ponterotto, and David Blustein) and current (Kwong-Liem Karl Kwan and Lawrence H. Gerstein) *IF* editors, and especially since 2000, an even greater number of international scholars have published their works in *TCP*. The authors of *IF* articles have been professionals residing in many countries (e.g., Turkey, the People's Republic of China, Spain, Norway, Taiwan, Japan, South Africa, Korea, India, Israel, and West Samoa/American Samoa), oftentimes writing about features of counseling in their home country.

Two other developments connected to *TCP* are important to mention. First, in 2007, to increase the likelihood that editorial board members were both competent in evaluating articles of an international nature and appreciative of the importance of publishing articles written by non-U.S. scholars, *TCP* added four persons to the board who had cross-cultural expertise and were born outside the United States. These individuals had ties with

Asia, Europe, and the Middle East. Three of these scholars lived outside the United States (Kwan & Gerstein, 2008).

The second new development connected to *TCP* is the fact that in 2008, a page in the beginning of each journal issue was devoted to displaying the journal's title, *The Counseling Psychologist,* in 24 different languages. This modification was implemented in an attempt to present *TCP* as a more inclusive, affirming, and welcoming periodical to counseling professionals residing throughout the world (Kwan & Gerstein, 2008).

One other important development that occurred in the 1980s must be highlighted. The Minnesota International Counseling Institute was launched in 1989 by the counseling psychology faculty (i.e., Thomas Skovholt, Sunny Hansen, John Romano, and Kay Thomas) affiliated with the University of Minnesota. International practitioners and scholars have attended this biennial Institute designed to address the science and practice of cross-cultural counseling.

In 1991, Paul Pedersen published a seminal article where he argued that culture is central to all counseling (Pedersen, 1991). Since that time, Pedersen has been considered one of the key leaders of the cross-cultural counseling movement. While Pedersen's 1991 publication had an impact on the counseling profession at the time, by the middle of the 1990s, it was clear that few accepted or understood an international focus for the field (Heppner & Gerstein, 2008).

This situation changed dramatically in the U.S. counseling psychology profession in the first decade of the 21st century (Heppner, Leong, & Chiao, 2008). During this time, greater systematic organizational efforts were put in place to embrace international issues, foster collaboration between United States and international counseling scholars, and share knowledge relevant to counseling psychology in the United States and abroad. In this regard, five of the six presidents of the APA Society of Counseling Psychology from 2003 to 2009 selected an international theme for their presidency. In 2003–2004, as president of this society, Louise Douce helped reenergize the counseling psychology profession's interest in international issues. Douce introduced a forum at the APA convention where counseling professionals interested in international topics could meet and discuss their interests and vision for the field. She also chose globalization of counseling psychology as her presidential theme (Douce, 2004). Douce claimed, "Counseling psychology can enhance the human condition in many ways by expanding from local and regional realities, not national politics. I envision a movement that transcends nationalism—including our own—and truly fosters a global village" (p. 145).

P. Paul Heppner, as the next president of the society in 2004–2005, focused on the internationalization of counseling psychology and the importance of becoming cross-culturally competent (Heppner, 2006). Consistent with this focus, he expanded the international scholar's breakfast and reception at the APA convention, first introduced by Douce during her presidency to encourage, in part, strengthening collaborative relationships between professionals living in different countries; an important need that was identified in a survey conducted on Division 17 members living outside the United States (Watkins, Lopez, Campbell, & Lew, 1986). Furthermore, in 2005, Heppner in collaboration with Lawrence H. Gerstein, launched the "International Section" within the society (http://www.internationalcounselingpsychology.org). Basically, the mission of this section is to encourage, promote, and facilitate a scientist-professional model of counseling psychology in international contexts in the United States and around the globe through research, service, teaching, training, policy development and implementation, and networking. Not surprisingly, in his presidential address, Heppner (2006) reported that "greater cross-cultural competence will promote a deeper realization that counseling occurs in a cultural context and will increase not only counseling effectiveness but also the profession's ability to address diverse mental health needs across different populations around the globe" (p. 148).

The next president of the society in 2005–2006, Roberta Nutt (2007), also embraced globalization as one of her themes. In fact, her presidential speech was titled "Implications of Globalization for Training in Counseling Psychology."

The second major initiative of Linda Forrest during her presidency of the society in 2007–2008 was the planning and implementation of the society's first ever "International Conference of Counseling Psychology," held in Chicago, Illinois, in March 2008. The theme of this highly successful conference was "Creating the Future: Counseling Psychologists in a Changing World." There were more than 1,400 attendees, including 109 international scholars from more than 40 countries. The number of attendees did not reflect, however, the many international students and scholars residing in the United States who attended the conference. Forrest (2008) reported that the "conference laid down a solid and healthy foundation for an international future for the Society of Counseling Psychology" (p. 8). It should be mentioned that in the planning of the 2001 Houston Counseling Psychology Conference, an international committee was also established to network with counseling psychologists from outside the United States and to encourage them to present and attend the conference (Fouad et al., 2004). While 1,052 individuals attended this conference, our impression was that the proportion of persons from countries other than the United States was rather small.

The more recent upsurge in the U.S. counseling and counseling psychology professions' activity connected to international pursuits is intimately tied to the rapid development and evolution of the U.S. multicultural counseling movement (for more details, see Heppner, Leong, & Chiao, 2008; Heppner, Leong, & Gerstein, 2008; Chapter 2, this volume). As the focus of this movement expanded in the late 1980s to incorporate meeting the needs and concerns of diverse populations, including all people of color, individuals of different ethnic origins and socioeconomic status, persons of various sexual orientations and ages, and individuals with different physical abilities and spiritual traditions, so it embraced serving international populations both in- and outside the United States. Multicultural counseling scholars also developed and introduced unique research paradigms and methodologies to study these populations. Furthermore, these scholars launched creative and dynamic training models designed to educate U.S. graduate students in counseling about culturally sensitive conceptual and intervention approaches that could be used to understand and effectively and appropriately assist such populations.

Since 2000, there has been a dramatic increase in the international activities of U.S. counselors and counseling psychologists (e.g., Gerstein, 2006; Gerstein & Ægisdóttir, 2005a, 2005b, 2005c; Heppner, 2006; Heppner & Gerstein, 2008; Heppner, Leong, & Chiao, 2008; Heppner, Leong, & Gerstein, 2008; Kwan & Gerstein, 2008; Leong & Blustein, 2000; Leong & Ponterotto, 2003; Leung, 2003; McWhirter, 1988a, 1988b, 1988c; Norsworthy & Gerstein, 2003; Pedersen & Leong, 1997; Ægisdóttir & Gerstein, 2005, 2010). A growing number of U.S. counselors and counseling psychologists have traveled abroad to experience and investigate different cultures, enrich themselves, and provide a host of educational (e.g., lectures, courses, workshops), research, and applied (e.g., counseling, consulting) services (see Heppner, Leong, & Chiao, 2008). As a result of this increase in travel outside the United States, counselors and counseling psychologists have developed and shared with others a much greater desire to pursue international issues. That is, they have shown more interest in collaborating with scholars, educators, researchers, practitioners, administrators, and government officials outside the United States. A sizable number of educators in U.S. counseling graduate programs have also turned their attention to training students to effectively serve international clientele, including preparing students to teach and consult overseas. Additionally, U.S. counseling scholars have disseminated information on how to conduct appropriate and valid cross-cultural research (Ægisdóttir et al., 2008), and they have published literature (Cheung, 2000; Gerstein & Ægisdóttir, 2005a, 2005b, 2005c, 2007; Leong & Ponterotto, 2003; Leung, 2003; Pedersen, 2003; Pedersen & Leong, 1997; Ægisdóttir & Gerstein, 2005) on the importance of counselors and counseling psychologists developing and demonstrating an appreciation, respect, and understanding of international cultures and models of psychology and counseling.

Without a doubt, the developments associated with the rising interest in international topics among U.S. counseling professionals can be traced to the enhanced ease of contact and communication (e.g., e-mail, Skype) between people residing in all four corners of the globe, and the knowledge, information, and cultural understanding resulting from such interactions (see Heppner, 1997; Heppner, Casas, Carter, & Stone, 2000; Heppner, Leong, & Chiao, 2008; Heppner, Leong, & Gerstein, 2008). These developments also emanate from the consequences of globalization and the rapidly growing population of international scholars and students associated with U.S. educational institutions. The rich interpersonal exchanges occurring in U.S. counseling training programs between international and U.S.-based individuals have contributed to the latter group acquiring a deeper appreciation and curiosity about cultures worldwide, a recognition to some extent about the function and status of the counseling professions outside the United States and to a lesser extent the role of psychological help seeking around the world. These interactions also have recently contributed to international scholars and students exploring and evaluating the cross-cultural relevance and validity of U.S.-derived counseling theories, methods, and strategies in their home countries. In fact, many counseling professionals around the world, including persons located in the United States, have voiced strong reservations about adopting U.S. counseling paradigms and interventions in other countries (Gerstein & Ægisdóttir, 2005a, 2005c, 2007; Heppner, 2006; Heppner, Leong, & Chiao, 2008; Leong & Ponterotto, 2003; Leung, 2003; Leong & Blustein, 2000; Pedersen, 2003; Pedersen & Leong, 1997). A growing number of serious concerns and questions have been raised about the cross-cultural validity and applicability of employing U.S. models with non-U.S. populations (Gerstein & Ægisdóttir, 2005a, 2005c, 2007; Leong & Blustein, 2000; Leong & Ponterotto, 2003; Leung, 2003; Marsella, 1998; Pedersen, 2003; Pedersen & Leong, 1997) and the ethnocentric nature of counseling psychology (Cheung, 2000; Heppner, 2006; Heppner, Leong, & Chiao, 2008; Heppner, Leong, & Gerstein, 2008; Leung, 2003; Leong & Leach, 2007; McWhirter, 2000; Norsworthy, 2006).

International Work of Non-U.S. Professionals: An Overview

The pursuit of international work has not only been the purview of U.S. psychologists and counseling professionals. Globalization has greatly enhanced opportunities for cross-national collaboration among counseling professionals worldwide. While we are unaware of an organized effort to internationalize the counseling profession outside the United States, counseling professionals throughout the world have engaged in a variety of international activities as counseling becomes an established field within and across national borders. Perhaps in Europe, there has been no need to launch a formal organized effort to internationalize the counseling profession because the borders of the European countries are so fluid. Europeans, including mental health professionals, often travel from country to country for pleasure and work, and they frequently speak multiple languages found in Europe. Given this reality, we suspect that European mental health professionals have a very different mind-set about internationalization as compared with their U.S. colleagues. That is, they have no need to formally internationalize the counseling profession since interacting with professionals from different European countries has been part and parcel of their existence for a very long time. Furthermore, European mental health professionals, as compared with U.S. professionals, have been engaged in the pursuit of cross-cultural research for many years. Therefore, there does not seem to be a systematic awakening among European mental health professionals to internationalize the counseling profession. In fact, European professionals have naturally embraced an international focus for a much longer period of time than U.S. counseling professionals who have more recently systematically organized an international agenda.

As stated earlier, U.S. counseling professionals have increasingly been engaged in collaborative international activities, including conducting research and scholarly work, providing training and service, and engaging in consultation (e.g., Gerstein, 2006; Heppner, 2006; Heppner, Leong, & Chiao, 2008; Norsworthy, 2006). Counseling professionals in other countries also frequently participate and collaborate. In fact, many local leaders have served as the "architects" of cross-border and cross-national activities. Furthermore, non-U.S. counseling professionals have performed numerous cross-cultural research studies and cross-national applied projects outside their own countries.

There are a multitude of channels through which non-U.S. counseling professionals have engaged actively in international work. First, there has been a great deal of academic activity for years in the Asian region involving counseling scholars from multiple countries. The Asian-Pacific Counseling and Guidance Association and the Chinese Association of Psychological Testing have been active for a long time and have routinely held conferences drawing scholars from several countries. Taiwanese counseling scholars have been particularly active in collaborating with their colleagues in other Asian countries. For instance, in 1997, Ping-Hwa Chen was invited to Hong Kong, China, and Singapore to discuss with their scholars how the

Taiwan school guidance system was developed (Chen, 1999). In 2008, the inaugural Asia Pacific Rim International Counseling Conference was held in Hong Kong, and the conference was co-organized by professional counseling associations in Hong Kong and Australia (Leung, 2008).

In Europe, counseling scholars from Italy have actively collaborated with researchers from other countries as well, particularly other European countries. In many ways, their level of cross-national collaboration has been far-reaching, such as the Bologna Project to promote international education at the undergraduate level. With the founding of the Laboratory for Research and Intervention in Vocational Guidance (LaRIOS) at the University of Padua more than 15 years ago, Italian counseling professionals began to conduct research studies on vocational psychology with scholars worldwide. For example, LaRIOS investigators performed research with Leon Mann of the University of Melbourne on decision making, self-efficacy beliefs, and coping strategies; with Sunny Hansen through the Minnesota International Counseling Institute on how to design supportive counseling services for students at the University of Padua; with John Krumboltz of Stanford University on career choice; with Scott Solberg and Kimberly Howard of the University of Wisconsin–Milwaukee on perceived support, self-efficacy beliefs, and school-career indecision; and with Robert Lent (University of Maryland) and Steven Brown (Loyola University) on the relationships between self-efficacy beliefs and job satisfaction. LaRIOS scholars have also conducted collaborative research on the relationships between self-regulation abilities, study abilities, school achievement, and levels of school-career indecision among middle and high school adolescents with Barry Zimmerman of the City University of New York; relationships between assertiveness, self-efficacy beliefs, and quality of life with Willem Arrindell of the University of Groningen (the Netherlands); problem-solving abilities with Puncky Heppner and Mary Heppner of the University of Missouri; the concept of work, study, and leisure time with David Blustein of Boston College and Hanoch Flum of Ben Gurion University (Israel); and coping strategies in young and old adolescents with Erica Frydenberg of Melbourne University (Australia).

Non-U.S. counseling scholars have also traveled to different countries to train and teach students and professionals. Professionals affiliated with LaRIOS, for instance, have trained psychologists, career service providers, and teachers in the Republic of Guinea-Bissau, Malta, and Singapore. Anthony Naidoo from Stellenbosch University in South Africa has been involved in the development and training of community psychologists in Mexico, Eritrea, and Norway as well. Moreover, with his colleagues, he took part in community and adolescent and male development programs in Mexico, Puerto Rico, Norway, the United

Kingdom, and Turkey. Furthermore, Naidoo has engaged in community service learning projects with international partners in the Congo DRC and the United States, and eco-therapy interventions with partners in the United States and Norway.

Finally, it is important to mention that there is an international group of scholars collaborating on research and other projects through the Life Design International Research Group. The members of this group are Salvatore Soresi (LaRIOS, Italy), Laura Nota (LaRIOS, Italy), Jean Guichard (Institut National d'Étude du Travail et d'Orientation Professionnelle—Conservatoire National des Arts et Métiers, Paris, France), Jean-Pierre Dauwalder (University of Lausanne, Switzerland), Raoul Van Esbroeck (Vrije Universiteit Brussels, Belgium), Jérôme Rossier (Institute of Psychology, University of Lausanne, Switzerland), and Mark Savickas (Behavioral Sciences Department, Northeastern Ohio University College of Medicine, the United States).

Counseling professionals from outside the United States have been heavily involved in the activities of international professional organizations as members, presenters, and leaders. For example, non-U.S. counseling professionals were instrumental in the effort to form the Counseling Psychology Division (Division 16) of the International Association of Applied Psychology (IAAP), and they also have served on the executive board of IAAP since its inception as the International Association of Psychotechnology in 1920, where its first Congress met in Geneva, Switzerland. Likewise, international counseling professionals have been actively involved in the International Association for Counselling, an organization that holds regular academic conferences (e.g., International Roundtable for the Advancement of Counselling) as well as publishing an international journal titled *International Journal for the Advancement of Counselling* (Harper, 2000; Lee, 1997). As of February 2009, the editorial board of this journal included counseling professionals from 21 countries. Moreover, international counseling professionals have been intimately associated with the Society of Vocational Psychology Section and the International Section of the Society of Counseling Psychology of the APA. Non-U.S. professionals can be members and leaders of the International Section. In fact, the bylaws of this group specify that the executive committee must include non-U.S.-based members in the elected role of section co-chair and membership co-chair.

International counseling professionals have regularly presented at numerous conferences outside their home country. For example, they have shared their work at the convention meetings of the International Union of Psychological Sciences Congress, International Association for Cross-Cultural Psychology (founded in 1972), International Association for Educational and

Vocational Guidance, APA, American Counseling Association, National Career Development Association, IAAP, International Conference on Psychology, Interamerican Congress of Psychology, European Congress of Psychology, World Congress for Psychotherapy, Asian American Psychological Association, and Society of Vocational Psychology.

A third prominent way that non-U.S. counseling professionals have engaged in scholarly activities around the world involves editorial responsibilities. International professionals have served as editors, associate editors, and members of editorial boards of many major counseling and psychology journals with an international focus. As a result, international counseling professionals have made important contributions to the development of the international counseling literature and the advancement of a scientific foundation for the entire profession (Skovholt, Hansen, Goh, Romano, & Thomas, 2005).

Counseling professionals from around the world have participated in international activities through relief work. Non-U.S. professionals have been actively involved in response efforts to natural disasters of a global magnitude, including providing mental health services, for instance, to victims and survivors of the 2004 (December 26) Tsunami in Southeast Asia (Chatterjee, 2005; Miller, 2005). Additionally, many mental health professionals, including psychiatrists, social workers, psychologists, and counselors have participated in a range of projects connected to the World Health Organization (WHO) and other nongovernment organizations (NGOs). International counseling professionals also provided psychosocial and psychological support to victims of the 2008 (May 12) Sichuan Earthquake in China via global-level organizations such as the United Nations Children's Fund (UNICEF, 2008) and the International Federation of Red Cross (2008). Through these international relief efforts and others, mental health professionals offered their expertise by developing culture-based, train-the-trainer programs aimed at strengthening local capacity to address post-trauma mental health concerns projected to become a heavy burden to the affected nations in the years to come (Miller, 2005). In an age where nations are no longer separated by geographic distance because of advances in communication technologies, counseling professionals have demonstrated through these efforts that they can effectively collaborate to assist and provide relief to persons who have experienced a natural and/or human disaster.

Collaboration among scholars from different corners of the world is not only important to provide effective relief in response to disasters, but such collaboration and increased opportunities for travel, learning, and disseminating information are extremely critical for the advancement of the science and practice of counseling and psychology. The results of effective collaboration have the potential to enhance the development of both universals (etics) in psychology and counseling and also the potential to stimulate the development of particulars (emics) or culture-specific information in psychology and counseling.

Unfortunately, though, it can be argued that the results of such collaboration and international projects designed to advance the science and practice of counseling are disseminated unilaterally. That is, these outcomes are more often than not published in the English language scholarly literature. Furthermore, when published in the non-English literature, these outcomes tend to go unnoticed in English-speaking countries such as the United States, and consequently, this work is often not read in many parts of the world. Stated more specifically, there is much more information available in the United States and English language literature about U.S. counseling professionals' work than there is about non-U.S. or non-English-speaking scholars' efforts in non-English-speaking countries. Taken together, these biases hinder the internationalization of counseling and psychological science (Draguns, 2001).

Despite these biases, a perusal of programs at various conventions and congresses in psychology around the world (e.g., Interamerican Congress of Psychology, European Congress of Psychology, Southeast Asia Psychology Conference, South African Psychology Congress) suggests that international collaboration and the sharing of knowledge are blooming. For instance, at the 2009 European Congress of Psychology (n.d.), there were numerous programs and keynote speeches focused on the dissemination of country-specific knowledge and reports of collaborative efforts among scholars from different countries in Europe. Furthermore, one aim of the European Federation of Psychologists' Associations (EFPA) founded in Germany in 1981 and that currently includes 34 member associations representing around 200,000 psychologists in Europe (EFPA, 2007) is to promote communication and cooperation between member associations in Europe. Another aim is to facilitate contacts with international bodies of psychology and related disciplines and to be an important source of advice to European institutions, government, political, social, and consumer organizations. Yet another aim is to disseminate psychological knowledge and professional skills to effectively assist European citizens (EFPA, 2007). Consistent with these aims, with the development of the European certificate in psychology (EuroPsy), opportunities for European psychologists to work and participate in other European countries have been greatly enhanced.

One goal of the Asian Psychological Association (APsyA), which was founded at the First Convention of the Asian Council of Psychologists in Jakarta, Indonesia, in 2005, is to encourage the development of psychology within Asian countries and to promote collaboration among Asian psychologists living in Asia. By recognizing the difference between the psychology of Western, more individualistic nations, and Eastern, more collectivistic nations, APsyA's goal is to encourage collaboration among interdisciplinary, cross-cultural, and interethnic individual psychologists to develop an Asian psychological paradigm designed to better comprehend and serve the unique needs of Asian people (Jaafar, n.d.).

Key Concepts and Terms: Definitions and Challenges

Before concluding this chapter with a discussion about the rationale, vision, and purpose of this book, it is essential to present operational definitions of concepts and terms found throughout this book. We also believe that it is critical to briefly highlight some of the challenges associated with these definitions. In fact, in the counseling and psychology literatures worldwide, these concepts and terms are inconsistently defined.

Mental Health Provider Titles and Functions

Throughout the world, there are major inconsistencies in the definition and use of the title *counselor* (Heppner & Gerstein, 2008), *psychologist* (Rosenzweig, 1982), and *counseling psychologist*. Professional counselors in the United States must hold a master's degree or higher in counselor education. Yet, counseling as it is known in the United States also does not exist in all parts of the world (Heppner, Leong, & Gerstein, 2008; Savickas, 2007). In the United States, according to the National Board of Certified Counselors (NBCC), counseling may be described as follows:

> A process whereby specially trained individuals provide (a) academic, career, or vocational guidance; (b) problem-solving support and expertise; (c) support and/ or expertise specific to certain biological threats; or (d) support and expertise to individuals, families, and communities as they strive toward optimum wellness. (see http://www.nbccinternational.org/home/about-professional-counseling)

In other parts of the world (e.g., India), the term *counseling* is used to denote the activities of many different diverse professionals (e.g., lawyers, bankers, financial advisors, physicians, nurses, indigenous healers, mental health practitioners). Furthermore, professional counselors are quite often located in school settings, and the standard professional training may be at the Bachelor's or Master's level. In this book, the use of the term *counselor* may refer to professionals who are trained in counselor education programs, or a counselor may refer to professionals or community members not part of the "counseling profession" as defined by NBCC who use counseling knowledge and skills in their work.

In many countries, there is no term for psychology or psychologist, and if there are, these terms do not mean the same as they do in Western nations (Abi-Hashem, 1997). The training and educational requirements to become a psychologist (Russell, 1984), counselor, or counseling psychologist vary greatly from country to country as well. In the United States, a person must have a doctoral degree to become a psychologist (see Figure 1.1). In South, Latin, and Central America, in contrast, an individual needs the equivalent of a bachelor's degree, while in Europe and many parts of Asia (e.g., Taiwan, China, Korea, and Japan), a master's degree or an equivalent diploma is required. In the early 1990s, Rosenzweig (1992) indicated that a master's degree was the modal credential for psychologists worldwide. This observation continues to be accurate in 2011.

While it is highly likely that a mental health provider and client in the United States understand the meaning of the term *counseling* and share similar assumptions about this meaning, in other countries, it cannot be assumed that both parties perceive this function the same way (Cheung, 2000). As a result, Cheung (2000) has argued, "Counseling must be deconstructed in the context of the culture in which it is offered" (p. 124).

Keeping in mind Cheung's (2000) warning, the definition of counseling we embrace and the one guiding this book is very broad and general (see Figure 1.1). We believe that this definition can capture the practice of counseling in many countries. Basically, counseling involves the use of diverse psychological interventions to assist individuals, groups, organizations, and systems with the achievement of their goals.

The discipline of counseling psychology, and the title *counseling psychologist,* also does not exist in many parts of the world (e.g., France, Argentina, India, Israel, Japan, Peru, the Netherlands, Iceland, El Salvador). Furthermore, where the terms do exist, they are very different and loosely defined (Heppner, Leong, & Gerstein, 2008; Savickas, 2007). The definition of counseling psychology adopted in the United States appears in Figure 1.1. This definition is quite specific, and it stresses an integration of science and practice guided by the importance of embracing culture, diversity, and human development to assist individuals and groups with a host of issues. This is the definition guiding the content in this book, but it is not necessarily the one employed by our colleagues in countries outside the United States.

A very clear definition of counseling psychology can be found in Hong Kong. According to Leung, Chan, and Leahy (2007), the Counseling Psychology Division of the Hong Kong Psychological Society has defined counseling psychology "as the application of psychological knowledge, psychotherapeutic skills, and professional judgment to facilitate enhanced human functioning and quality of life" (p. 53). Similarly, a precise and descriptive definition can be found in Canada. Citing the Colleges of Psychologists of Ontario, which is the body that licenses psychologists in Canada, Young and Nicol (2007) reported that counseling psychology "is the fostering and improving of normal human functioning by helping people solve problems, make decisions, and cope with stresses of everyday life" (p. 21). In China, in contrast, there is no highly specific definition of counseling psychology. It is simply viewed as psychological helping (Chang, Tong, Shi, & Zeng, 2005). In South Africa, the definition is also not very specific (Savickas, 2007). Watson and Fouche (2007) claimed that counseling psychology has a positive and solution focus with an emphasis on health and well-being. The definition of counseling psychology in Australia is also broadly construed as helping persons and groups with acute, developmental, and normal challenges across the life span (Pryor & Bright, 2007). As Savickas (2007) observed and we concur, regardless of the definition of counseling psychology or counseling psychologist employed throughout the world, it appears that most definitions appear to "share the root conception that counseling psychology concentrates on the daily life adjustment issues faced by reasonably well-adjusted people, particularly as they cope with career transitions and personal development" (pp. 183–184).

Defining Culture

A long and even more extensive debate exists in anthropology and cross-cultural psychology about the definition of culture. In anthropology, most scholars have been influenced, however, by Tyler's definition introduced in 1871. Tyler stated that culture is a "complex whole which includes knowledge, belief, art, morals, law, custom, and any other capabilities and habits acquired by man as a member of society" (Moore, 1997, p. 17). Therefore, culture is seen as a set of learned behaviors and ideas human beings acquire as members of a society or a specific group. Such behaviors and ideas, however, do not result from nature (biology) but from the socialization or enculturation process (Gerstein, Rountree, & Ordonez, 2007). Most anthropologists also claim that there are four basic components of a culture: (1) it is socially transmitted through enculturation; (2) knowledge (people share enough knowledge that they can behave in ways that are acceptable and meaningful to others, so that they do not constantly misunderstand one another); (3) there are shared behavioral regularities or patterns; and (4) there are shared collective experiences of a specific group (Gerstein, Rountree, & Ordonez, 2007).

Ho (1995) also discussed a definition of culture from an anthropological perspective. He indicated that culture can be conceptualized externally or internally. Ho argued that for counseling psychologists, the internalized culture acquired through enculturation is more relevant to practice. He defined internalized culture "as the cultural influences operating within the individual that shape (not determine) personality formation and various aspects of psychological functioning" (p. 5). Examples of internalized culture are gender, psychological maturity, and identification with a class. Furthermore, Ho reported that subjective culture as conceptualized by Triandis (1972) could be considered internalized culture with examples being worldview, cognitive map, and life space.

Cross-cultural psychologists have also introduced definitions of culture. Segall, Lonner, and Berry (1998), for example, claimed that historically, culture was conceptualized as something external to the individual, a shared approach to life by individuals interacting in a common group and through the processes of enculturation and socialization transmitted from generation to generation. Additionally, Segall et al. reported that in the late 1990s because of the cognitive approaches, individuals were no longer seen as "pawns or victims of their cultures but as cognizers, appraisers, and interpreters of them" (p. 1104). Instead, culture was thought to emerge from transactions between persons and their environment.

In the counseling professions, a number of scholars have offered definitions of culture. For instance, Pedersen (1993) presented a broad definition of culture that is very different from the ones mentioned above. He stated that culture includes demographic (e.g., age, gender), status (e.g., social, economic), and ethnographic (e.g., ethnicity, nationality) variables along with affiliations (formal and informal). In contrast, Sue and Sue (2003) defined culture as "all those things that people have learned in their history to do, believe, value, and enjoy. It is the totality of ideals, beliefs, skills, tools, customs, and institutions into which each member of society is born" (p. 106). Finally, Ponterotto, Casas, Suzuki, and Alexander (1995) concluded that for most counseling scholars, culture is a learned system of meaning and behavior passed from one generation to the next.

Given the diversity in how anthropologists, cross-cultural psychologists, and counseling professionals define culture, there are many obvious conceptual, methodological, and applied challenges inherent to the practice and science of counseling within and outside the U.S. borders. These challenges can become even more magnified when engaging in cross-cultural counseling. For the purposes of this book, therefore, the definition of culture to which we subscribe can be found in Figure 1.1. This definition, based on the work of Tyler, is drawn from the anthropology literature discussed at the beginning of this section.

Defining Cultural Psychology

In general, though there is some inconsistency in the definition of cultural psychology, it can be defined as a field dedicated to enhancing an understanding of individuals within their cultural context by employing concepts that are meaningful within the particular culture of interest (Adamopoulos & Lonner, 2001). For the purposes of this book, we employ this definition (see Figure 1.1). Triandis (2000) claimed that cultural psychologists frequently investigate cultures other than their own, often relying on ethnographic methods tied to cultural anthropology. Studying the meaning of constructs (emic) in a culture is of greatest interest to cultural psychologists, and they refute the notion that culture and cultural variables are independent of the individual. Instead, they view culture as an integral, critical, and inseparable part of the human mind (Adamopoulos & Lonner, 2001). For further detailed discussion about cultural psychology, including methodological strategies employed, see Chapter 5.

Defining Indigenous Psychology

According to Kim (1990), *indigenous psychology* is psychological knowledge that emerges from the target culture rather than knowledge that comes directly or indirectly from another location. Although admittedly, today there are many ways that most cultures are affected by outside influences, the focus of indigenous psychology is on developing a knowledge base that evolves from this process constructed for the individuals in the specific culture (Kim, 1990); that is, "behavior as seen from people's own viewpoint" (Brislin, 1990, p. 28). This knowledge is acquired by scholars from the target culture (Adamopoulos & Lonner, 2001). The definition just mentioned is used consistently in the psychology literature and will be employed (see Figure 1.1) in this book. (For a more detailed discussion of indigenous psychology, see Chapter 5.) The main purpose of indigenous psychology is to establish a knowledge base that has meaning within a specific culture (e.g., Kim, Park, & Park, 2000). This approach embraces "insiders" (emic) as well as "outsiders" (etic) viewpoints, and it also advocates the use of both qualitative and quantitative methodologies (Kim, Yang, & Hwang, 2006).

Indigenous psychologies have dramatically increased worldwide (Allwood & Berry, 2006). In part, psychology can be considered quite new in some parts of the world and reinvented (Pedersen, 2003; Yang, 1997; Yang, Hwang, Pedersen, & Daibo, 2003) or reinvigorated in other locations. Furthermore, in a number of regions of the world, the issue of the relevance of constructs and strategies to the culture is driving the development of indigenous forms of psychology (Sinha & Holtzman, 1984). Therefore, it is not surprising that indigenous psychologies are developing mostly in non-Western countries (Allwood & Berry, 2006). According to Pedersen (2003), "Indigenous psychology is not a universal psychology but rather reminds us that psychological principles cannot be assumed to be universally similar" (p. 401).

Indigenous practices and models of counseling are critical, therefore, to the development of the counseling and counseling psychology professions worldwide (Leung, 2003), if in fact unique models and strategies that are culturally appropriate and effective are to be established and employed. As stated earlier, some authors (e.g., Leung, 2003) have claimed that theories and strategies of counseling psychology in the United States are indigenous to the U.S. cultures. Therefore, serious questions can be raised about the suitability of these theories and strategies to other cultures and countries. Indigenous paradigms of counseling, in contrast, would be much better suited to reflect and capture the unique cultural values, norms, and behaviors of each culture or country.

Defining Transcultural Psychology

Another term that is sometimes found in the psychology literature but more often found in the psychiatry and nursing literature is *transcultural psychology*. According to Hiles (1996), transcultural psychology is interested in making certain that psychological results and theories derived in one culture are applicable in other cultures rather than the naïve, uncritical transference of one culture to another without recognition of the specific context (see Figure 1.1). Transcultural application involves critically determining when to apply psychological concepts, findings, and practices across cultures.

Defining Multicultural Counseling

As will become clear in Chapter 2, the line between cross-cultural counseling and multicultural counseling has been and continues to be ambiguous. Some authors have used the two terms interchangeably as if they are equivalent. In fact, early on in the multicultural counseling literature, authors (e.g., LaFromboise & Foster, 1992; Sue, 1981; Vontress, 1979) used the term *cross-cultural counseling* and not multicultural counseling to describe the work of a mental health professional serving a client from a different culture, ethnicity, and/or country. Originally, even the multicultural counseling competencies were called *cross-cultural competencies* (see Sue, Arredono, & McDavis, 1992).

In this chapter, we will stress the point that multicultural counseling and cross-cultural counseling have many shared values and goals, yet they also differ in their foci and applications. Nonetheless, the two approaches complement each other and provide invaluable perspectives in counseling that serve to delineate culture-related issues within and beyond geographic and national boundaries.

In the 1970s and early 1980s, when the impact of culture and issues related to cultural bias were being discussed in the counseling literature, the term *cross-cultural counseling* was often used. Yet when the term *multicultural counseling* and *multiculturalism* started to gain attention, cross-cultural counseling was used less frequently. Indeed, into the 1990s, multicultural counseling had become the preferred term among many scholars. As suggested by Sue et al. (1998),

> Originally called "cross-cultural counseling/ therapy," this usage has become progressively less popular and has been superseded by the term MCT (Multicultural Counseling and Therapy). Because it is inclusive, MCT may mean different things to different people (racial/ethnic minorities emphasis, sexual orientation emphasis, gender emphasis, and so on); thus it is very important for us to specify the particular populations we are referring. (p. 13)

The history of multicultural counseling is closely connected to social and political movements in the United States, such as the civil rights movement. The multicultural movement in counseling began in the 1960s and 1970s and challenged the cultural bias behind the Eurocentric counseling theories and practice. It also called attention to forces of racism, discrimination, and prejudice that had caused much injustice in the U.S. mental health delivery system as well as in the larger social and cultural system.

There are many definitions of multicultural counseling that, for the most part, share more similarities than differences. Jackson (1995) defined multicultural counseling as "counseling that takes place between or among individuals from different cultural backgrounds" (p. 3). Smith (2004) offered a broader definition and suggested that, "multicultural counseling and psychology refers not merely to working with diverse populations, but to an approach that accounts for the influences of culture and power in any therapeutic relationship" (p. 4). The definition we embrace and the one guiding this book can be found in Figure 1.1. Basically, this definition takes into consideration the unique cultural background of mental health professionals and their clientele and the universality of their experiences and culture so that professionals can provide culturally effective, appropriate, and sensitive services. Recent formulations of multicultural competencies have underscored the importance of an advocacy and social justice perspective (Enns & Sinacore, 2005; Goodman et al., 2004; Toporek, Gerstein, Fouad, Roysircar-Sodowsky, & Israel, 2006; Vera & Speight, 2003). Accordingly, it has been suggested that multicultural counseling should include in its repertoire of interventions advocacy, actions, and personal empowerment that engage clients as co-participants to confront oppressive forces in their environments and systems, including racism, discrimination, prejudice, and social injustice. Thus, in many ways, even the content of multicultural counseling is indigenous to the U.S. cultural context. Regardless of the definition, multicultural counseling is fully anchored on the ideals of multi-culturalism that emphasizes the value of diversity and the moral obligation to treat individuals from diverse cultural groups with respect and dignity (e.g., Fowers & Richardson, 1996; Sue et al., 1998).

Multicultural counseling in an international context could take many forms and also address culture-specific issues. The literature on multicultural counseling has served as an important starting point for international scholars to expand or build new frameworks to focus on multicultural issues salient to their particular geographic areas. Multicultural counseling could also be synthesized with a cross-cultural perspective, where the concept of culture is studied more globally across national borders.

Defining Multicultural Psychology

In the *Encyclopedia of Multicultural Psychology* (Jackson, 2006), the term *multicultural psychology* appears to be defined as an umbrella field that encompasses a diverse group of sub-disciplines (e.g., cross-cultural psychology, multicultural counseling, and race psychology) in psychology. Members of this field use research methodologies and training strategies to understand the role of culture in human behavior and to generate results to accomplish this task. Many different populations in- and outside the United States are the focal point of investigation. According to Jackson, the main assumption of multicultural psychology is that to understand differences between people, it is best to study culture and not race.

The APA (2003) multicultural guidelines offer a very different perspective on multicultural psychology. These guidelines indicate that multicultural psychology focuses primarily on the influence of race, racism, ethnic culture, and/or xenophobia on psychological constructs (e.g., attitudes, psychological processes, behaviors). For the purpose of this book, we embrace (see Figure 1.1) the definition of multicultural psychology found in the APA guidelines.

Defining Cross-Cultural Psychology

A distinctive feature of cross-cultural counseling is its close alignment with the field of cross-cultural psychology. Cross-cultural psychology was defined by Berry et al. (1992) as, "the study of similarities and differences in individual psychological functioning in various cultural and ethnic groups; of the relationships between psychological variables and sociocultural, ecological, and biological variables; and of current changes in these variables" (p. 2). There are many definitions of cross-cultural psychology in the literature. In general, these definitions are inconsistent and tend to focus on different features. Lonner and Adamopoulos (1997) reviewed various definitions of cross-cultural psychology and identified the following themes: (a) It (cross-cultural psychology) is interested in understanding the nature and reasons behind human diversity and universals at the level of the individual; (b) it uses research methodologies that allow researchers to study in the widest range of cultural contexts and settings where human behavior occurs; (c) it assumes that culture is one of the critical factors contributing to individual differences in behavior; (d) it involves comparisons of behavior occurring in two or more cultural settings; and (e) its ultimate goal is the development of psychology that would become increasingly "universal" in its scope and application. Throughout this book, we rely on a definition of cross-cultural psychology (see Figure 1.1) based on the writing of Adamopoulos and Lonner (2001). This definition takes into account the influence of culture on behavior toward the goal of establishing an inclusive universal psychology. Our definition also stresses comparative research rather than research performed in one country or with one culture.

Defining Cross-Cultural Counseling

The themes often linked with cross-cultural psychology have also become salient features of cross-cultural counseling. In fact, cross-cultural counseling derived its knowledge base from the rich research literature of cultural and cross-cultural psychology (Leung & Chen, in press; Leung & Hoshmand, 2007). Draguns (2007) argued that cross-cultural counseling is concerned with accurately understanding the culture-specific and universal aspects of human problems as well as the process of helping. Furthermore, Pedersen (2000) reported that in cross-cultural counseling, all behavior should be understood from the context of one's culture. Sue et al. (1992) and Lonner (1985) even claimed that all counseling is cross-cultural. What is inherent in this description is that mental health professionals need to cross the boundaries of culture or disentangle culture to reach the person or client.

Some writers (e.g., Pedersen, 1995) have indicated that cross-cultural counseling is concerned with cross-border cultural transitions, culture- and reverse-culture shocks, the process of acculturation, along with comparisons of individuals across national borders to facilitate accurate cultural understanding in counseling encounters. Another common description of cross-cultural counseling that can be extrapolated from the literature is that it is the science and practice (e.g., direct service, consultation, training, education, prevention) of counseling devoted to investigating and establishing the common and unique features of the culture-behavior interaction of persons residing in at least two different countries. Yet another description we extrapolated from the literature is that cross-cultural counseling is the investigation of the relevance and validity of specific theories, strategies, and research paradigms of counseling employed in a similar fashion in two or more countries through an in-depth examination of the cultural and epistemological underpinnings of each country. Cross-cultural counseling also aims at the development of a counseling profession that is relevant internationally (Leung, 2003; Savickas, 2007). In general, the phrase *cross-cultural counseling* has frequently been employed to capture the international and national application of counseling strategies across cultures (Pedersen, 2004; Pedersen, Draguns, Lonner, & Trimble, 2002).

Given the historic inconsistent use and definition of the term *cross-cultural counseling,* we offer a new definition of this phrase (see Figure 1.1) that frames the discussion found in this book. Our definition indicates that cross-cultural counseling incorporates universal and indigenous theories, strategies, and research paradigms of counseling and help seeking based on the cultural and epistemological assumptions of countries around the world.

Defining Cross-National Counseling

The term *cross-national counseling* has been used in the counseling literature by a few authors. At times, scholars have used the term to discuss collaboration between professionals across borders. Others have discussed conducting research on two or more nationalities as cross-national counseling. Until now, however, this term has not been defined. No doubt, the lack of an operational definition for cross-national counseling and the apparent use of this term to refer to various activities has contributed to potential confusion and misunderstanding among counseling professionals. To facilitate a clearer understanding of the use of this term in this book, we introduce a specific definition for cross-national counseling (see Figure 1.1). This definition assumes that cross-national counseling involves mental health professionals from at least two countries collaborating on some professional activity such as consultation or program development.

Defining Transnational

Finally, at times, the term *transnational* will be used in this book. This term originates in the feminist literature. We have offered a definition of transnational in Figure 1.1. In general, this term has been defined as the worldwide intersections of nationhood, race, ethnicity, gender, sexuality, and economic status with an emphasis on the elimination of global north/south hierarchies by embracing and valuing the multiplicity of cultures, languages, experiences, and voices (Mohanty, 2003).

Overview, Rationale, and Vision of Book

The chapters in this book first appeared in Part One of our earlier publication, the *International Handbook of Cross-Cultural Counseling: Cultural Assumptions and Practices Worldwide* (Gerstein et al., 2009). These chapters were slightly revised for the current volume, *Essentials of Cross-Cultural Counseling*. We have shortened and structured this new book to provide a more accessible publication for understanding and potentially functioning effectively cross-culturally, cross-nationally, and in international settings. Additionally, we wanted to publish a briefer book that discusses the essential core concepts linked with cross-cultural practice, research, theory, and training so it could be easily used in the classroom as a supplementary text in, for instance, multicultural, cross-cultural, and research design courses. Therefore, this new book presents a wide repertoire of research, theoretical, and professional issues and a broader perspective regarding the appropriate roles and activities of mental health professionals around the world. It also addresses numerous issues affecting diverse populations and the relevance of counseling and psychology globally. In many chapters, our authors critically discuss the relevance and validity of adopting U.S. counseling theories and approaches in other countries. As such, the appropriateness of cultural assumptions and strategies derived in the United States are analyzed, critiqued, and questioned. Ultimately, we hope that this book will contribute, in part, to helping counselors, psychologists, and other mental health professionals throughout the world become more effective when performing international, cross-national, and cross-cultural work.

Each chapter in this book is co-authored by at least one of the book co-editors along with other scholars. Chapters 1 to 8 provide a systematic and comprehensive discussion and analyses about various conceptual, methodological, professional, and practice issues connected to the pursuit of international activities. Topics include, for instance, the similarities and differences of multicultural and cross-cultural psychology and counseling; the status of the counseling profession in- and outside the United States;

U.S. counseling models exported worldwide; methodological issues when studying culture; the internationalization of the counseling profession; and benefits, challenges, and outcomes of collaboration among counseling professionals across borders. The final chapter of this book discusses ethical issues tied to international work, future directions for international work (e.g., theory, research, training, and practice), recommendations concerning cross-cultural counseling competencies, how to integrate international issues into the counseling training program, and strengths, challenges, and opportunities of international collaboration.

We are hopeful that this book will make a very unique contribution to the scholarly literature in psychology and counseling. This book is intended for counseling graduate programs, students, practitioners, educators, researchers, program planners, policymakers, trainers, consultants, and administrators worldwide. We believe that this book could be used as a core resource for graduate students, purchased at the beginning of their program and used throughout their graduate training. This brief book also may be used as a supplementary text for graduate level courses, such as multicultural counseling, diversity counseling, introduction to counseling, research design, professional issues seminars, practica, and cross-cultural psychology. In programs that do have an international or cross-cultural counseling class, this book could serve as the primary text. We hope that this book will be a resource and inspiration for counselors, psychologists, and other mental health professionals around the world who are interested in various aspects of international, cross-national, and cross-cultural work. For instance, professionals and educators in fields related to counseling, such as cross-cultural psychology, social work, clinical psychology, education, psychiatry, psychological anthropology, and psychiatric nursing, may find this book useful.

For readers interested in a more extensive resource about counseling practices around the world, we suggest our earlier book, the *International Handbook of Cross-Cultural Counseling: Cultural Assumptions and Practices Worldwide* (Gerstein et al., 2009). The chapters in Part II of this handbook describe counseling models and practices across nine regions of the world, including East Asia (Japan, Taiwan, South Korea, and China), Southeast Asia (Singapore and Malaysia), South Asia (Pakistan and India), Central Asia (Kyrgyzstan), Europe (Italy, Great Britain, Ireland, Iceland, Sweden, France, the former USSR, and Greece), the Middle East (Israel, United Arab Emirates, and Turkey), the Americas and the Caribbean (Canada, Colombia, Venezuela, Argentina, Ecuador, and Puerto Rico), South and West Africa (South Africa and Nigeria), and Oceania (Australia). More specifically, these chapters focus on the background of the country, relevant cultural and epistemological assumptions, the use of counseling services, indigenous models of psychology and counseling, and the use of Western models of counseling and psychology. Moreover, these chapters include discussion of salient norms, values, attitudes, and behaviors underlying particular cultures and/or countries and how these constructs relate to various aspects of counseling, including help seeking.

Conclusion

There is a great need to recognize and embrace the different forms of counseling around the world. Through this book, we hope that readers will acquire a deeper understanding and respect for the importance of comprehending the cultural assumptions that may guide counseling and help seeking behaviors in different countries. Examining the cultural values and practices of persons in diverse countries can lead to a richer perspective about various approaches to counseling not often reported in the scholarly literature (e.g., Cheung, 2000; Pedersen & Leong, 1997). This in turn can lead to further development and refinement of effective, indigenous counseling models and strategies, while contributing to a comprehensive base of psychological knowledge about human behavior that is critical for effectively engaging in counseling around the globe (Heppner, 2006; Heppner, Leong, & Chiao, 2008; Heppner, Leong, & Gerstein, 2008). More important, through exposure to indigenous and shared models of counseling, there is the potential of successfully confronting the challenge of cultural encapsulation (Wrenn, 1962) since increased awareness can result in the identification of one's biases and the discovery of new frameworks (Pedersen & Leong, 1997), worldviews, and approaches toward others.

As stated early on in this chapter, the European countries dominated psychology in the late 19th century with U.S. psychology following suit in the post–World War II years. A major shift appears to be occurring in psychology with a more equally balanced arsenal of power shared by the psychology professions throughout the world (Cole, 2006). For U.S. psychologists, as they learn about psychology elsewhere, they will be more equipped to comprehend the limits of the science, practice, and professional development attributes of psychology in the States, and in so doing, they will be better prepared to assist persons in the United States (Mays, Rubin, Sabourin, & Walker, 1996) and in other countries.

Though we appear to be in a renaissance period of counseling around the world with counseling professionals outside the United States closely scrutinizing their practices and theories, and U.S. professionals questioning the cross-cultural validity and applicability of their strategies and methodologies, it remains to be seen if a strong and truly indigenous global counseling movement can be maintained and strengthened. The chapters in this book attest to the importance of becoming much more cognizant and supportive of this movement and the strength, creativity, talents, and determination of counseling professionals worldwide to make certain that the movement is successful. Ultimately, the success of a dynamic indigenous, cross-cultural, and cross-national counseling movement can greatly enhance our conceptual understanding of common and unique aspects of behavior and enrich the strategies we employ in our counseling, research, and training. At the same time, such a movement will affirm some of the core principles and philosophies of counseling endorsed throughout the world: that is, understanding, respecting, and embracing cultural values, norms, and behaviors regardless of person, ethnicity, nationality, or country. The science and practice of counseling worldwide can only benefit from such an outcome, as can the citizens of this planet.

Chapter Questions

1. It has been argued that there is a Eurocentric and even U.S. centric bias connected to the profession of counseling and psychology worldwide. Discuss what needs to occur in the next 5 to 10 years to overcome these biases. Support your argument and use examples to clarify your argument.

2. There are similarities and differences in multicultural, cross-cultural, and cross-national counseling. Discuss how well some often used counseling theories and approaches (e.g., Cognitive-Behavioral, Person Centered, & Emotion Focused) address these similarities and differences.

3. Ten years from now will there be a need for multicultural counseling or will it only be necessary to employ cultural, cross-cultural, and cross-national approaches to counseling theory, research, and practice? Support your argument and use examples to clarify your argument.

References

Abi-Hashem, N. (1997). Reflections on international perspectives in psychology. *American Psychologist, 52,* 569–573.

Adamopoulos, J., & Lonner, W. J. (2001). Culture and psychology at a crossroad: Historical perspective and theoretical analysis. In D. Matsumoto (Ed.), *Handbook of culture and psychology* (pp. 11–34). New York: Oxford University Press.

Allwood, C. M., & Berry, J. W. (2006). Origins and development of indigenous psychologies: An international analysis. *International Journal of Psychology, 41,* 243–268.

American Psychological Association. (2003). Guidelines on multicultural education, training, research, practice, and organizational change for psychologists. *American Psychologist, 58,* 377–402.

Ardila, R. (1982). International psychology. *American Psychologist, 37,* 323–329.

Ardila, R. (1993). Latin American psychology and world psychology: Is integration possible? In U. Kim & J. Berry (Eds.), *Indigenous psychologies: Research and experience in cultural context* (pp. 170–176). Newbury Park, CA: Sage.

Arnett, J. J. (2002). The psychology of globalization. *American Psychologist, 57,* 774–783.

Arnett, J. J. (2008). The neglected 95%: Why American psychology needs to become less American. *American Psychologist, 63,* 602–614.

Berlyne, D. E. (1968). American and European psychology. *American Psychologist, 23,* 447–452.

Berry, J. W., Poortinga, Y. H., Segall, M. H., & Dasen, E. R. (1992). *Cross-cultural psychology: Research and applications.* Cambridge, UK: Cambridge University Press.

Bochner, S. (1999). Cultural diversity within and between societies: Implications for multicultural social systems. In P. B. Pedersen (Ed.), *Multiculturalism as a fourth force* (pp. 19–60). Washington, DC: Taylor & Francis.

Bohm, D. (1980). *Wholeness and the implicate order.* London: Routledge.

Bozarth, J. D. (1985). Quantum theory and the personcentered approach. *Journal of Counseling and Development, 64,* 179–182.

Brandt, L. (1970). American psychology. *American Psychologist, 25,* 1091–1093.

Brehm, S. S. (2008). Looking ahead: The future of psychology and APA. *American Psychologist, 63,* 337–344.

Brislin, R. W. (1990). Applied cross-cultural psychology: An introduction. In R. W. Bristin (Ed.), *Applied cross-cultural psychology* (pp. 9–33). Newbury Park, CA: Sage.

Brown, L. S. (1997). The private practice of subversion: Psychology as tikkun olam. *American Psychologist, 52,* 449–462.

Chang, D. F., Tong, H., Shi, Q., & Zeng, Q. (2005). Letting a hundred flowers bloom: Counseling and psychotherapy in the People's Republic of China. *Journal of Mental Health Counseling, 27,* 104–116.

Chatterjee, P. (2005). Mental health care for India's tsunami survivors. *Lancet, 365,* 833–834.

Chen, P. H. (1999). Towards professionalism: The development of counseling in Taiwan. *Asian Journal of Counseling, 6,* 21–48.

Cheung, F. M. (2000). Deconstructing counseling in a cultural context. *The Counseling Psychologist, 28,* 123–132.

Cole, M. (1977). About this special issue. *American Psychologist, 32,* 903–904.

Cole, M. (2006). Internationalism in psychology: We need it now more than ever. *American Psychologist, 61,* 904–917.

David, H. P. (1960). Reciprocal influences in international psychology: A summary report of the 1959 APA Symposium. *American Psychologist, 15,* 313–315.

David, H. P., & Swartley, W. M. (1961). Toward more effective international communication in psychology. *American Psychologist, 16,* 696–698.

Denmark, F. L. (1998). Women and psychology: An international perspective. *American Psychologist, 53,* 465–473.

Douce, L. A. (2004). Globalization of counseling psychology. *The Counseling Psychologist, 32,* 142–152.

Draguns, J. G. (2001). Toward a truly international psychology: Beyond English only. *American Psychologist, 56,* 1019–1030.

Draguns, J. G. (2007). Universal and cultural threads in counseling individuals. In P. B. Pedersen, J. G. Draguns, W. J. Lonner, & J. E. Trimble (Eds.), *Counseling across cultures* (6th ed., pp. 21–36). Thousand Oaks, CA: Sage.

Enns, C. Z., & Sinacore, A. L. (Eds.). (2005). *Teaching and social justice: Integrating multicultural and feminist theories in the classroom.* Washington, DC: American Psychological Association.

European Congress of Psychology. (n.d.). *The 11th European Congress of Psychology.* Retrieved February 19, 2009, from http://www.ecp2009.no/

European Federation of Psychologists' Associations. (2007). *Activity plan 2007–2009 of the executive council of EFPA to the general assembly.* Prague, Czech Republic: Author.

Evans, R. B., & Scott, F. J. D. (1978). The 1913 International Congress of Psychology: The American Congress that wasn't. *American Psychologist, 33,* 711–723.

Fleishman, E. A. (1999). Applied psychology: An international journey. *American Psychologist, 54,* 1008–1016.

Forrest, L. (2008). *Reflections on the international counseling psychology conference.* American Psychological Association Society of Counseling Psychology Newsletter, *Spring,* 1, 7, 8.

Fouad, N. A., McPherson, R. H., Gerstein, L., Blustein, D. L., Elman, N., Helledy, K. I., et al. (2004). Houston, 2001: Context and legacy. *The Counseling Psychologist, 32,* 15–77.

Fowers, B. J., & Richardson, F. C. (1996). Why is multiculturalism good? *American Psychologist, 51,* 609–621.

Fretz, B. R. (1999). Polishing a pearl and a diamond. *The Counseling Psychologist, 27,* 32–46.

Friedman, T. L. (2000). *The Lexus and the olive tree: Understanding globalization.* New York: Anchor.

Friedman, T. L. (2005). *The world is flat: A brief history of the twenty-first century.* New York: Farrar, Straus, & Giroux.

Gerstein, L. H. (2006). Counseling psychologists as international social architects. In R. L. Toporek, L. H. Gerstein, N. A. Fouad, G. Roysircar-Sodowsky, & T. Israel (Eds.), *Handbook for social justice in counseling psychology: Leadership, vision, and action* (pp. 377–387). Thousand Oaks, CA: Sage.

Gerstein, L. H., & Bennett, M. (1999). Quantum physics and mental health counseling: The time is . . . ! *Journal of Mental Health Counseling, 21,* 255–269.

Gerstein, L. H., Heppner, P. P., Ægisdóttir, S., Leung, S. A., & Norsworthy, K. L. (2009). *International handbook of cross-cultural counseling: Cultural assumptions and practices worldwide.* Thousand Oaks, CA: Sage Publications.

Gerstein, L. H., Rountree, C., & Ordonez, M. A. (2007). An anthropological perspective on multicultural counselling. *Counselling Psychology Quarterly, 20*, 375–400.

Gerstein, L. H., & Ægisdóttir, S. (Guest Eds.). (2005a). Counseling around the world [Special issue]. *Journal of Mental Health Counseling, 27*, 95–184.

Gerstein, L. H., & Ægisdóttir, S. (Guest Eds.). (2005b). Counseling outside of the United States: Looking in and reaching out [Special section]. *Journal of Mental Health Counseling, 27*, 221–281.

Gerstein, L. H., & Ægisdóttir, S. (2005c). A trip around the world: A counseling travelogue! *Journal of Mental Health Counseling, 27*, 95–103.

Gerstein, L. H., & Ægisdóttir, S. (2007). Training international social change agents: Transcending a U.S. counseling paradigm. *Counselor Education and Supervision, 47*, 123–139.

Goodman, L. A., Liang, B., Helms, J. E., Latta, R. E., Sparks, E., & Weintraub, S. R. (2004). Training counseling psychologists as social justice agents: Feminist and multicultural principles in action. *The Counseling Psychologist, 32*, 793–837.

Harper, F. D. (2000). Challenges to counseling professionals for the new millennium [Editorial]. *International Journal for the Advancement of Counselling, 22*, 1–7.

Heppner, P. P. (1997). Building on strengths as we move into the next millennium. *The Counseling Psychologist, 25*, 5–14.

Heppner, P. P. (2006). The benefits and challenges of becoming cross-culturally competent counseling psychologists: Presidential address. *The Counseling Psychologist, 34*, 147–172.

Heppner, P. P., Casas, J. M., Carter, J., & Stone, G. L. (2000). The maturation of counseling psychology: Multifaceted perspectives from 1978–1998. In S. D. Brown & R. W. Lent (Eds.), *Handbook of counseling psychology* (3rd ed., pp. 3–49). New York: Wiley.

Heppner, P. P., & Gerstein, L. H. (2008). International developments in counseling psychology. In E. Altmaier & B. D. Johnson (Eds.), *Encyclopedia of counseling: Changes and challenges for counseling in the 21st century* (Vol. 1, pp. 260–266). Thousand Oaks, CA: Sage.

Heppner, P. P., Leong, F. T. L., & Chiao, H. (2008). A growing internationalization of counseling psychology. In S. D. Brown & R. W. Lent (Eds.), *Handbook of counseling psychology* (4th ed., pp. 68–85). Hoboken, NJ: Wiley.

Heppner, P. P., Leong, F. T. L., & Gerstein, L. H. (2008). Counseling within a changing world: Meeting the psychological needs of societies and the world. In W. B. Walsh (Ed.), *Biennial review in counseling psychology* (pp. 231–258). Thousand Oaks, CA: Sage.

Hiles, D. (1996). *Cultural psychology and the centreground of psychology.* Paper presented at the XXVI International Congress of Psychology, August 16–21, Montreal, Quebec, Canada.

Ho, D. Y. F. (1995). Internalized culture, culturocentrism, and transcendence. *The Counseling Psychologist, 23*, 4–24.

Hunter, W. S., Miles, W. R., Yerkes, R. M., & Langfeld, H. S. (1946). Committee on international planning. *American Psychologist, 1*, 123–124.

International Federation of Red Cross and Red Crescent Societies. (2008, June). *China: Sichuan earthquake.* Retrieved February 25, 2009, from http://www.ifrc.org/docs/appeals/08/MDRCN00309.pdf

Jaafar, J. L. S. (n.d.). The second convention of the Asian Psychological Association: A message from the president elect of the 2nd convention. Retrieved February 19, 2009, from http://umweb.um.edu.my/apsya/

Jackson, M. L. (1995). Multicultural counseling: Historical perspectives. In J. G. Ponterotto, J. M. Casas, L. A. Suzuki, & C. M. Alexander (Eds.), *Handbook of multicultural counseling* (pp. 3–16). Thousand Oaks, CA: Sage.

Jackson, Y. (Ed.). (2006). *Encyclopedia of multicultural psychology.* Thousand Oaks, CA: Sage.

Kelman, H. C., & Hollander, E. P. (1964). International cooperation in psychological research. *American Psychologist, 19,* 779–782.

Kennedy, S., Scheirer, J., & Rogers, A. (1984). The price of success: Our monocultural science. *American Psychologist, 39,* 996–997.

Kim, U. (1990). Indigenous psychology: Science and applications. In R. W. Bristin (Ed.), *Applied cross-cultural psychology* (pp. 142–160). Thousand Oaks, CA: Sage.

Kim, U., Park, Y. S., & Park, D. H. (2000). The challenge of cross-cultural psychology: The role of indigenous psychologies. *Journal of Cross-Cultural Psychology, 31,* 63–75.

Kim, U., Yang, K. S., & Hwang, K. K. (2006). Indigenous and cultural psychology: Understanding people in context. New York: Springer.

Kwan, K.-L. K., & Gerstein, L. H. (2008). Envisioning a counseling psychology of the world: The mission of the international forum. *The Counseling Psychologist, 36,* 182–187.

LaFromboise, T. D., & Foster, S. L. (1992). Cross-cultural training: Scientist-practitioner model and methods. *The Counseling Psychologist, 20,* 472–489.

Lee, C. C. (1997). The global future of professional counseling: Collaboration for social change. *International Journal of Intercultural Relations, 21,* 279–285.

Leong, F. T. L., & Blustein, D. L. (2000). Toward a global vision of counseling psychology. *The Counseling Psychologist, 28,* 5–9.

Leong, F. T. L., & Leach, M. M. (2007). Internalizing counseling psychology in the United States: A SWOT analysis. *Applied Psychology: An International Review, 56,* 165–181.

Leong, F. T. L., & Ponterotto, J. G. (2003). A proposal for internationalizing counseling psychology in the United States: Rationale, recommendations, and challenges. *The Counseling Psychologist, 31,* 381–395.

Leung, S. A. (2003). A journey worth traveling: Globalization of counseling psychology. *The Counseling Psychologist, 31,* 412–419.

Leung, S. A. (2008, July). *Indigenization and internationalization in counseling: Contradiction or complementation.* Keynote address delivered at the Inaugural Asia Pacific Rim International Counseling Conference, Hong Kong.

Leung, S. A., Chan, C. C., & Leahy, T. (2007). Counseling psychology in Hong Kong: A germinating discipline. *Applied Psychology: An International Review, 56*(1), 51–68.

Leung, S. A., & Chen, P-W. (in press). Developing counseling psychology in Chinese communities in Asia: Indigenous, multicultural, and cross-cultural considerations. *The Counseling Psychologist.*

Leung, S. A., & Hoshmand, L. T. (2007). Internationalization and international publishing: Broadening the impact of scholarly work in counseling. *Asian Journal of Counselling, 14,* 141–154.

Lonner, W. J. (1985). Issues in testing and assessment in cross-cultural counseling. *The Counseling Psychologist, 13,* 599–614.

Lonner, W. J., & Adamopoulos, J. (1997). Culture as antecedent to behavior. In J. W. Berry, Y. H. Poortinga, & J. Pandey (Eds.), *Handbook of cross-cultural psychology: Theory and method* (Vol. 1, pp. 43–83). Boston: Allyn & Bacon.

Lucas, C. (1985). Out at the edge: Notes on a paradigm shift. *Journal of Counseling and Development, 64,* 165–172.

Marsella, A. J. (1998). Toward a "global-community psychology": Meeting the needs of a changing world. *American Psychologist, 53,* 1282–1291.

Mays, V. M., Rubin, J., Sabourin, M., & Walker, L. (1996). Moving toward a global psychology: Changing theories and practice to meet the needs of a changing world. *American Psychologist, 51,* 485–487.

McWhirter, J. J. (1988a). Counseling psychology and the Fulbright Program: The Australian connection. *The Counseling Psychologist, 16,* 303–306.

McWhirter, J. J. (1988b). The Fulbright Program in counseling psychology. *The Counseling Psychologist, 16,* 279–281.

McWhirter, J. J. (1988c). Implications of the Fulbright Senior Scholar Program for counseling psychology. *The Counseling Psychologist, 16,* 307–310.

McWhirter, J. J. (2000). And now, up go the walls: Constructing an international room for counseling psychology. *The Counseling Psychologist, 28,* 117–122.

McWhirter, P. T., & McWhirter, J. J. (2009). Historical antecedents: Counseling psychology and the Fulbright Program. Unpublished manuscript.

Miller, G. (2005). The tsunami's psychological aftermath. *Science, 309,* 1030–1033.

Moghaddam, F. M. (1987). Psychology in the three worlds: As reflected by the crisis in social psychology and the move toward indigenous third-world psychology. *American Psychologist, 42,* 912–920.

Mohanty, C. T. (2003). *Feminism without borders: Decolonizing theory, practicing solidarity.* Durham, NC: Duke University Press.

Moore, J. D. (1997). *Visions of culture.* Thousand Oaks, CA: Sage.

Norsworthy, K. L. (2006). Bringing social justice to international practices of counseling psychology. In R. L. Toporek, L. H. Gerstein, N. A. Fouad, G. Roysircar-Sodowsky, & T. Israel (Eds.), *Handbook for social justice in counseling psychology: Leadership, vision, and action* (pp. 421–441). Thousand Oaks, CA: Sage.

Norsworthy, K. L., & Gerstein, L. (2003). Counseling and building communities of peace: The interconnections. *International Journal for the Advancement of Counseling, 25*(4), 197–203.

Nutt, R. L. (2007). Implications of globalization for training in counseling psychology: Presidential address. *The Counseling Psychologist, 35,* 157–171.

Pawlik, K. (1992). Psychologie international: Aufgaben und Chancen [International psychology: Tasks and chances]. *Psychologie in Osterreich, 12,* 84–87.

Pawlik, K., & d'Ydewalle, G. (1996). Psychology and the global commons: Perspectives of international psychology. *American Psychologist, 51,* 488–495.

Pedersen, P. (1993). The multicultural dilemma of white cross-cultural researchers. *The Counseling Psychologist, 21,* 229–232.

Pedersen, P. (1995). The five stages of culture shock: Critical incidents around the world. Westport, CT: Greenwood Press.

Pedersen, P., Draguns, J., Lonner, W., & Trimble, J. (2002). *Counseling across cultures* (5th ed.). Thousand Oaks, CA: Sage.

Pedersen, P. B. (1991). Multiculturalism as a generic approach to counseling. *Journal of Counseling and Development, 70,* 6–12.

Pedersen, P. B. (2000). Cross-cultural counseling. In A. E. Kazdin (Ed.), *Encyclopedia of psychology* (Vol. 2, pp. 359–361). Washington, DC: American Psychological Association.

Pedersen, P. B. (2003). Culturally biased assumptions in counseling psychology. *The Counseling Psychologist, 31,* 396–403.

Pedersen, P. B. (2004). Cross-cultural counseling. In W. E. Craighead & C. B. Nemeroff (Eds.), *The concise Corsini encyclopedia of psychology and behavioral science* (3rd ed., pp. 236–237). Hoboken, NJ: Wiley.

Pedersen, P. B., & Leong, F. (1997). Counseling in an international context. *The Counseling Psychologist, 25,* 117–122.

Peoples, J., & Bailey, G. (1994). *Humanity: An introduction to cultural anthropology* (3rd ed.). Minneapolis, MN: West.

Ponterotto, J. G., Casas, J. M., Suzuki, L. A., & Alexander, C. M. (Eds.). (1995). *Handbook of multicultural counseling.* Thousand Oaks, CA: Sage.

Pryor, R. G. L., & Bright, J. E. H. (2007). The current state and future direction of counseling psychology in Australia. *Applied Psychology: An International Review, 56*(1), 7–19.

Ritchie, P. L. J. (2008). Annual report of the International Union of Psychological Science (IUPsyS). *International Journal of Psychology, 43,* 929–935.

Rosenzweig, M. R. (1982). Trends in development and status of psychology: An international perspective. *International Journal of Psychology, 17,* 117–140.

Rosenzweig, M. R. (1984). U.S. psychology and world psychology. *American Psychologist, 39,* 877–884.

Rosenzweig, M. R. (1992). Psychological science around the world. *American Psychologist, 47,* 718–722.

Rosenzweig, M. R. (1999). Continuity and change in the development of psychology around the world. *American Psychologist, 54,* 252–259.

Russell, R. W. (1984). Psychology in its world context. *American Psychologist, 39,* 1017–1025.

Savickas, M. L. (2007). Internationalisation of counseling psychology: Constructing cross-national consensus and collaboration. *Applied Psychology: An International Review, 56*(1), 182–188.

Schultz, E. A., & Lavenda, R. H. (2001). *Cultural anthropology: A perspective on the human condition.* London: Mayfield.

Segall, M. H., Lonner, W. J., & Berry, J. W. (1998). Cross-cultural psychology as a scholarly discipline: On a flowering of culture in behavioral research. *American Psychologist, 53,* 1101–1110.

Sexton, V. S., & Misiak, H. (1984). American psychologists and psychology abroad. *American Psychologist, 39,* 1026–1031.

Sinha, D., & Holtzman, W. H. (Eds.). (1984). The impact of psychology on Third World development [Special issue]. *International Journal of Psychology, 19,* 3–192.

Skovholt, T., Hansen, S., Goh, M., Romano, J., & Thomas, K. (2005). The Minnesota International Counseling Institute (MICI) 1989–Present: History, joyful moments, and lessons learned. *International Journal for the Advancement of Counselling, 27,* 17–33.

Smith, R. J. (1983). On Ardila's "International Psychology." *American Psychologist, 38,* 122–123.

Smith, T. B. (2004). *Practicing multiculturalism: Affirming diversity in counseling and psychology.* Boston: Allyn & Bacon.

Sue, D. W. (1981). Critical incidents in cross-cultural counseling. In D. W. Sue (Ed.), *Counseling the culturally different* (pp. 259–291). New York: Wiley.

Sue, D. W., Arredono, P., & McDavis, R. J. (1992). Multicultural counseling competencies and standards: A call to the profession. *Journal of Multicultural Counseling and Development, 20,* 64–89.

Sue, D. W., Carter, R. T., Casas, J. M., Fouad, N. A., Ivey, A. E., Jensen, M., et al. (1998). *Multicultural counseling competencies: Individual and organizational development.* Thousand Oaks, CA: Sage.

Sue, D. W., & Sue, D. (2003). *Counseling the culturally diverse: Theory and practice.* New York: Wiley.

Sue, D. W., & Torino, G. C. (1994). Racial-cultural competence: Awareness, knowledge, and skills. In R. T. Carter (Ed.), *Handbook of racial-cultural psychology and counseling: Vol. 2. Training and practice* (pp. 3–18), New York: Wiley.

Takooshian, H. (2003). Counseling psychology's wide new horizons. *The Counseling Psychologist, 31,* 420–426.

Tanaka-Matsumi, J. (2004). Japanese forms of psychotherapy: Naikan therapy and Morita therapy. In U. P. Gielen, J. M. Fish, & J. G. Draguns (Eds.), *Handbook of culture, therapy, and healing* (pp. 277–292). Mahwah, NJ: Lawrence Erlbaum.

Toporek, R. L., Gerstein, L. H., Fouad, N. A., Roysircar-Sodowsky, G., & Israel, T. (Eds.). (2006). *Handbook for social justice in counseling psychology: Leadership, vision, and action.* Thousand Oaks, CA: Sage.

Triandis, H. C. (1972). *The analysis of subjective culture.* New York: Wiley.

Triandis, H. C. (2000). Dialectics between cultural and cross-cultural psychology. *Asian Journal of Social Psychology, 3,* 185–195.

Trimble, J. E. (2001). A quest for discovering ethno-cultural themes in psychology. In J. G. Ponterotto, J. M. Casas, L. A. Suzuki, & C. M. Alexander (Eds.), *Handbook of multicultural counseling* (2nd ed., pp. 3–13). Thousand Oaks, CA: Sage.

United Nations Children's Fund. (2008, November). Six month report: China earthquake emergency. Retrieved February 25, 2009, from http://www.unicef.org.hk/sichuan/6monthsrpt_e.pdf

United Nations Economic and Social Survey of Asia and the Pacific. (1999). *Part two: Asia and the Pacific into the twenty-first century.* Bangkok, Thailand: Poverty and Development Division.

United Nations Population Division. (2007). *World population prospects: The 2006 revision.* New York: United Nations.

Vera, E. M., & Speight, S. L. (2003). Multicultural competence, social justice, and counseling psychology: Expanding our roles. *The Counseling Psychologist, 31,* 253–272.

Vontress, C. E. (1979). Cross-cultural counseling: An existential approach. *Personnel and Guidance Journal, 58,* 117–122.

Watkins, C. E., Jr., Lopez, F. G., Campbell, V. L., & Lew, D. E. (1986). Facilitating the involvement of Division 17 members living outside the United States. *The Counseling Psychologist, 14,* 592–593.

Watson, M. B., & Fouche, P. (2007). Transforming a past into a future: Counseling psychology in South Africa. *Applied Psychology: An International Review, 56*(1), 152–164.

Wheatley, M. J. (2006). *Leadership and the new science: Discovering order in a chaotic world* (3rd ed.). San Francisco: Berrett Koehler.

Wrenn, C. G. (1962). The culturally encapsulated counselor. *Harvard Educational Review, 32,* 111–119.

Yang, K. S. (1997). Indigenising Westernized Chinese psychology. In M. H. Bond (Ed.), *Working at the interface of cultures: Eighteen lies in social science* (pp. 62–76). New York: Routledge.

Yang, K. S., Hwang, K. K., Pedersen, P. B., & Daibo, I. (Eds.). (2003). *Progress in Asian social psychology: Conceptual and empirical contributions.* Westport, CT: Praeger.

Young, R. A., & Nicol, J. J. (2007). Counselling psychology in Canada: Advancing psychology for all. *Applied Psychology: An International Review, 56*(1), 20–32.

Ægisdóttir, S., & Gerstein, L. H. (2005). Reaching out: Mental health delivery outside the box. *Journal of Mental Health Counseling, 27,* 221–224.

Ægisdóttir, S., & Gerstein, L. H. (2010). International counseling competencies: A new frontier in multicultural training. In J. C. Ponterotto, J. M. Casas, L. A. Suzuki, & C. A. Alexander (Eds.), *Handbook of multicultural counseling* (3rd ed., pp. 175–188). Thousand Oaks, CA: Sage.

Ægisdóttir, S., Gerstein, L. H., & Çinarbaş, D. C. (2008). Methodological issues in cross-cultural counseling research: Equivalence, bias, and translations. *The Counseling Psychologist, 36,* 188–219.

Chapter Two

The Intersection of Multicultural and Cross-National Movements in the United States

A Complementary Role to Promote Culturally Sensitive Research, Training, and Practice

P. Paul Heppner, Stefanía Ægisdóttir, Seung-Ming
Alvin Leung, Changming Duan, Janet E. Helms,
Lawrence H. Gerstein, and Paul B. Pedersen

This chapter focuses on the multicultural movement as well as the *cross-national* movement in the U.S. counseling profession. As will become clearer in the pages to follow, the term *cross-national movement*, as compared with *cross-cultural movement*, in our opinion, more accurately characterizes the internationalization of the counseling profession in the United States. It is not uncommon for graduate students and professionals in counseling and counseling psychology to be confused about the similarities and differences between "multicultural," "cross-cultural," and "cross-national" issues. Are they one and the same? Or do they coexist side by side? Are they rivals? As discussed in Chapter 1 (this volume), these are often confusing questions, in part because of the changing definitions as well as the introduction of new terms over time. Unfortunately, the multicultural and cross-national movements in counseling, and the larger discipline of psychology, have not enjoyed a consensus of the meaning of its labels (Olson, Evans, & Shoenberg, 2007).

The purpose of this chapter is threefold. First, the chapter aims to promote greater understanding of the differences and similarities of the U.S. multicultural and cross-national movements. The history and evolution of these movements will be very briefly sketched, including associated foci, goals, and competencies. Briefly, the U.S. multicultural movement refers to the evolution of thought related to understanding the cultural context within all aspects of the U.S. counseling profession (research, practice, and training). The cross-national movement in the U.S. counseling profession refers to the evolution of thought about culturally sensitive collaboration about all aspects of the counseling profession among counseling professionals across countries. Although we present these movements separately, it is important to understand that they are not in reality separate movements but rather that the lines are blurred and a Venn diagram of scholars associated with each movement would overlap significantly. Second, the chapter will discuss the historical and current uneasy tensions that sometimes exist between the U.S. multicultural and cross-national movements in the U.S. counseling profession. These tensions are a function of many events, including the histories of these movements, the motivations of scholars for joining these movements, shifting resources, the shrinking of time and space, especially in the last decade, and the ever-changing evolution of terms and worldviews of leaders involved in these movements. It is very important to address these tensions and to be clear that in our view it is neither desirable nor possible for one movement to replace the other.

The third purpose of this chapter is to propose a complementary role between the multicultural and cross-national foci in promoting culturally sensitive research and applied interventions in the U.S. counseling professions. We suggest that each movement has the same long-term goal of increasing cultural awareness and sensitivity to create more applicable research and promote more effective counseling practices in the counseling profession around the world.

The U.S. Multicultural Movement in Counseling

The past few decades have witnessed a multicultural movement in the United States that has, in many ways, revolutionized the entire specialty of counseling in the country. From being literally nonexistent some 40 years ago, multicultural counseling and psychology has become an established specialty (Ponterotto, 2008) and has been viewed as "the fourth force in counseling" (Pedersen, 1999b). Today, one can hardly find a textbook or an issue of any professional journal in the field of counseling and counseling psychology that does not include chapters or articles that directly address multicultural issues or have chapters or articles on any topic without integrating multicultural issues. In this section, we provide a very brief overview of the history of the U.S. multicultural movement in the counseling profession. In this chapter, the *U.S. multicultural movement in counseling* refers to the evolution of thought (in research, practice, and training) related to the conceptualization of the unique cultural context of both the helping professional and his or her clientele to more accurately assess, understand, develop, and implement helpful interventions (see Ponterotto, 2008).

The multicultural movement, however, did not occur easily or quickly (see, e.g., Casas, 1984; Heppner, Casas, Carter, & Stone, 2000; Jackson, 1995; Ponterotto, Casas, Suzuki, & Alexander, 2001); instead, it has been a journey, a no-return journey. Ponterotto (2008) outlined the growth of multicultural counseling and psychology as being born in the 1960s, experiencing its establishment as a specialty in the 1980s, maturing and expanding in the 1990s, and growing beyond borders and disciplines in the most recent decade. Although in many ways the process was nonlinear, with many "bumps and curves in the road," this chronological view highlights a developmental process of the multicultural movement in counseling and psychology. The advancement of this movement is not only reflected in its developmental maturity but also in its diversification and growth of younger branches so as to now encompass not only U.S. racial ethnic minorities but a very broad range of marginalized groups (e.g., women, persons of different sexual orientations, older adults, individuals with physical challenges), in resonance with the societal pulses, and in its organizational and systemic contexts.

Prior to 1960, only a few counseling articles addressed racial issues, and when they did, it was primarily in relation to African Americans (Jackson, 1995). Additionally, in the 1940s and 1950s, minorities, including African Americans, were not actively involved in what was then known as the personnel and guidance movement (Jackson, 1995), which was connected to the American Personnel and Guidance Association (APGA), now called the American Counseling Association (ACA). The birth of a multicultural movement in the United States was greatly affected by the civil rights movement in the 1960s (Neville & Carter, 2005). The nationwide racial upheavals led to substantial debate regarding the "counseling needs of culturally different clients, as well as the efficacy of services available to certain populations" (Robinson & Morris, 2000, p. 239). The discussion at the time mainly focused on racial issues, particularly African-American-related issues, recognizing that racism had led to the "covert and overt racist practices for several decades" (Robinson & Morris, 2000, p. 239) by the counseling profession, psychological organizations, and mental health systems.

Also at that time, Wrenn (1962) warned of the dangers of a "culturally encapsulated counselor" who was unaware and insensitive to the cultural worldview of clients. Although his words were very clear, his message was neither widely understood nor followed.

During the 1960s, there was a dramatic increase in the racial and cultural diversity of counselors, resulting in greater attention being paid to diverse populations of clients (Aubrey, 1977). In fact, in 1966, the APGA adopted a policy urging counselors to serve culturally disadvantaged individuals (Hoyt, 1967), and in 1968, the Association of Black Psychologists was formed. Furthermore, William Banks led a campaign in 1969 at the APGA Conference to establish an Office of Non-White Concerns in the Association (Jackson, 1995). Later, in 1972, this office was transformed into a division of the APGA called the Association for Non-White Concerns. This organization changed its name in 1985 to the Association for Multicultural Counseling and Development (AMCD). Not surprisingly, this association embraced all counselors of color and focused on helping all persons of color (Jackson, 1995). In the 1970s, the AMCD launched the first counseling journal devoted to multicultural issues, the *Journal of Non-White Concerns* (now called the *Journal of Multicultural Counseling and Development* [*JMCD*]). Three special issues in the 1970s of APGA's flagship journal, *Personnel and Guidance Journal,* also focused on multicultural issues and for the first time were guest edited by Paul Smith and Derald Wing Sue, counseling professionals of color (Jackson, 1995).

Formal attempts were also begun for the first time in the 1960s within the American Psychological Association (APA) to raise awareness of the needs of U.S. racial and ethnic minorities. For instance, in the late 1960s, African American psychologists called for attention to racial issues, the elimination of racist themes in APA journals, and the establishment of programs for addressing racial concerns (Guthrie, 1998). To respond to such calls, the APA created the Ad Hoc Committee on Equality of Opportunity in Psychology in 1963 and the Commission on Accelerating Black Participation in Psychology in 1968. The APA also held the Vail Conference (in 1973), where the organization took steps to encourage the psychology profession to prepare students to function in a multiracial society (Korman, 1974)—affirmative action programs and diverse training programs became associated with basic ethical obligations. These were examples of structural changes that preceded the formation of APA Division 45, Society for the Psychological Study of Ethnic Minority Issues, in the late 1970s.

Interest in multicultural counseling, or what was then sometimes also called cross-cultural counseling, increased substantially in the 1970s. During the 1970s, the academy in psychology (which had been largely responsible for the popular racial inferiority theories for a sizable portion of the last century) started to pay more attention to the "culturally different" or "minorities" (Jackson, 1995) and their psychological needs (Sue, 1977). Research on cross-racial and multicultural issues in counseling emerged on university campuses, and the dialogue about the role of race in the counseling process started to appear in counseling journals (e.g., Vontress, 1971). Multicultural researchers and theorists openly recognized that the mainstream counseling models and theories had failed not only to meet the needs of African Americans but also all racial/ethnic minority clients (Sue, 1977; Vontress, 1971). Moreover, a significant amount of empirical evidence became available that racial minorities were extremely underrepresented among both the mental health providers and mental health service recipients (Atkinson & Thompson, 1992).

There had been a growing awareness of inequalities and discrimination around gender, sexual orientation, and people with disabilities, as well as children, adolescents, and older adults in the United States (see Heppner et al., 2000). For example, events with the second wave of the feminist movement that dealt with both legal and cultural inequality, as well as the gay rights movement in the 1960s through the 1980s (especially the monumental event of homosexuality being removed from their list of mental disorders by the American Psychiatric Association in 1973; Rothblum, 2000), all contributed significantly to the broadening of the scope of equality and the multicultural movement. Thus, the notion of *multicultural counseling* was also strengthened and mutually complemented by voices of other social groups who shared similar experiences of discrimination and prejudice. In aggregate, these voices challenged the counseling profession to examine its core values and to reformulate its conceptualization and practice to accommodate diversities in the population, including culture, gender, sexual orientation, and physical challenges (see Jackson 1995, for more details). By the turn of the 20th century, multicultural counseling had evolved to favor a broad definition of culture, to include demographic (e.g., gender), status (e.g., economic), and ethnographic (e.g., nationality) variables (e.g., Pedersen, 1999a; Sue et al., 1998), based on the rationale that "the broad definition of culture is particularly important in preparing counselors to deal with the complex differences among clients from every cultural group" (Pedersen, 1999a, p. 5). However, it is fair to say there has been considerable disagreement about the theoretical relation between counseling and culture (Pedersen, 2003).

Moreover, during the 1980s and 1990s, multicultural issues were centrally reflected in the priorities and activities of professional organizations. For example, in the late 1990s, multicultural counseling competency requirements were written into the practice and training standards of the AMCD (American Association for Counseling and Development, now known as the ACA), APA Divisions 17 (Society of Counseling Psychology) and 45 (Society for the Psychological Study of Ethnic Minority Issues; Ridley & Kleiner, 2003), and the APA (e.g., APA, 1993). Driven by the quest for knowledge to serve the culturally and racially different, theorists and researchers achieved significant and unprecedented progress in multicultural issues in the 1980s and 1990s. The term *multicultural counseling* began to appear in the counseling literature more frequently; the literature also grew extensively during this period, including numerous journal articles, handbooks (e.g., Ponterotto, Casas, Suzuki, & Alexander, 1995), and scholarly journals devoted to publishing empirical and conceptual articles on multicultural counseling (e.g., *Journal of Multicultural Counseling and Development*). Numerous theories were developed in the areas of racial identity, acculturation, worldviews, and values (Ponterotto, 2008). These theories provided tools for understanding not only between-group differences among different races/cultures but also within-group differences. Additionally, these theories enabled the examination of complex intrapersonal and interpersonal processes (i.e., multicultural competencies) through which counselors can engage in culturally sensitive counseling (Constantine, Miville, & Kindaichi, 2008).

With these advancements in multicultural studies, the multicultural competence movement emerged; for example, Sue, Arredondo, and McDavis (1992) presented the first tripartite model of multicultural competence, which emphasized the role of awareness, knowledge, and skills in multicultural competence. This model was first published in the *JMCD* and the competencies identified by these authors were drawn, in part, from a position paper, "Cross-cultural Counseling Competencies," produced by APA Division 17 (Sue et al., 1982), and the *APA Guidelines for Providers of Psychological Services to Ethnic, Linguistic, and Culturally Diverse Populations* (APA, 1991).

Research addressing the counseling needs of women, men, and individuals of different sexual orientations have burgeoned since the 1980s (Betz & Fitzgerald, 1993), and age and disability have also started gaining attention from the multicultural research community. With the recognition that the U.S. society has been oppressive to many individuals, a most recent expansion of the multicultural movement has emerged: social justice counseling (Warren & Constantine, 2007). More recently, social class has also been recognized as an individual identity that leads to unearned privileges or disadvantages and deserves professional attention (see Liu & Ali, 2008). In 2008, social justice was depicted as "the overarching umbrella that guides our profession" (Sue & Sue, 2008, p. 292).

In the 2000s, multicultural counseling has become a major area of scholarly inquiry as well as a major force in counseling (Pedersen, 1999c). Multiculturalism has become a mainstream value in professional organizations such as the ACA and APA (Heppner et al., 2000). Clearly, the multicultural movement has traveled a long way and become a diversified and inclusive area of counseling and counseling psychology. Its advancement has also reflected the political and cultural climate of the society. Although many would agree there has been an increased awareness and commitment to diversity issues over the last 40 years, many would also say there has "often been tension and many of the changes have not come easily" (Heppner et al., 2000, pp. 30–31), and clearly there is still a long way to go (see, e.g., Heppner et al., 2000; Jackson, 1995; Ponterotto, 2008; Ponterotto et al., 1995, 2001; Sue & Sue, 2008).

The Growing Cross-National Movement in the U.S. Counseling Profession

In this section, we provide a very brief overview of the history of the growing cross-national movement of counseling psychology in the United States (see Heppner, Leong, & Chiao, 2008, for more details). The *cross-national movement in the U.S. counseling profession* refers to the evolution of thought related to culturally sensitive collaboration among counseling professionals across countries, including sharing knowledge related to research, practice, and service. In essence, although the inclusion of international perspectives began in the 1940s (Savickas, 2007), there has been a relatively slow growth in U.S. counseling psychology until the beginning of the 21st century (Heppner, Leong, & Chiao, 2008). Since 2000, however, there has been quite an accelerated interest in cross-national initiatives. For example, there is an increasingly supportive infrastructure within several U.S. professional counseling psychology associations (e.g., the International Section was established in 2005 within the Society of Counseling Psychology), a rising number of scholarly publications on international topics as well as international samples in the professional journals, growing interest in training international students and promoting cross-cultural competencies in all students, and greater cross-national communication and collaboration (see Heppner, Leong, & Chiao, 2008). The level of change in all the developments just mentioned, however, has been relatively small and in many ways still in its infancy compared with the U.S. multicultural counseling movement. The change in the internationalization of the counseling profession has been a function of the synergy of a number of factors, such as (a) social, economic, political, and environmental events and forces; (b) the advances in the U.S. multicultural movement; (c) pioneering leaders and scholars who conceptualized the utility of internationalizing counseling psychology; (d) a critical mass of voices articulating the profound role of culture in the work of counseling professionals in the United States and around the globe; and

(e) structural changes within professional organizations that promote cultural perspectives (see Heppner, Leong, & Chiao, 2008).

Some of the earliest cross-national efforts occurred in the 1950s and 1960s as U.S. counseling psychologists were asked to consult with leaders in other countries to help international colleges develop a similar counseling profession. For example, after World War II, a number of U.S. counseling leaders (e.g., W. Lloyd, E. G. Williamson, D. Super, H. Borow, and L. Brammer) served as consultants to the Japanese government. Similarly, in the 1960s, counseling psychology leaders (e.g., C. G. Wrenn, F. Robinson) provided consultation to establish the counseling profession in England. In the 1960s, Donald Super and his colleagues also began to engage in international research on work values connected to career choice. Beginning in the early1980s, the second wave of counseling psychologists going abroad were most often Fulbright scholars who taught and/or conducted research for 3 to 12 months in other countries (see Hedlund, 1988; Heppner, 1988; McWhirter, 1988; Nugent 1988; Skovholt, 1988).

Other early efforts to increase cross-cultural communication within the counseling profession began in the mid-1960s with the creation of a new journal, the *International Journal for the Advancement of Counseling* (*IJAC*). This journal has provided a major arena for scholarly exchanges on issues of guidance and counseling from international perspectives. Similarly, then-editor Fretz began the International Forum in *The Counseling Psychologist* (*TCP*) to promote communication about international topics. Although Fretz's call was clear, the message was not widely received, with the vast majority of the articles being written by U.S. scholars describing their experiences as Fulbrighters or visiting scholars.

During these early years, it was not uncommon for counseling psychologists to question the value of such international experiences. For example, McWhirter (2000) wrote that "my professional colleagues were supportive and happy for me, but many could not understand why a counseling psychologist would want to take his family to Turkey for anything other than a brief tourist trip, and some even questioned that" (p. 117). The motivations of counseling psychologists interested in international issues were also often questioned; McWhirter (2000) described an incident where a colleague presumed the motivation for such international work to be "only looking for an excuse for foreign travel" (p. 118). Such attitudes and beliefs undoubtedly affected the development of the international movement in the counseling profession. Clearly ahead of the times, also in the 1980s, the Minnesota International Counseling Institute was created by counseling psychology faculty at the University of Minnesota (e.g., T. Skovholt, S. Hansen, J. Romano, K. Thomas). This institute provided (and continues to offer) a biennial gathering of international psychological and educational professionals that promoted scholarly exchanges among counseling professionals from around the world.

Although there was an increased focus on multicultural issues within the counseling profession during the 1990s (see Casas, 1984; Heppner et al., 2000; Jackson, 1995; Ponterotto, 2008; Watkins, 1994), an increased focus on international topics was less evident within U.S. counseling psychology (see Heppner, Leong, & Chiao, 2008). Also at this time, the cross-cultural movement in psychology, which emphasized comparative research across cultures, was very active, but relatively few U.S. counseling psychologists seemed to be actively involved in this specialty.

Paul Pedersen published a landmark article in 1991 (more fully articulated in 1999) in which he proposed that culture, defined broadly, is generic to all counseling; his conceptualization of culturally focused counseling emphasized the centrality of the cultural context within all dimensions of the counseling profession, including both multicultural counseling and cross-cultural counseling across two countries. Nonetheless, the discipline of U.S. psychology, including the counseling profession, continued to be characterized as a white middle-class enterprise "conceived in English, thought about in English, written about in English, and taking into account problems relevant to Anglo-Saxon culture" (Ardila, 1993, pp. 170–171).

It is important to note, however, that during the 1990s, a number of individuals in the U.S. counseling profession who would later become vocal proponents of the cross-national movement were being affected greatly by the growing U.S. multicultural counseling movement. More specifically, the worldview of many of these individuals was becoming more culture-centered (see Pedersen, 1999a) and, in essence, gaining multicultural competencies that would later be extended to cross-national contexts and thus serve as the foundation of a culture-centered cross-national movement in U.S. counseling psychology. In this way, the U.S. multicultural movement was very important in promoting cultural sensitivities in the work of some members of the counseling profession that would later serve as the foundation to examine the utility of the cultural context cross-nationally.

At the dawn of the 21st century, advances in communication, transportation, manufacturing, and technology began to alter the world greatly, most notably the Internet, which dramatically changed the flow of information and resources and modified radically our relationships, our recreation, and the way we work and play. With the shrinking of space-time, the world has not only become increasingly interconnected but interdependent along numerous dimensions (e.g., economically, environmentally; Friedman, 2005). Moreover, the cross-cultural understanding of values and customs of different societies became a key to survival and success (Friedman, 2005). During this time, many university leaders worldwide began to articulate the need for universities to prepare students who would have relevant cultural skills to contribute to the societal needs around the globe (Heppner, Leong, & Chiao, 2008). In short, counseling faculty at many U.S. universities were reinforced to extend their work into international contexts, and communication within the counseling profession began to greatly increase worldwide.

In the late 20th and early 21st centuries, more authors who were also actively involved in the U.S. multicultural movement articulated the failure of U.S. counseling psychology to incorporate cross-cultural perspectives in their work (e.g., Cheung, 2000; Gerstein & Ægisdóttir, 2005a; Heppner, 2006; Leong & Ponterotto, 2003; Leong & Blustein, 2000; Leung, 2003; Marsella, 1998; Pedersen & Leong, 1997). For example, Cheung (2000) wrote aptly,

> The meaning of counseling may seem obvious to American psychologists. The understanding of its meaning by American clients is assumed. In another cultural context, however, counseling may imply a different nature of relationship to both the provider and the recipient. Counseling needs to be deconstructed in the context of the culture in which it is offered. (p. 124)

Similarly, but more recently, Arnett (2008) argued that American psychology has focused on 5% of the world's population and neglected the other 95%.

In 1997, the incoming editor of *TCP*, P. Paul Heppner, observed that the increased internationalization of the world not only suggested the need for change in the education and training of the next generation of U.S. counseling psychologists but also a shift from viewing the counseling profession in the United States as an insular enterprise to a part of a larger global movement (Heppner, Leong, & Chiao, 2008). After some policy and structural changes (e.g., forum editors and reviewers with cross-cultural sensitivities and well versed in international issues), a number of articles appeared in *TCP* in the next 6 years that more fully articulated a strong rationale for internationalizing U.S. counseling psychology, the pervasiveness of cultural influences across all dimensions of the counseling profession (particularly culturally encapsulated assumptions within the prevailing counseling theories and practices), descriptions and examples of the state of counseling professions in other countries, obstacles and challenges prohibiting change in the profession, and recommendations for internationalizing U.S. counseling psychology (e.g., Cheung, 2000; Heppner, 2006; Leong & Blustein, 2000; Leong & Ponterotto, 2003; McWhirter, 2000; Pedersen & Leong, 1997).

By the first part of the 21st century, therefore, numerous scholars had articulated the need to attend to the cultural context in U.S. counseling psychology and abroad and to be mindful of simply transporting empirical findings and theories from the United States to other countries with a different cultural context (e.g., Cheung, 2000; Leong & Ponterotto, 2003; Heppner, 2006; Leung, 2003; Marsella, 1998; Segall, Lonner, & Berry, 1998). Moreover, the emphasis on the cultural context reiterated and built on similar messages from within the multicultural movement in the United States (Heppner, Leong, & Chiao, 2008). The previous conceptualization of internationalization as "helping" our international colleagues had begun to fade, and a host of scholars were developing qualitatively different cross-national collaborative relations (e.g., Lent, Brown, Nota, & Soresi, 2003; also see Chapters 7 and 8, this volume). A number of training programs launched curriculums aimed at enhancing cross-cultural competencies that were built on the established U.S. multicultural counseling competencies (e.g., Alexander, Kruczek, & Ponterotto, 2005; Friedlander, Carranza, & Guzman, 2002; Heppner & Wang, 2008). These efforts were significant in that not only did they represent some of the earliest formal international education immersion programs but even signified inclusion of cross-cultural competencies into the cultural education of future counseling professionals.

In addition, it is only in the last decade that there has been some increase in the number of publications, including international topics and samples of counseling outside the United States (e.g., Gerstein & Ægisdóttir, 2005a, 2005b, 2007; Heppner, 2006; Heppner, Leong, & Gerstein, 2008; Kwan & Gerstein, 2008; Leong & Blustein, 2000; Leong & Ponterotto, 2003; Leong & Savickas, 2007; Pedersen, Draguns, Lonner, & Trimble, 2008; Ægisdóttir & Gerstein, 2005). Even though the counseling field has seen an increased interest in international topics, publications on international samples in contemporary journals appear at an alarmingly low rate. For instance, Gerstein and Ægisdóttir (2007) found that international topics only accounted for about 6% of publications between the years 2000 and 2004 in four U.S. counseling journals.

The 21st century also witnessed an increasing number of counseling psychologists with different types of cross-national experiences. For instance, 112 counseling psychologists received 127 Fulbright Senior Scholar grants across 77 universities in 45 countries (McWhirter & McWhirter, 2009), more counseling psychologists had work-related experiences abroad, and the number of international students receiving graduate degrees in counseling from U.S. training programs also began to increase (see Heppner, 2006). Additionally, by 2005, 152 international counseling and student development specialties from 40 countries had participated in the Minnesota International Counseling Institute (Skovholt, Hansen, Goh, Romano, & Thomas, 2005).

In 2002 in Singapore, F. Leong, M. Savickas, P. Pedersen, I. Gati, and R. Young spearheaded the beginning of Division 16 (Counseling Psychology) in the International Association of Applied Psychology, marking the advent of a global counseling psychology organization within applied psychology.

Furthermore, in 2003, L. Douce, as president of the APA Society of Counseling Psychology, chose globalization as her presidential theme. In 2 of the next 3 years, the succeeding presidents of the Society (P. Heppner and R. Nutt) also had a significant focus on international issues (see Heppner, Leong, & Chiao, 2008). In 2008, President L. Forrest organized the first International Conference on Counseling Psychology, which was held in Chicago, Illinois. This conference underscored the importance of understanding the role of culture, having respect for the international professional community, and promoting international collaboration as key processes of internationalization.

Other organizations also hosted international conferences for the first time. For example, in 2003, the Society of Vocational Psychology, a section within APA Division 17, held its first international conference in Coimbra, Portugal, followed by another in Canada 2 years later. Additionally, the Association for University and College Counseling Center Directors (AUCCCD) started to internationalize its work in counseling centers (see Heppner, Leong, & Chiao, 2008). Moreover, in 2004, the APA approved the Resolution on Culture and Gender Awareness in International Psychology, which was similar to the APA multicultural guidelines (APA, 2003) but different in that it focused on international aspects of psychology. This resolution called for the development of a multicultural mind-set and the need to increase cross-cultural competencies in international psychology. In short, at the beginning of the 21st century, major counseling psychology professional organizations and the APA began to internationalize their focus and establish structures in their organizations to promote greater international collaboration.

At the same time, the counseling profession was growing rapidly around the globe. Subsequently, numerous descriptions of the history and current status of counseling professions in a wide array of countries were published, such as Gerstein and Ægisdóttir (2005a, 2005b), Leong and Savickas (2007), and Heppner, Leong, and Gerstein (2008). These and additional international articles published in *TCP* and other U.S. journals significantly increased the amount of information available about the state of the counseling profession around the world (Heppner, Leong, & Gerstein, 2008). In brief, the counseling profession was vigorously growing worldwide at the beginning of the 21st century, with different identities, various training, accreditation, and credentialing standards, and a wide array of professional service delivery models to address a broad range of societal needs across diverse cultures. In essence, not only was the counseling profession active worldwide, there were also systematic efforts to promote collaboration among counseling professionals across countries (Heppner, Leong, & Chiao, 2008; Heppner, Leong, & Gerstein, 2008).

Uneasy Tensions Between the Multicultural and Cross-National Movements

Although there are many commonalities in the U.S. multicultural and cross-national movements, there have been points of divergence and tensions between these two approaches that are important to discuss. To some extent, the tensions are not only mired in definitional issues of the terms tied to these movements but also complicated by definitions that have changed over time (see Chapter 1, this volume). In this section, we will refer to the broader multicultural movements in education as well as the larger profession of psychology. In addition, we will also refer to the smaller multicultural counseling movement as well as the cross-national movement in counseling; the former has undoubtedly contributed to the establishment of the foundation and greatly affected the conceptualization of the cultural framework of the latter in the United States. Moreover, both the multicultural and cross-national movements in the U.S. counseling profession have been influenced by the larger multicultural movements in education and psychology.

Historically, the broad U.S. multicultural education movement emerged from the civil rights movement of the 1960s and 1970s, and it was motivated by social justice and equality (Banks, 2004; Olson et al., 2007). Similarly, although the larger multicultural psychology movement (as well as the multicultural counseling movement) has expanded to include a variety of socio-demographic populations, it also began as a movement to incorporate principles of race, racism, and ethnic culture into the psychological literature (including the counseling literature). It was primarily a movement instigated by people of color (Helms, Henze, Mascher, & Satiani, 2005; Miville, 2008). Moreover, multicultural psychology and counseling focused on what the U.S. scholars were not doing well and critiqued the existing mono-cultural theories and counseling frameworks and in a way was operating from a position of lower power.

Conversely, the U.S. cross-national movement in counseling initially focused on transporting U.S. counseling psychology to other countries in the 1950s and 1960s (e.g., establishing U.S.-based counseling models in Japan). Thus, the movement started with what Western psychologists did well and could offer to other countries; thus, the early cross-national counseling psychologists operated from positions of power, which is often the case today (see Chapters 7 and 8 of this volume for additional discussions on this issue). Isolated concerns were expressed over the homogeneous exportation of this knowledge and values to other countries with varying degrees of cultural dissimilarity (see Wrenn, 1962, and Chapter 1 of this volume). At this time, there was little connection with and little influence from the larger cross-cultural psychology movement. In the last two decades, the cross-national movement has been influenced by the need to address the growing interrelatedness across the globe (Olson et al., 2007), and been motivated primarily by the need to learn more about different cultures around the world. More recently, grounded in part in the U.S. multicultural counseling movement, the cross-national movement has also focused on the quest to promote the development of culturally contextual knowledge bases in the counseling profession. Initially, the majority of the scholars in the U.S. cross-national movement in counseling had been white, but this is increasingly less so. Pedersen (2003) observed that the motivation for studying cultural similarities and differences has over time evolved from a defense of colonization to a demonstration of political activism, to the development of affirmative action and/or the justification of elitism, toward a more interdependent global perspective.

Historically, there has been a tendency to view the larger U.S. multicultural psychology and cross-cultural psychology as separate approaches with little overlap. The historical backgrounds, motivations, and often differing worldviews of these approaches have played a role in some of the tension between these two movements. Conversely, at this time, the U.S. multicultural counseling movement and the cross-national movement in the counseling profession share more commonalities, particularly a similar focus on examining the cultural context, and an emphasis on cultural complexities within counseling. Yet some of the old tensions between these movements still remain. We focus briefly on three areas of tension: (1) omissions and ambiguities related to the lack of integration of multicultural counseling into the cross-national movement in counseling, (2) applications of methodologies within U.S. psychology to non-dominant racial and cultural groups, and (3) implications arising from resource limitations.

Omissions and Ambiguities

One source of tension has been the lack of recognition and integration of the larger multicultural psychology movement with the cross-cultural psychology movement and to a lesser extent the movements within the U.S. multicultural counseling with cross-national approaches in counseling. Previously, when psychologists (mostly non-minority) discussed internationalizing psychology or had been rewarded for their efforts to internationalize psychology, one rarely found references to the growing body of literature that has given race and ethnic culture a place in U.S. American psychology (e.g., Kaslow, 2000).

Multicultural psychology, as discussed in the APA multicultural guidelines (APA, 2003), pertains primarily to the effects of race, racism, ethnic culture, and/or xenophobia on psychological constructs (e.g., attitudes, psychological processes, behaviors). Additional aspects of human diversity, including gender, social class, and sexual orientation, are covered in other APA guidelines or position papers. The effects of race and ethnic culture have been studied, discovered, and used as the basis of interventions in primarily U.S. American minority psychology. Helms and Richardson (1997), for instance, contended that the term *multiculturalism* shifts psychologists' focus from the power dynamics associated with the sociopolitical constructs of race and racism to less emotionally laden socio-demographic categories, such as socioeconomic status. There is also the concern that the power dynamics of racism may become even more problematic as psychologists attempt to internationalize psychology because it may be wrongly assumed that oppression of ethnic minorities and/or immigrant groups is not racism.

In addition, prior to the diversification of U.S. psychology, the tendency was to study white (i.e., dominant group) people's reactions to people of color and/or to use white Americans as the normalcy standard against which the minority-status groups were compared as a means of quantifying the minorities' levels of abnormality. Thus, research that focused primarily on anti-black racism reflected this first tendency, and the "deficit model," reflected in concepts such as the "achievement gap," reflected the other. The parallel, especially in cross-cultural psychology, is evident in the study of dominant or host groups' biases toward immigrant groups and the use of host cultures to define appropriate behavioral standards for the so-called immigrant groups.

Although it is the case that U.S. psychology has not incorporated multicultural principles as fully as it should, there are now enough multicultural scholars to make it harder to ignore the effects of racial/cultural discrimination and biases on victims as well as beneficiaries of these societal dynamics. However, a concern is that as psychologists engaged in the U.S. exportation of psychology to other countries, they will not have the skills to also export the fairness principles of multicultural psychology if they have not been adequately trained in the discipline (Giorgis & Helms, 1978). In short, the concern is that as the concept of multiculturalism has an ambiguous meaning in some quarters of the internationalization efforts, there is a greater danger of imposing dominant cultures onto members of subordinated cultures (see Chapter 4 of this volume for further discussions of concerns about exportation).

Using Methodologies to Impose Cultures

One legacy of cross-cultural psychology is the knowledge regarding the mechanics of translating assessment tools for use across cultures and countries. The concept of cultural equivalence or ensuring that instruments are measuring the same phenomena across countries emanates from cross-cultural psychologists and is an acknowledgment of the importance of addressing cultural factors in research designs (see Chapter 5, this volume). In the past, though, *cultural equivalence* was narrowly defined by U.S. psychologists as being synonymous with linguistic equivalence (American Educational Research Association [AERA], APA, National Council on Measurement in Education, 1999, Chapter 5; Peña, 2007). Therefore, it is the perception of many U.S. minority scholars that this narrow focus on just linguistic equivalence or meaning of constructs, using sophisticated statistical techniques, has resulted in negligence of issues such as bias related to using traditional U.S. methodologies in assessing non-dominant racial and cultural groups within the United States (e.g., Heppner, 2006; Heppner, Leong, & Chiao, 2008; Quintana, Troyano, & Taylor, 2001; Ægisdóttir, Gerstein, & Çinarbaş, 2008). Multicultural theorists in the United States have also been strong advocates for requiring researchers and practitioners to recognize and change the racial/cultural power dynamics in the counseling and psychology research and treatment processes (Helms et al., 2005). Therefore, some multicultural counseling scholars in the United States are concerned that U.S. cross-cultural psychologists will erroneously equate methodological or statistical sophistication with attention to racial/cultural factors and, as a result, wrongly conclude that the latter do not matter. In essence, there has been a history of not recognizing the extent to which U.S. scholars have inappropriately imposed their own racial and cultural socialization perspectives on research participants and not adequately considered the socialization experiences and worldviews of their research participants and clients (also see discussion in Chapter 5, this volume).

Shifting Resources

Historically, calls for inclusion of race in psychology have resulted in emotionally laden reactions, which U.S. psychologists have managed by making race invisible. Helms et al. (2005) reported that most psychology training programs, professional associations, and journals have predominantly white memberships who either have been reluctant to focus on racial matters or do not know how to do so in ways that are respectful of the interracial and/or intercultural dynamics of research participants and those who study them. Mak, Law, Alvidrez, and Perez-Stable (2007) reviewed 379 NIMH-funded clinical trials that were published between 1995 and 2004 and found that racial/ethnic and/or gender analyses could not be conducted in more than half of them. That is, very few financial resources had been allotted to focus on examining the mental health concerns of African American, Latino/Latina American, Asian American, and Asian American/Pacific Islander (ALANA) populations.

Some U.S. scholars within the larger multicultural psychology and multicultural counseling movements are concerned that the burgeoning focus on international populations threatens to remove even these limited resources from native U.S. minority-status populations. Such diminished resources might not only be limited to financial resources but may also include access to psychological education as well. It is already the case that students born in other countries outnumber their ALANA counterparts in U.S. colleges and universities. As the focus of educational systems shifts to active recruitment of international students, and affirmative action programs in the United States disappear, so may a multicultural psychology that is relevant to the life circumstances of native-born ALANA populations. In short, some scholars are concerned that the limited resources available for enriching multicultural psychology and multicultural counseling in the United States are rapidly being shifted to internationalizing initiatives in psychology and counseling in a manner that denies the existence of race and culture as important aspects of how people function worldwide.

In sum, the tensions and concerns between scholars in both the U.S. multicultural psychology and cross-cultural psychology movements, as well as between U.S. scholars in the multicultural and cross-national counseling movements, deserve examination and discussion. It is important to address these concerns and to disentangle the foci of different psychology groups involved in cross-national activities (e.g., cross-cultural psychology, cultural psychology, and the U.S. cross-national movement in the counseling profession). Much more examination and understanding of the tensions is needed to move the profession toward a more integrated culture-centered approach within the profession. In the next section, we identify many commonalities between the multicultural and cross-national movements in counseling and the larger discipline of psychology and suggest complementary roles of these two schools of thought.

A Complementary Role to Promote Culturally Sensitive Research, Training, and Practice

Although there may be different perspectives about the definitions, foci, and constructs associated with multicultural psychology, multicultural counseling, cross-cultural psychology, and the more recent cross-national movement in counseling, there also are many important areas of convergence. What follows is a discussion of the complementary roles of the U.S. multicultural and cross-national movements within the counseling profession (see Heppner, Leong, & Chiao, 2008) and of how such integration may enhance culturally sensitive research, practice, and training in the counseling field.

Both the U.S. multicultural and cross-national schools of thought in counseling focus on understanding human behavior in the cultural context and strive to make the important role of culture more visible and transparent across a wide range of behaviors. These range from help seeking, counseling theory, and the counseling process, to issues related to language, power, and privilege. Thus, both movements focus on behaviors and psychological processes within a larger environmental context. Moreover, the importance of a person's worldview is emphasized and, relatedly one's ability to understand others from different cultures. Therefore, both movements are concerned with issues of cultural bias and ethnocentrism (e.g., Cheung, 2000; Leong & Blustein, 2000; Norsworthy, 2006). For example, many U.S. multicultural scholars have discussed cultural biases in the counseling process (e.g., ethnocentric counseling theories) and in testing (Sue & Sue, 2008). Scholars in both movements strive to reduce bigotry and stereotyping in counseling theory, research, and practice, and promote a core value of appreciating differences, and the assumption that being different does not imply being "less than" or "inferior" but simply being different. In fact, differences are not only to be tolerated but valued and celebrated.

Also shared by the multicultural and cross-national movements is a developmental perspective in conceptualizing behavior and psychological processes, such that starting at an early age, one learns to view his or her world in a socially constructed manner. For instance, it is understood that individuals can learn and internalize a racist or sexist worldview; moreover, biases, stereotypes, and prejudices can be unlearned over time. Thus, both schools promote the value of intercultural learning (see Olson et al., 2007). Specifically, both movements have emphasized the necessity of increasing one's awareness and knowledge of one's own values, cultural socialization processes, and worldview, as well as greater knowledge of others who have different worldviews and experiences. Moreover, both movements have emphasized the utility of a host of culturally sensitive skills, particularly interpersonal skills, to enhance and improve inter-group communication and the ability to interact appropriately, comfortably, and effectively with individuals from different cultural groups. Both schools of thought, therefore, insist that cultural competencies be articulated and synthesized into U.S. counseling training programs and the respective ethical codes (e.g., Heppner, Leong, & Chiao, 2008; Heppner, Leong, & Gerstein, 2008; Marsella & Pedersen, 2004; Pedersen, 2007; Ægisdóttir & Gerstein, 2010).

In essence, there seems to be a great deal of commonality between the foci of the U.S. multicultural and cross-national movements within the counseling profession. Because of the growing appreciation in the United States of cultural contexts in shaping individuals' behavior and psychological processes, there is an immense possibility for these two areas of inquiry, or schools of thought, to inform each other. We will briefly discuss how the common goals of U.S. multicultural movement and cross-national movement in counseling cannot only complement each other but also have a bidirectional influence on each other in theory, research, practice, and training.

Training

There are very significant needs to train the next generation of counseling professionals to be culturally competent not only with diverse U.S. populations (including international populations) but also with populations around the world (see Ponterotto et al., 1995, 2001; Sue & Sue, 2008). Moreover, there is a growing need to train culturally competent scholars to cross boundaries and collaborate with colleagues from other countries. In essence, the common training focus on behavior as an act-in-context not only suggests an opportunity to collaborate across these two schools of thought but also potentially to enhance cultural training outcomes by exposing counseling students to both multicultural and cross-cultural training strategies (see Heppner, Leong, & Chiao, 2008).

Although great strides have been made in multicultural training, Constantine et al. (2008) indicated that there remain a number of questions about the effectiveness of multicultural training. The challenge is not only how to define and assess multicultural competencies (see Constantine et al., 2008) but also how to promote it in the next generations of counselors. Based on some of the literature on multicultural and cross-cultural training experiences, there seems to be a synergistic effect on trainee cultural competencies when students receive training aimed at both multicultural and cross-cultural competencies. For example, there is some evidence within the multicultural training literature that exposure may be an important activity to reduce ethnocentric worldviews (Kiselica, 1998). Similarly, research on study abroad and immersion programs, even less than 4 weeks in duration, has suggested that such programs can have powerful effects on students, most notably leading to further engagement in cross-cultural experiences (see Fischer, 2009). Other data indicate that brief but intense cross-cultural immersion programs deepen cultural awareness and enhance cultural sensitivities, as well as broaden participants' worldviews (Chien et al., 2008; Huang et al., 2008). Two- to four-week immersion programs, for instance, with multiple contacts of extended duration each day may provide students with an opportunity to explore more deeply a new cultural context, especially within cross-cultural interpersonal relationships. Furthermore, such intense immersions may deepen students' sensitivity to the cultural context in new or different ways compared with studying various multicultural issues while in their home culture. And, more important, it is highly possible that the previous multicultural competencies and mind-set of students allow them to benefit maximally from such cross-cultural immersion. To further explore the effect of such cultural immersion experiences, qualitative methodologies and single-subject methodologies may be useful. Such research strategies may not only provide a richer understanding of the impact of different types of cultural training but may also provide information about the additive and cumulative effects of different training activities over time. Marsella and Pedersen (2004) and Ægisdóttir and Gerstein (2010) suggested a wide array of international education activities that could be examined and compared with the various multicultural training approaches currently in use in U.S. counseling training programs.

Research

There is no doubt that counseling research programs conducted on U.S. multicultural populations and populations in other countries may inform one another. For example, a legacy that multicultural counseling theorists, researchers, and practitioners have contributed to psychology is the alternative paradigms for conceptualizing racial and cultural factors (Pedersen, Crethar, & Carlson, 2008). In particular, the focus on replacing socio-demographic categories (e.g., race) with psychological racial (e.g., racial identity) and ethnic cultural (e.g., cultural values) constructs and related variables has been a major contribution of multicultural psychology and multicultural counseling. Such contributions have many implications for how minority-status groups are studied in other cultural contexts by international colleagues or cross-national researchers in the counseling profession. Conversely, the research on nationalists (non-U.S.) living in other countries where they are not socially oppressed based on race may provide additional insight into how culture can shape non-racist behavior, as well as how social oppression operates in harming its victims.

Another example pertains to two closely related topics, applied problem solving and coping (e.g., Folkman & Moskowitz, 2004; Heppner, Witty, & Dixon, 2004; Somerfield & McCrae, 2000). Overall, U.S. scholars have added greatly to this line of research over the years. However, Heppner (2008) maintained that U.S. scholars have tended to approach coping and applied problem solving in a culture-blind manner, overlooking or ignoring the cultural context in most of the research studies in this area. This omission is serious because the cultural context affects all aspects of applied problem solving and coping (see Heppner, 2008). As a result, the existing body of literature on this topic does not tell the whole story but rather has greatly oversimplified the many complexities and nuances within coping across different U.S. cultural groups. When a coping inventory was developed based on Asian values and theories, very different factors emerged that were not included in U.S. coping inventories (see Heppner et al., 2006). These Asian-based findings might provide useful information for future investigations aimed at understanding Asian American coping strategies. For example, the unique cultural strategies found in Taiwan will provide more valid information about coping among other U.S. cultural groups that adhere to collectiv-istic values and customs. Similarly, research findings on the racial stress of African Americans (Utsey & Ponterotto, 1996) might be applicable to other cultural groups in countries outside the United States. Moreover, conducting culturally sensitive research not only in the United States but in many cultures and countries will greatly expand the depth and richness of the counseling and psychology knowledge base and may further stimulate the development of theoretical models that more accurately depict how people respond to stressful life events around the world (Heppner, 2008).

In short, U.S.-based multicultural research and cross-national research that examines human behavior across different cultural contexts has the potential to expand our conceptualizations of psychological processes and their interaction with culture (e.g., ethnic identity, racial identity, self-construal, applied problem solving and coping). Therefore, integrating research findings found in the United States and abroad has a great poten-tial to broaden our current understanding of how culture affects individu-als' behavior and psychological processes. Moreover, as researchers across the globe become aware of each others' research interests and activities, more cross-national collaboration may occur. This will greatly enhance counseling research around the world.

Practice

There are also many ways in which the intersection of the U.S. mul-ticultural movement and cross-national movements in counseling can enhance counseling practice. For example, the aim of the APA multicul-tural guidelines has been to promote culturally sensitive practice (as well as education, training, and research) in counseling minority populations in the United States (APA, 2003; Arredondo et al., 1996; Sue et al., 1992). The underlying principles included (a) studying and valuing the social-ization processes of people in their cultural contexts, (b) examining the adverse effects of minority status on individuals (i.e., power dynamics), and (c) recognizing that studying and providing services to people belonging to minority cultural groups requires an understanding of the counseling professional's own racial and cultural dynamics. These principles are the foundation of an array of multicultural counseling competency guidelines. These guidelines for culturally sensitive counseling services (and research) in the United States may also be useful in counseling a cross-national clientele. An asset of multicultural counseling is that if psychologists learn how to apply its principles properly, multicultural counseling can potentially diversify counseling worldwide and thereby reveal unacknowledged strengths of disenfranchised populations while alleviating the psychological damage caused by racism and xenophobia. In essence, because all behaviors are learned and displayed in a cultural context (e.g., African Americans or international students studying within the United States, a Hakka woman in Taiwan), it is essential that all those in the counseling professions accurately understand the cultural context with which they are engaged.

Moreover, "If practitioners are to understand traditional African Americans, Chinese Americans, Japanese Americans, and Mexican Americans, they must first understand traditional Africans, Chinese, Japanese, and Mexican cultures" (Henderson, Spigner-Littles, & Milhouse, 2006, p. vii). For instance, research on Asians' experiences in Asia may enhance the understanding of the cultural adjustment of Asians in the United States; their behaviors can be understood in relation to cultural socialization in both cultures. Such inquiry may help researchers understand the processes of cultural preservation and acculturation of ethnic minorities in the United States. It may also provide information about the existence and consequences of cultural value shifts among Asians in Asia, which have been occurring in recent years in many Asian countries as the result of exposure to Western cultures. Similarly, if practitioners in South Korea are to understand U.S. expatriates, they must also understand the U.S. cultural contexts from where their ex-pat clients were socialized.

In sum, there is a great deal of potential for the U.S. multicultural and cross-national movements in counseling to enrich one another. These two schools of thought have many common goals. A concerted collaboration between these two movements can enhance the sophistication of counseling research worldwide, expand the complexities of current knowledge and theoretical models, increase the range of counseling interventions, and, in essence, enhance counseling effectiveness across a range of populations in the United States and beyond.

Despite the benefits just mentioned, there are also some limitations in the cross-fertilization of U.S. multicultural and cross-national movements in counseling. Leung and Chen (in press) identified three limitations in applying U.S. multicultural counseling internationally. They argued that, first, U.S. multicultural counseling is founded on the ideals, principles, and philosophical beliefs behind the U.S. political and social system. These include the definitions of social justice, equality, cultural democracy, and human rights, which are often highly culturally laden. Multiculturalism in the United States has been associated with many politically charged terms such as *affirmative action, quotas, civil rights, discrimination, reverse discrimination, racism, sexism,* and *political correctness* (Smith, 2004; Sue et al., 1998). These are unique terms with meanings and implications derived from racial relationships in the United States and the history of its social and political system. Leung and Chen (in press) maintained that the U.S.-based multicultural counseling literature should not be "exported" to other countries without modification and contextual adaptation. The principles (e.g., equality, justice) behind multicultural counseling might be universal, yet the meaning, operational definitions, and timing and pace of implementation of these principles may vary across cultures and contexts. Leung and Chen (in press) suggested that, second, multicultural counseling in the United States explored populations and issues that are specific to the U.S. contexts. It focused mostly on ethnic and cultural groups in the United States, such as African Americans, Hispanics, Asian Americans, and Native American Indians, and on the cultural and political dynamics triggered by majority-minority relationships. As such, multicultural counseling does not address issues that are salient to ethnic groups and cultural minorities in regions around the world who might have a different majority-minority relationship history. Leung and Chen (in press) observed that, moreover, research studies on multicultural counseling have focused mostly on samples in the United States and very few research studies published in U.S. journals employed international samples (Arnett, 2008; Ægisdóttir et al., 2008). Hence, findings and conceptualization derived from these studies have limited generalization to different ethnic and cultural groups around the world. Finally, studies on U.S. samples (minority and majority groups), the research questions examined, the theories tested and developed, and the methods used are highly grounded in the U.S. cultural context and worldview. Similarly, the social and political reality in other countries needs to be considered in understanding psychological processes.

Conclusion

Multicultural and cross-national foci in the counseling profession have similar core values, and there is substantial overlap between the two areas of inquiry in both theory and practice—most notably understanding behavior within cultural contexts. Not surprisingly, many scholars in the counseling profession have participated in both movements. As Pedersen observed, "Each of us is guided by our own 1,000 cultural teachers, some domestic and some from other countries" (personal communication, February 26, 2009). Therefore, scholars have called for "culturally informed counseling" (Pedersen, 2008). The focus tying these two perspectives together is not only an increased understanding of cultural differences but also valuing cultural differences and diversity. Moreover, both approaches emphasize the need for intercultural learning and the necessity of cultural competencies of counseling researchers, trainers, and practitioners. We contend that the differences that exist between the two perspectives should be viewed as mutually enriching and complementary rather than evidence of rivalry. It is neither desirable nor possible for one movement to replace the other. Yet it is important to not ignore the tensions between these two movements but rather continue this dialogue to promote greater integration and extension of the many important views and conceptualizations emerging from these two perspectives about how culture affects individual functioning around the world.

A significant challenge with integrating the U.S. multicultural and cross-national movements in the counseling profession involves changing definitions of what we do and the introduction of new terms over time as well as a broad array of differing perspectives on culture and its influence (see Pedersen, 2003). Pedersen (2008) suggested that ultimately, counseling and psychology theories require an understanding of every behavior in the cultural context in which that behavior was learned and displayed. Thus, the ultimate objective of culture-centered counseling is accuracy. This includes not only an accurate assessment, meaningful understanding, and appropriate interventions for our clients but also an acknowledgment of the culturally learned assumptions of oneself as a counselor and the assumptions on which counseling is based (Pedersen, 2008). Both the U.S. multicultural counseling movement and a culture-focused cross-national movement can promote progress toward this end. Together, the counseling profession has a much better chance of being successful.

Chapter Questions

1. What are the most important take-away messages you learned about the intersection of multicultural and cross-national movements in the United States?

2. Describe how you might integrate all the cultural and cross-national approaches in your future work (e.g., research, practice, training) to promote cultural awareness in our profession.

3. What are potential advantages and disadvantages of including both multicultural and cross-national approaches in the work of counselors and counseling psychologists? Do you think the advantages outweigh the disadvantages? Why or why not?

4. List and compare the differences and similarities of the U.S. multicultural and cross-national movements. What do you see as the most significant differences and similarities?

References

Alexander, C. M., Kruczek, T., & Ponterotto, J. G. (2005). Building multicultural competencies in school counselor trainees: An immersion experience. *Counselor Education and Supervision, 44,* 255–266.

American Educational Research Association, American Psychological Association, National Council on Measurement. (1999). *Standards for educational and psychological testing.* Washington, DC: American Educational Research Association.

American Psychological Association. (1991). *Guidelines for providers of psychological services to ethnic, linguistic, and culturally diverse populations.* Washington, DC: Author.

American Psychological Association. (1993). Guidelines for providers of psychological services to ethnic, linguistic, and culturally diverse populations. *American Psychologists, 48,* 45–48.

American Psychological Association. (2003). Guidelines on multicultural education, training, research, practice, and organizational change for psychologists. *American Psychologist, 58,* 377–402.

Ardila, R. (1993). Latin American psychology and world psychology. In U. Kim & J. Berry (Eds.), *Indigenous psychologies* (pp. 170–176). Newbury Park, CA: Sage.

Arnett, J. J. (2008). The neglected 95%: Why American psychology needs to become less American. *American Psychologist, 63,* 602–614.

Arredondo, P., Toprek, R., Brown, S. P., Jones, J., Locke, D. C., Sanchez, J., et al. (1996). Operationalization of the multicultural counseling competencies. *Journal of Multicultural Counseling and Development, 24,* 42–78.

Atkinson, D. R., & Thompson, C. E. (1992). Racial, ethnic and cultural variables in counseling. In S. D. Brown & R. W. Lent (Eds.), *Handbook of counseling psychology* (pp. 349–382). New York: Wiley.

Aubrey, R. F. (1977). Historical development of guidance and counseling and implications for the future. *Personnel and Guidance Journal, 55,* 288–295.

Banks, J. A. (2004). Multicultural education: Historical development, dimensions, and practice. In J. A. Banks & C. A. McGee Banks (Eds.), *Handbook of research on multicultural education* (pp. 3–29). San Francisco: Jossey-Bass.

Betz, N., & Fitzgerald, L. F. (1993). Individuality and diversity: Theory and research in counseling psychology. *Annual Review of Psychology, 44,* 343–381.

Casas, J. M. (1984). Policy, training, and research in counseling psychology: The racial/ethnic minority perspective. In S. D. Brown & R. W. Lent (Eds.), *Handbook of counseling psychology* (pp. 785–831). New York: Wiley.

Cheung, F. M. (2000). Deconstructing counseling in a cultural context. *The Counseling Psychologist, 28,* 123–132.

Chien, W.-Y., Chou, L.-C., Lai, P.-H., Lee, Y.-H., Chen, C.-L., Ting, S.-H., et al. (2008, August). The benefits and challenges of being the BCCIP visitors. In P. P. Heppner & L.-F. Wang (Cochairs), *Multiple benefits of a bidirectional cross-cultural immersion program.* Symposium presented at the annual meeting of the American Psychological Association, Boston, MA.

Constantine, M. G., Miville, M. L., & Kindaichi, M. M. (2008). Multicultural competence in counseling psychology practice and training. In S. D. Brown & R. W. Lent (Eds.), *Handbook of counseling psychology* (pp. 141–158). Hoboken, NJ: Wiley.

Fischer, K. (2009, March 6). Study Abroad directors adjust programs in response to recession. *Chronicle of Higher Education,* pp. 25–26.

Folkman, S., & Moskowitz, J. T. (2004). Coping: Pitfalls and promise. *Annual Review of Psychology, 55,* 745–774.

Friedlander, M. L., Carranza, V. E., & Guzman, M. (2002). International exchanges in family therapy: Training, research, and practice in Spain and United States. *The Counseling Psychologist, 30,* 314–329.

Friedman, T. L. (2005). *The world is flat: A brief history of the twenty-first century.* New York: Farrar, Straus, & Giroux.

Gerstein, L. H., & Ægisdóttir, S. (Guest Eds.) (2005a). Counseling around the world [Special issue]. *Journal of Mental Health Counseling, 27,* 95–184.

Gerstein, L. H., & Ægisdóttir, S. (2005b). Counseling outside of the United States: Looking in and reaching out. *Journal of Mental Health Counseling, 27,* 221–281.

Gerstein, L. H., & Ægisdóttir, S. (2007). Training international social change agents: Transcending a U.S. counseling paradigm. *Counselor Education and Supervision, 47,* 123–139.

Giorgis, T. W., & Helms, J. E. (1978). Training international students from developing nations as psychologists: A challenge for American psychology. *American Psychologist, 33,* 945–951.

Guthrie, R. V. (1998). *Evan the rat was white: A historical view of psychology.* Needham Heights, MA: Allyn & Bacon.

Hedlund, D. E. (1988). Counseling psychology and the Zambian Fulbright program. *The Counseling Psychologist, 16,* 288–292.

Helms, J. E., Henze, K. T., Mascher, J., & Satiani, A. (2005). Ethical issues when white researchers study ALANA and immigrant people and communities. In J. E. Trimble & C. Fisher (Eds.), *Handbook of ethical research with ethno-cultural populations and communities* (pp. 299–324). Thousand Oaks, CA: Sage.

Helms, J. E., & Richardson, T. Q. (1997). How multiculturalism obscures race and culture as differential aspects of counseling competency. In H. Coleman & D. Pope-Davis (Eds.), *Multicultural counseling competencies* (pp. 60–79). Thousand Oaks, CA: Sage.

Henderson, G., Spigner-Littles, D., & Milhouse, V. H. (2006). *A practitioner's guide to understanding indigenous and foreign cultures.* Springfield, IL: Charles C Thomas.

Heppner, P. P. (1988). Cross-cultural outcomes of a research Fulbright in Sweden. *The Counseling Psychologist, 16,* 297–302.

Heppner, P. P. (1997). Building on strengths as we move into the next millennium. *The Counseling Psychologist, 25,* 5–14.

Heppner, P. P. (2006). The benefits and challenges of becoming cross-culturally competent counseling psychologists. *The Counseling Psychologist, 34,* 147–172.

Heppner, P. P. (2008). Expanding the conceptualization and measurement of applied problem solving and coping: From stages to dimensions to the almost forgotten cultural context. *American Psychologist, 63,* 803–816.

Heppner, P. P., Casas, J. M., Carter, J., & Stone, G. L. (2000). The maturation of counseling psychology: Multifaceted perspectives, 1978–1998. In S. D. Brown & R. W. Lent (Eds.), *Handbook of counseling psychology* (pp. 3–49). New York: Wiley.

Heppner, P. P., Heppner, M. J., Lee, D.-G., Wang, Y.-W., Park, H.-J., & Wang, L.-F. (2006). Development and validation of a collectivistic coping styles inventory. *Journal of Counseling Psychology, 53,* 107–125.

Heppner, P. P., Leong, F. T. L., & Chiao, H. (2008). The growing internationalization of counseling psychology. In S. D. Brown & R. W. Lent (Eds.), *Handbook of counseling psychology* (pp. 68–85). New York: Wiley.

Heppner, P. P., Leong, F. T. L., & Gerstein, L. H. (2008). Counseling within a changing world: Meeting the psychological needs of societies and the world. In W. B. Walsh (Ed.), *Biennial review in counseling psychology* (pp. 231–258). Thousand Oaks, CA: Sage.

Heppner, P. P., & Wang, L.-F. (2008, March). *The multiple benefits of a bidirectional cross-cultural immersion program.* Invited pre-conference presentation at the International Counseling Psychology Conference, "Creating the Future: Counseling Psychologists in a Changing World," Chicago, IL.

Heppner, P. P., Witty, T. E., & Dixon, W. A. (2004). Problem-solving appraisal and human adjustment: A review of 20 years of research utilizing the Problem Solving Inventory. *The Counseling Psychologist, 32,* 344–428.

Hoyt, K. B. (1967). Attaining the promise of guidance for all. *Personnel and Guidance Journal, 45,* 624–630.

Huang, P.-C., Chao, J.-C., Chou, Y.-C., Chang, Y.-P., Chu, S.-Y., & Wang, L.-F. (2008, August). Cross-cultural competence development of the BCCIP. In P. P. Heppner & L.-F. Wang (Cochairs), *Multiple benefits of a bidirectional cross-cultural immersion program.* Symposium presented at the annual meeting of the American Psychological Association, Boston, MA.

Jackson, M. L. (1995). Multicultural counseling: Historical perspectives. In J. G. Ponterotto, J. M. Casas, L. A. Suzuki, & C. M. Alexander (Eds.), *Handbook of multicultural counseling* (pp. 3–16). Thousand Oaks, CA: Sage.

Kaslow, F. W. (2000). Establishing linkages through international psychology: Dealing with universalities and uniquenesses. *American Psychologist, 55,* 1377–1388.

Kiselica, M. S. (1998). Preparing Anglos for the challenges and joys of multiculturalism. *The Counseling Psychologist, 26,* 5–21.

Korman, M. (1974). National conference on levels and patterns of professional training in psychology: The major themes. *American Psychologist, 29,* 441–449.

Kwan, K.-L. K., & Gerstein, L. H. (2008). Envisioning a counseling psychology of the world: The mission of the International Forum. *The Counseling Psychologist, 36,* 182–187.

Lent, R. W., Brown, S. D., Nota, L., & Soresi, S. (2003). Testing social cognitive interest and choice hypotheses across Holland types in Italian high school students. *Journal of Vocational Behavior, 62,* 101–118.

Leong, F. T. L., & Blustein, D. L. (2000). Toward a global vision of counseling psychology. *The Counseling Psychologist, 28,* 5–9.

Leong, F. T. L., & Ponterotto, J. G. (2003). A proposal for internationalizing counseling psychology in the United States: Rationale, recommendations, and challenges. *The Counseling Psychologist, 31,* 381–395.

Leong, F. T. L., & Savickas, M. L. (2007). Introduction to special issue on international perspectives on counseling psychology. *Applied Psychology: An International Review, 56,* 1–6.

Leung, S. A. (2003). A journey worth traveling: Globalization of counseling psychology. *The Counseling Psychologist, 31,* 412–419.

Leung, S. A., & Chen, P.-W. (in press). Developing counseling psychology in Chinese communities in Asia: Indigenous, multicultural, and cross-cultural considerations. *The Counseling Psychologist.*

Liu, R. M., & Ali, S. R. (2008). Social class and classism: Understanding the psychological impact of poverty and inequality. In S. D. Brown & R. W. Lent (Eds.), *Handbook of counseling psychology* (pp. 159–175). Hoboken, NJ: Wiley.

Mak, W. W. S., Law, R. W., Alvidrez, J., & Perez-Stable, E. J. (2007). Gender and ethnic diversity in NIMH funded clinical trials: Review of a decade of published research. *Administration and Policy in Mental Health and Mental Health Services Research, 34,* 497–503.

Marsella, A. J. (1998). Toward a "global-community psychology": Meeting the needs of a changing world. *American Psychologist, 53,* 1282–1291.

Marsella, A. J., & Pedersen, P. B. (2004). Internationalizing the counseling psychology curriculum: Toward new values, competencies, and directions. *Counseling Psychology Quarterly, 17,* 413–423.

McWhirter, J. J. (1988). The Fulbright program in counseling psychology. *The Counseling Psychologist, 16,* 279–281.

McWhirter, J. J. (2000). And now, up go the walls: Constructing an international room for counseling psychology. *The Counseling Psychologist, 28,* 117–122.

McWhirter, P. T., & McWhirter, J. J. (2009). *Historical antecedents: Counseling Psychology and the Fulbright Program.* Unpublished manuscript.

Miville, M. (2008). Race and ethnicity in school counseling. In H. L. K. Coleman & C. Yeh (Eds.), *Handbook of school counseling* (pp. 177–194). New York: Routledge.

Neville, H. A., & Carter, R. T. (2005). Race and racism in counseling psychology research, training, and practice: A critical review, current trends, and future directions. *Counseling Psychologist, 33,* 413–418.

Norsworthy, K. L. (2006). Bringing social justice to international practices of counseling psychology. In R. L. Toporek, L. H. Gerstein, N. A. Fouad, G. Roysircar-Sodowsky, & T. Israel (Eds.), *Handbook for social justice in counseling psychology: Leadership, vision, and action* (pp. 421–441). Thousand Oaks, CA: Sage.

Nugent, F. A. (1988). Counseling psychology and the West German Fulbright program. *The Counseling Psychologist, 16,* 293–296.

Olson, C. L., Evans, R., & Shoenberg, R. F. (2007). *At home in the world: Bridging the gap between internationalization and multicultural education.* Dupont Circle, Washington, DC: American Council on Education.

Pedersen, P., & Leong, F. (1997). Counseling in an international context. *The Counseling Psychologist, 25,* 117–122.

Pedersen, P. B. (1991). Multiculturalism as a generic approach to counseling. *Journal of Counseling & Development, 70,* 6–12.

Pedersen, P. B. (1999a). *Culture-centered counseling interventions: Striving for accuracy.* Thousand Oaks, CA: Sage.

Pedersen, P. B. (Ed.). (1999b). *Multiculturalism as a fourth force.* Philadelphia: Taylor & Francis.

Pedersen, P. B. (Ed.). (1999c). *Multicultural counseling as a fourth force.* Philadelphia: Taylor & Francis.

Pedersen, P. B. (2003). The multicultural context of mental health. In T. B. Smith & P. S. Richards (Eds.), *Practicing multiculturalism* (pp. 17–32). Boston, MA: Allyn & Bacon.

Pedersen, P. B. (2007). Ethics, competence, and professional issues in cross-cultural counseling. In P. B. Pedersen, J. G. Draguns, W. J. Lonner, & J. E. Trimble (Eds.), *Counseling across cultures* (pp. 5–20). Thousand Oaks, CA: Sage.

Pedersen, P. B. (2008). Ethics, competence, and professional issues in cross-cultural counseling. In P. B. Pedersen, J. G. Draguns, W. J. Lonner, & J. E. Trimble (Eds.), *Counseling across cultures* (pp. 5–20). Thousand Oaks, CA: Sage.

Pedersen, P. B., Crethar, H. C., & Carlson, J. (2008). *Inclusive cultural empathy: Making relationships central in counseling and psychotherapy.* Washington, DC: American Psychological Association.

Pedersen, P. B., Draguns, J. G., Lonner, W. L., & Trimble, J. E. (Eds.). (2008). *Counseling across cultures* (6th ed.). Thousand Oaks, CA: Sage.

Peña, E. D. (2007). Lost in translation: Methodological considerations in cross-cultural research. *Child Development, 78,* 1255–1264.

Ponterotto, J. G. (2008). Theoretical and empirical advances in multicultural counseling and psychology. In S. D. Brown & R. W. Lent (Eds.), *Handbook of counseling psychology* (pp. 121–140). Hoboken, NJ: Wiley.

Ponterotto, J. G., Casas, J. M., Suzuki, L. A., & Alexander, C. M. (Eds.). (1995). *Handbook of multicultural counseling.* Thousand Oaks, CA: Sage.

Ponterotto, J. G., Casas, J. M., Suzuki, L. A., & Alexander, C. M. (Eds.). (2001). *Handbook of multicultural counseling.* Thousand Oaks, CA: Sage.

Quintana, S. M., Troyano, N., & Taylor, G. (2001). Cultural validity and inherent challenges in quantitative methods for multicultural research. In J. G. Ponterotto, J. M. Casas, L. A. Suzuki, & C. M. Alexander (Eds.), *Handbook of multicultural counseling* (pp. 604–630). Thousand Oaks, CA: Sage.

Ridley, C. R., & Kleiner, A. J. (2003). Multicultural competence: History, themes, and issues. In D. B. Pope-Davis, H. L. K. Coleman, W. Ming, & R. L. Toporek (Eds.), *Handbook of multicultural competencies in counseling and psychology* (pp. 3–20). Thousand Oaks, CA: Sage.

Robinson, D. T., & Morris, J. R. (2000). Multicultural counseling: Historical context and current training considerations. *Western Journal of Black Studies, 24,* 239–253.

Rothblum, E. D. (2000). Somewhere in Des Moines or San Antonio: Historical perspectives on lesbian, gay, and bisexual health. In R. M. Perez, K. A. DeBord, & K. J. Bieschke (Eds.), *Handbook of counseling and psychotherapy with lesbian, gay, and bisexual clients* (pp. 57–80). Washington, DC: American Psychological Association.

Savickas, M. L. (2007). Internationalization of counseling psychology: Constructing cross-national consensus and collaboration. *Applied Psychology: An International Review, 56,* 182–188.

Segall, M. H., Lonner, W. J., & Berry, J. W. (1998). Cross-cultural psychology as a scholarly discipline: On a flowering of culture in behavioral research. *American Psychologist, 53,* 1101–1110.

Skovholt, T., Hansen, S., Goh, M., Romano, J., & Thomas, K. (2005). The Minnesota International Counseling Institute (MICI) 1989-present: History, joyful moments, and lessons learned. *International Journal for the Advancement of Counseling, 27,* 17–33.

Skovholt, T. M. (1988). Searching for reality. *The Counseling Psychologist, 16,* 282–287.

Smith, T. B. (2004). *Practicing multiculturalism: Affirming diversity in counseling and psychology.* Boston: Allyn & Bacon.

Somerfield, M. R., & McCrae, R. R. (2000). Stress and coping research: Methodological challenges, theoretical advances, and clinical applications. *American Psychologist, 55,* 620–625.

Sue, D. W., Arredondo, P., & McDavis, R. J. (1992). Multicultural counseling competencies and standards: A call to the profession. *Journal of Multicultural Counseling and Development, 20,* 64–88.

Sue, D. W., Bernier, Y., Durran, A., Feinberg, L., Pedersen, P. B., Smith, E. J., et al. (1982). Position paper: Cross-cultural counseling competencies. *The Counseling Psychologist, 10,* 45–52.

Sue, D. W., Carter, R. T., Casas, J. M., Fouad, N. A., Ivey, A. E., Jensen, M., et al. (1998). *Multicultural counseling competencies: Individual and organizational development.* Thousand Oaks, CA: Sage.

Sue, D. W., & Sue, D. (2008). *Counseling the culturally diverse: Theory and practice.* Hoboken, NJ: Wiley.

Sue, S. (1977). Community mental health services to minority groups: Some optimism, some pessimism. *American Psychologist, 32,* 616–624.

Utsey, S. O., & Ponterotto, J. G. (1996). Development and validation of the Index of Race-Related Stress. *Journal of Counseling Psychology, 43,* 490–501.

Vontress, C. E. (1971). Racial differences: Implication to rapport. *Journal of Counseling Psychology, 18,* 7–13.

Warren, A. K., & Constantine, M. G. (2007). Social justice issues. In M. G. Constantine (Ed.), *Clinical practice with people of color* (pp. 231–242). New York: Teachers College Press.

Watkins, C. E., Jr. (1994). On hope, promise, and possibility in counseling psychology or some simple, but meaningful observations about our specialty. *The Counseling Psychologist, 22,* 315–334.

Wrenn, C. G. (1962). The culturally encapsulated counselor. *Harvard Educational Review, 32,* 111–119.

Ægisdóttir, S., & Gerstein, L. H. (2005). Reaching out: Mental health delivery outside the box. *Journal of Mental Health Counseling, 27,* 221–224.

Ægisdóttir, S., & Gerstein, L. H. (2010). International counseling competencies: A new frontier in multi-cultural training. In J. C. Ponterotto, J. M. Casas, L. A. Suzuki, & C. A. Alexander (Eds.), *Handbook of multicultural counseling* (3rd ed., pp. 175–188). Thousand Oaks, CA: Sage.

Ægisdóttir, S., Gerstein, L. H., & Çinarbaş, D. C. (2008). Methodological issues in cross-cultural counseling research: Equivalence, bias, and translations. *The Counseling Psychologist, 36,* 188–219.

Chapter Three

The Counseling Profession In- and Outside the United States

Lawrence H. Gerstein, P. Paul Heppner, Rex Stockton, Frederick T. L. Leong, and Stefanía Ægisdóttir

As will become apparent from this chapter and practically every other chapter in this book, the counseling profession is much larger than any one country (Heppner, 2006). And, contrary to the belief of some, the profession outside the United States is thriving, making important discoveries about human behavior and the science and practice of counseling, and effectively meeting the needs of the clients being served. Furthermore, the counseling profession outside the United States has much to offer professionals in the United States, and it is incumbent on U.S. counselors and counseling psychologists, and for counseling professionals worldwide for that matter, to actively acquire knowledge about the field as it is practiced elsewhere (Heppner, Leong, & Gerstein, 2008).

This chapter begins by discussing the counseling movement in the United States and how it has evolved to embrace an international focus and agenda. Following this, it is argued that the counseling profession is quite vibrant and active in more than one specific country, that is, the United States. Next, the chapter addresses the importance of counselors and counseling psychologists developing a strong cross-cultural sensitivity to effectively perform in diverse cultures and in different countries. The current status of the internationalization of the counseling profession is then discussed. Challenges revolving around defining various important terms and concepts in the field of counseling are covered next. The chapter ends with a presentation of various trends and challenges for counseling professionals worldwide and some recommendations for addressing these challenges.

The Counseling Profession Exists Beyond One Country

In the sense of human beings listening to and assisting one another, counseling has been practiced in some form or another throughout history. It could be associated with a hypothesized genetic predisposition toward altruism. Some writers (e.g., Torrey, 1972) have drawn comparisons between witchdoctors and psychiatrists or psychotherapists. Torrey in his classic book, *The Mind Game: Witchdoctors and Psychiatrists,* argued that these individuals rely on similar philosophies and strategies to help people. That is, these helpers are effective when the persons they assist are instilled with hope, have faith in their provider's talents, believe in the treatment, expect positive outcomes, share the same worldview, and experience a similarity in how the helper cognitively and perceptually approaches the world. While it is true that people from the same culture are more likely to embrace a similar worldview, and cognitive and perceptual style, these factors and the others mentioned by Torrey are all critical in his view to the outcome of a healing relationship, be it with a witchdoctor or a psychiatrist.

Counseling as a formal discipline, however, is now just a hundred years old with the launching of the vocational guidance movement, whereas natural healers or witchdoctors as Torrey called them have been around since ancient times. Beginning in the United States, counseling spread to Great Britain and Europe, and then expanded throughout the world (Stockton, Garbelman, Kaladow, & Terry, 2007). The process of international expansion has been greatly aided through the efforts of national and international organizations dedicated to the helping profession.

Perhaps more than any other individual, Hans Hoxter was responsible for the development of counseling worldwide (Ivey, 2003). He was personally responsible for helping found two international organizations, the International Association of Educational and Vocational Guidance (IAEVG) in 1950 and the International Roundtable for the Advancement of Counselling (IRTAC) in 1966. In 1997, IRTAC was renamed as the International Association for Counselling (IAC).

Hoxter was a remarkable man, one of the truly great figures in the counseling movement. He was a contemporary of other luminaries in counseling and psychology such as Jean Piaget, Leona Tyler, and Gilbert Wrenn (Ivey, 2003). His special talent was to bring people and organizations together. For example, he worked to gain consultative status with organizations such as the United Nations, UNESCO, and many other international organizations of this caliber (Borgen, 2003). IAC continues to bring together professionals from around the world in their annual meetings that are held in various countries each year. In addition, IAC members can be part of a "working group" that interacts throughout the year, reporting on their activities at the annual meeting. These meetings provide a venue that facilitates exchange between individuals around the world. Another effective mechanism for the exchange of ideas, practices, and research is through the *International Journal for the Advancement of Counselling* published by the IAC. This is a valuable resource for articles from professionals worldwide. Among its other accomplishments, the founding of counseling organizations nationally, in several countries, has been a direct result of the influence of IAC.

National organizations, particularly in the West, have begun to develop an international focus. Examples of this include the National Board of Certified Counselors (NBCC), which is a national certification organization. NBCC, however, operates with a broad counseling mission (see Chapter 7, this volume). This organization established NBCC International (NBCC-I) in 2003 "to strengthen counseling and highlight counseling needs throughout the world" (NBCC, 2009). Not long after its founding, the Southeast Asia tsunami of 2004 occurred, and NBCC-I became active in collaboration with other groups, including the World Health Organization (WHO), in providing support to mental health professionals who offered counseling services to those affected by the tsunami. Currently, through a series of international conferences, NBCC-I brings together counselors and other helping professionals throughout the world.

The American Counseling Association (ACA) that serves as an umbrella structure for counselors in the United States through both its divisions and individual members has had a major influence on the development of counseling internationally. Particularly after World War II, influential U.S. counselors who were ACA members, primarily university faculty, began to travel to other countries and to serve as a resource for those interested in counseling.

Various divisions of ACA such as the Association for Multicultural Counseling and Development (AMCD), National Career Development Association (NCDA), and other divisions that became active in international outreach also encouraged these individual efforts. In some ACA divisions, there is a formal committee structure for international activities. Also, the ACA publication, the *Journal of Counseling and Development,* at times, features articles with an international focus. The annual ACA conference brings together many international counselors who interact with colleagues from the United States and other countries throughout the world. In addition to the informal connections that are made at receptions for international visitors, various convention programs also provide a venue for international speakers who both contribute to the knowledge base and stay current with the professional developments of their Western counterparts (e.g., U.S. counselors).

The American Psychological Association (APA) has a long-standing interest and involvement in international activities as well. There is an Office of International Affairs in the national headquarters, an International Division (52), and substantial international activity in many of the other divisions, including Division 17, the Society of Counseling Psychology (see Chapter 1, this volume).

Counseling psychology in the United States has a long and distinguished history (see reviews by Blocher, 2000; Borgen, 1984; Heppner, 1990; Heppner, Casas, Carter, & Stone, 2000; Meara & Myers, 1999; Scott, 1980; Whiteley, 1980, 1984). In 1946, Division 17 (then called Personnel and Guidance Psychology) of the APA was founded. The historic establishment of Division 17 was in many ways the cumulative confluence of the vocational guidance, mental hygiene, and psychometric movements, all of which began in the early 1900s. Just 7 years later, in 1953, the division name was changed to Counseling Psychology; in 2002, the name was changed once again to the Society of Counseling Psychology. The division has maintained its position within the larger APA for now more than 60 years, at one point having more than 3,000 members within the division and another 11,000 counseling psychologists in other divisions of the APA. "Although Division 17 formally represents organized counseling psychology [in the United States], the profession has now evolved beyond any one organization" (Heppner et al., 2000, p. 37) and currently includes very important collaborative relations with several other organizations such as the Council of Counseling Psychology Training Programs (which has today considerable strength within U.S. professional psychology) as well as the Association of Counseling Center Training Agencies (which also has evolved into a strong force within organized psychology). The combined efforts of these and other professional groups represent a very strong voice for counseling psychology in the United States (Heppner et al., 2000). In 2005, an International Section of Division 17 was formed by more than 150 international and U.S.-based counseling professionals to provide a voice for individuals specifically interested in international issues. The overall mission of this section continues to be encouraging, promoting, and facilitating a scientist-professional model of counseling psychology in international contexts in the United States and worldwide through research, service, teaching, training, policy development and implementation, and networking. The members of the section interact through a newsletter, listserv, and Web site (http://www.internationalcounselingpsychology.org).

Major national conferences followed the founding of the Counseling Psychology Division initially in 1951 with the Northwestern Conference and later with conferences such as the Greystone Conference (1964), Georgia Conference (1987), Houston Conference (2001), and Chicago Conference (2008); the latter of which was the historic first International Counseling Psychology Conference held in the United States. In addition, doctoral training in counseling psychology has received a great deal of attention over the years, with initial accreditation of doctoral training programs more than 50 years ago (1952); as of this writing, there are more than 70 APA-accredited doctoral programs in counseling psychology in the United States. Moreover, in the 1980s, a standardized credentialing or licensing system was begun in every state in the United States. Counseling psychologists have also maintained an active program of empirical research for more than 50 years with increasing "methodological sophistication and rigor, and providing important new knowledge that is furthering the development of theories and practice relevant to counseling psychology" (Heppner et al., 2000, p. 37). The combination of long-standing strong professional organizations within U.S. counseling psychology, an active and growing sophistication of evidence-based knowledge, a wide array of accredited training programs, and a respectable and standardized credentialing system had led to the perception that "counseling psychology [in the United States] is strong, vibrant, politically active, and expanding" (Heppner et al., 2000, p. 37).

In fact, in 2005, Heppner, then president of the Society of Counseling Psychology of the APA proclaimed, "It is a great time to be a counseling psychologist. We have strong knowledge bases and practice skills, and we have strong professional organizations" (Heppner, 2006, p. 170). In essence, the counseling psychology profession in the United States has evolved from the late-19th-century vocational guidance movement to a strong, mature, vibrant, politically correct, active, and expanding profession (Heppner et al., 2000). For many years, it seemed that the heart of counseling psychology was Division 17 (Society of Counseling Psychology) of the APA. As was stated earlier, Division 17 was established in 1946, and for quite a long time it represented organized counseling psychology. The U.S. counseling psychology profession, however, has now evolved beyond any one organization, and it includes viable, active, and politically strong groups such as the Council of Counseling Psychology Training Programs, the Association of Counseling Center Training Agencies, the Academy of Counseling of Psychology, the Council of the Specialty of Counseling Psychology, and other organizations (see Heppner et al., 2000). Although there is considerable overlap in the membership of the Society of Counseling Psychology and some of the other counseling organizations mentioned earlier (e.g., ACA, ICA), there has not been a great deal of direct organizational coordination and collaboration. Given the great needs for consultation, training, and on-the-ground service, it is hoped that more official contact between various counseling organizations throughout the world will be forthcoming in the near future.

Perhaps for a variety of reasons, it may seem to some people that counseling psychology is a U.S. discipline (Heppner, Leong, & Chiao, 2008; Leung, 2003; McWhirter, 1988). It must be stressed, however, that while counseling psychology as a specialized formally recognized discipline or a professional label is not common outside the United States, the services provided by counseling psychologists in the United States certainly are offered by individuals (e.g., general psychologists, guidance counselors, clergy, nurses, social workers, physicians, fortunetellers) living in other countries. Moreover, as Pedersen (2005) so eloquently stated, "The functions of counseling have been practiced for thousands of years and are not merely an invention of the last century or two" (p. xi). Similarly, sometimes erroneously U.S.-based counseling psychologists assume that counseling psychology in the United States is the most advanced or most well-developed specialty across the globe (Heppner, Leong, & Chiao, 2008). In fact, for the most part, many U.S. counseling psychologists have not received much exposure to the counseling professions in other countries. We are so encapsulated in the United States, we lack awareness of the implications, and our international colleagues sometimes get annoyed with our ignorance combined with our individualistic perspectives (Heppner, 2007). Our sense, as well, is that frequently U.S. counseling psychologists are oblivious to the counseling professions in other countries and know very few, if any, international counseling scholars. This lack of exposure and knowledge, however, is understandable for many reasons. In general, U.S. training programs do not offer much information about counseling and counseling psychology outside the United States. There is lack of information about the functions of organized counseling outside the United States that is published in U.S. counseling journals (especially, prior to 2005). Furthermore, U.S. libraries typically do not subscribe to foreign counseling and psychology journals. The lack of exposure to and perhaps the lack of ability of U.S. scholars to read publications not written in the English language also contribute to U.S. counseling professionals being oblivious to the profession in other countries. Also, in the United States, prior to 2000, there was a general lack of international focus in counseling and counseling psychology beyond the U.S. borders. In fact, many international scholars, especially before the year 2005, experienced difficulties when trying to publish or present at professional conferences on issues relevant to populations outside the United States (e.g., Leung, 2003; Ægisdóttir & Gerstein, 2010).

Nonetheless, the lack of exposure in the United States to counseling professions around the world is quite unfortunate because it represents a tremendous loss to U.S. counseling psychologists and counselors. The many chapters in the *International Handbook of Cross-Cultural Counseling: Cultural Assumptions and Practices Worldwide* (Gerstein, Heppner, Ægisdóttir, Leung, & Norsworthy, 2009) from numerous countries indicate the development of a broad range of knowledge acquired from around the world. Not only had such knowledge been unavailable to U.S. counseling professionals until the publication of this handbook, a lack of information about counseling and psychology worldwide also meant less awareness and comprehension about different cultural contexts and what this meant for counseling. These limitations not only restrict U.S. counseling psychologists' knowledge base but also their worldview and understanding of humanity around the globe.

The current economic recession in the United States, beginning in the year 2008, that has expanded worldwide, reminds us about how interconnected countries are in modern times. With economic globalization and increased technology, many countries and cultures have experienced greater pressure toward cultural change than ever before. Such change can be perceived as positive and negative. Oftentimes, societies are resistant to economic, social, and political changes and hang on to cultural traditions sometimes beyond their original intent. Berry (1997), for instance, describing the power of culture stated that "individuals generally act in ways that correspond to cultural influences and expectations" (p. 6). It is also true that even the most ancient of societies is not static in their beliefs and practices. Sometimes very slowly, but in other places quite rapidly, change occurs, be it positive or negative. For instance, current technology, such as cell phones and the Internet, makes instant communication between individuals who are geographically separated possible. This can enhance the sharing of ideas, worldviews, and ways of living.

Migration to cities and tourism are additional factors that expose cultures to change. Sadly, the forced migration as a result of wars also brings about rapid change and social disruption. We suspect that when societies go through rapid change, the climate for counseling develops. Then, counseling services, formal or informal, provide solace and guidance that are often interrupted and even destroyed.

It is difficult to keep up with the exponential expansion of counseling worldwide. Counseling is a natural progression as countries develop a resource base and begin to react to profound demographic changes. "When a nation lacks the financial and organizational capital to reinvest in the country, mental health and other services tend to remain underdeveloped—despite the need for these services that is often present in such times of crisis" (Stockton et al., 2007, p. 80). Fortunately, though, this lack of resources is sometimes mitigated by the contributions of nongovernmental organizations (NGOs) or foreign government assistance that provides assistance for counseling services. Thus, from an early-20th-century beginning by either internal development or external aid, counseling has become a worldwide phenomenon, and U.S. counseling professionals must accept this reality and actively develop a much broader and richer understanding of the diverse cultures and countries around the globe.

The Importance of Cross-Cultural Sensitivity

Almost 50 years ago, Gilbert Wrenn (1962) raised concerns about counselors' cross-cultural insensitivities in a landmark book, *The Counselor in a Changing World.* Wrenn was particularly concerned about counselors' inability to understand others from a different culture, and in essence, he warned of the dangers of cultural encapsulation. "Although Wrenn's message was clear about the importance of counselors' understanding of their own worldviews and how these may affect their work with clients from different cultures, it was not widely received" (Heppner, Leong, & Chiao, 2008, p. 69). This notion of being insensitive to other's worldviews, or ethnocentrism, has been suggested as perhaps "the biggest impediment" (Marsella & Pedersen, 2004, p. 414) to the internationalization of the counseling profession. In fact, many scholars have identified ethnocentrism as a major challenge (e.g., Cheung, 2000; Gerstein, 2006; Heppner, 2006; Heppner, Leong, & Chiao, 2008; Kwan & Gerstein, 2008; Leong & Blustein, 2000; Leong & Leach, 2007; Leong & Ponterotto, 2003; Leung, 2003; Marsella, 1998; McWhirter, 2000; Norsworthy, 2006; Pedersen & Leong, 1997; Segall, Lonner, & Berry, 1998).

Ethnocentrism is particularly problematic because "when we are unaware of cultural issues, it is difficult to know what we do not know" (Heppner, Leong, & Chiao, 2008, p. 77). And, when counseling professionals are unaware of the cultural context in their interactions with international colleagues, their lack of awareness significantly affects their understanding, sensitivity, and appropriate responses (Heppner, Leong, & Chiao, 2008). Sometimes, the lack of cross-cultural awareness of U.S. counseling psychologists and counselors is overlooked, and our international colleagues simply dismiss our responses as innocent and uninformed behavior coming from outsiders or foreigners who just lack cultural knowledge. In addition, sometimes the emphasis on individualism within the dominant Eurocentric culture in the United States can also result in a more self-centered orientation in contrast to more collectivistic cultures. And sometimes the combination of perceived cultural insensitivity and individualism will result in serious negative perceptions of U.S. scholars, ranging from annoyance to frustration to anger. As Heppner (2006) noted, "It is all too easy to offend our international colleagues" (p. 169). Because cross-cultural insensitivities, slights, and disrespectful behavior often occur without the U.S. counseling professionals' awareness, they often continue their insensitive actions and may never get corrected. Such ongoing negative consequences can inhibit or even curtail cross-cultural and cross-national collaboration.

As a greater number of U.S. counseling psychologists and counselors perform work beyond their geographical borders, though, their awareness of their limited knowledge about the world's cultures and its implications for counseling may increase. A very strong statement about the information available about cultures worldwide was voiced by Arnett (2008). He persuasively argued that psychological research published in six premier APA journals focused primarily on Americans who make up less than 5% of the world's population. Therefore, the currently published research in the premier U.S. journals has ignored the remaining 95% of the world's population. The same can be said about research in counseling and counseling psychology. Gerstein and Ægisdóttir (2007) found that counseling journals included few studies on international populations and topics. Based on his review, Arnett concluded that the "mainstream of American Psychology has so far been largely oblivious to international contributions and remains largely an insular enterprise" (p. 603). And, unfortunately, this conclusion also applies to the U.S. counseling and counseling psychology professions. Leung (2003) even stated that it is possible for U.S. counseling psychology students to obtain a PhD without ever reading an international article!

Current Status of Internationalization of the Counseling Profession

Recently, a number of scholars have reported on the breadth and depth of the counseling profession across the globe (e.g., Gerstein & Ægisdóttir, 2005a, 2005b; Heppner & Gerstein, 2008; Heppner, Leong, & Gerstein, 2008; Leong & Savickas, 2007; Stockton et al., 2007). In essence, the counseling profession is growing rapidly worldwide, not only in size but stature. The counseling profession is developing at different rates in non-Western countries, and while it is a very specialized field in the United States, in other countries, where psychology is poorly established, many types of professionals and paraprofessionals who have received little to no training are offering counseling services (Cheung, 2000).

Although there are many cross-national similarities and differences in the identity and credentials of counselors and counseling psychologists and in the breadth and function of their professional associations (Heppner & Gerstein, 2008; Heppner, Leong, & Gerstein, 2008), the cumulative impact of our international colleagues and their professional groups worldwide is revealing, informative, exciting, and inspiring. Moreover, the recent development of an International Division of Counseling Psychology (Division 16) in the International Association of Applied Psychology, the oldest applied psychology association in the world, is very exciting and indicates the growing internationalization of the counseling profession.

Furthermore, the first *International Handbook of Cross-Cultural Counseling* (Gerstein et al., 2009) confirmed there is much to learn from counseling professionals around the world. This includes learning about shared and indigenous perspectives in counseling and psychology worldwide, current research findings and conceptual models, and unique strategies of psychology and counseling practice around the globe. In fact, it is our opinion that an opportunity to learn from our international colleagues is one of the most exciting new developments within the counseling specialty. We also anticipate that increased international collaboration will have the potential to change the entire face of counseling and counseling psychology forever. As Heppner (2006) claimed, international contact and collaboration will "enhance the sophistication of our research, expand our knowledge bases, increase the range of counseling interventions, and in essence, increase counseling effectiveness across a wide range of populations" (p. 169). Clearly, U.S. counseling professionals can benefit greatly from an understanding of counseling in other countries and cultures.

Definitional Challenges for the Counseling Profession

As reported in Chapter 1 of this volume, the definitions for *counseling, counselor,* and *counseling psychologist* are not consistent throughout the world. Neither is there consistency in current uses of these terms nor the required credentials to use one of these professional titles. In the United States and in Canada, a doctoral degree is required to be eligible to obtain the title of "counseling psychologist." In other parts of the world, counseling psychology is a master's- or bachelor's-level profession, or such a professional title may not even exist. Moreover, what is considered professional counseling in the United States and Canada does not necessarily reflect how professional counseling is practiced elsewhere. For example, in Great Britain, an attorney or a legal representative is also a counselor. In the United States, there are financial counselors, genetic counselors, nutritional counselors, home improvement counselors, and executive coaches/counselors. Therefore, it is critical to differentiate professional counseling and counselors from other types of services and providers. Stated differently, it is essential to clarify and stipulate what professional counseling is and what it is not.

Regardless of how counseling is defined around the world, individuals in every country and culture still have to cope with emotional and physical suffering. Such suffering can come in different forms and can be experienced quite differently from culture to culture and from country to country. As Frank and Frank (1993) reported in their classic book *Persuasion and Healing: A Comparative Study of Psychotherapy,* from a Western perspective, many individuals are struggling with feelings of demoralization. However, as Tyler, Brome, and Williams (1991) so eloquently stated, there are many ways to be human. They proposed that their ethnic validity model of psychotherapy is predicated on the assumption "that there are a variety of ways of being human and these ways are not directly translatable into one another" (p. 25). Similarly, extrapolating from Tyler et al.'s model, there are also many forms of healing in the world, including professional counseling, to match these multiple ways of being human.

In the United States and many other Western countries, there is a strong Cartesian (Descartes) dualistic philosophy and methodology of intervention, be it psychological or otherwise. For instance, if a person in the United States is clinically depressed, he or she will tend to seek help from a mental health professional (e.g., counselor, counseling psychologist, psychiatrist). If on the other hand, an individual in the United States is having a heart problem, he or she will visit a cardiologist. In general then, persons in the United States prefer to see a medical doctor for problems with their bodies and a mental health professional for concerns about their minds.

In many other cultures or countries, a person in need will seek out a "helper" who offers services to treat a broad range of problems. Such helpers conceptualize individuals in terms of their whole body, mind, and spirit. They embrace a holistic approach to caring for others integrating intervention strategies such as communication, rituals, herbs, touch, and prayer. In general, it would appear that in many Western countries, especially the United States, mental health professionals gravitate to a dualistic, analytic approach (treat the mind not the body; treat the body and not the mind), while in the East (Asia) and parts of South, Latin, and Central America, they embrace a holistic, integrated approach (treat both the mind and the body). It is important to note also that persons' help-seeking behavior is greatly influenced by the health service system of each country regardless of its grounding in a dualistic or holistic philosophy.

There are also some important distinctions that can be stated about differences in the way mental health professionals in the West think about and approach counseling. U.S. counseling professionals, in general, are very practical and pragmatic. Many believe that all the problems experienced by clients are solvable. Furthermore, being pragmatic, U.S. counseling professionals are not as interested in philosophical issues and challenges. They approach their work as problem solvers frequently using functional approaches such as cognitive-behavioral therapy, dialectic therapy, and solution-focused therapy. In contrast, mental health professionals in Europe, in general, are much more interested in philosophical issues and challenges, and as such, they value discussions with their clients about meaning and purpose. They also believe that not all problems are solvable. European counselors and psychologists are also baffled by the extensive use in the United States of educational and other tests in counseling. Counseling in Europe, therefore, is often about phenomenological exploration and finding meaning. Therefore, existential therapy based on the writings of Rollo May and Victor Frankl often guides the work of European mental health professionals.

Not surprisingly, the educational training programs for mental health professionals in the United States and Europe stress different bodies of knowledge and skills. In the United States, there is a heavy emphasis on the acquisition and enactment of various skills. In Europe, in contrast, there is an extensive focus on philosophy and the establishment of a rich conceptual framework and ability to think and express thoughts. In fact, it is not uncommon to be just trained in one or very few theoretical frameworks. Moreover, in European counseling training programs, students sit for essay examinations not multiple choice tests. Additionally, in Europe, graduate students rarely take classes. Instead, there is an apprenticeship model of learning, where the student has individual meetings with a professor and/or participates in informal discussions with other students at locations apart from campus. In Great Britain, for example, a graduate student in counseling receives a highly personalized and individualized education.

While generalizations often lead to misunderstandings and conflicts, sometimes they help capture the essence of situations. Given this caveat, European mental health professionals frequently perceive U.S. mental health professionals as technicians and mechanical, while professionals in the United States often view their European counterparts as philosophers. If these stereotypes are even somewhat accurate, then it follows that individuals who earn a PhD in counseling/counseling psychology in Europe have obtained a Doctorate of Philosophy, whereas persons earning a similar degree in the United States have obtained a Doctorate of Pragmatism!

Given the observations stated above, at the most basic level, counseling professionals around the world, particularly U.S. counseling professionals, must acquire information on the unique and common function of counseling and the shared and specific roles of mental health professionals in different countries. Speaking at an IAC conference, Hoxter (1998) defined counseling as follows:

> A method of relating and responding to others with the aim of providing them with opportunities to explore, clarify, and work towards living in a more personally satisfying and resourceful way . . . and may be used in widely different contexts and settings. (p. 29)

There are a variety of other definitions promulgated by professional organizations, including the APA Society of Counseling Psychology, Division 17, as well as professional societies in various other countries. The central theme of each definition though is *the counselor as a helping professional.*

Since professional counseling as we think of it today began in the United States, and has grown rapidly throughout the world, there is sometimes an assumption, as stated earlier, that a Western or U.S. model of counseling has to be the most desired one. A Western or U.S. style of counseling, however, may clash with local or national cultural traditions that are highly significant to the populace. Emavardhana (2005) noted that the Western concept of counseling, for example, often emphasizes the importance of the individual, which can run counter to the more traditional beliefs in community prevalent in many developing world societies. The role of the family, including extended family, clan, and tribe cannot be overemphasized. T. Dodson, who has worked extensively in Latin America, concurs and comments on the common bonds of cultural values regarding family that exist within Latin America: "A counselor would be wise to consider the family impact of the change process that an individual is going through while going through a counseling experience" (personal communication, January 24, 2009).

This emphasis on the communal is exemplified in a story related by L. Levers (personal communication, January 19, 2009), who was asked to counsel an influential African male who had been kidnapped and then later rescued. She agreed to meet the individual at his home, which was in effect a compound. She was surprised that not only was the client present for the meeting but many members of his extended family and friends were also in attendance. Rather than a 1-hour session, the counseling lasted throughout the day, and meals were even served. Levers reported that despite her initial surprise, the event went well and the client felt relief.

As Bradley (2000) has noted, cultural misunderstandings can occur through nonverbal ways, as well. This became very apparent early in the career of one of the co-authors of this chapter, Rex Stockton, when he was on sabbatical leave in Spain and also attending a conference in Holland. Stockton's Spanish colleagues would place themselves physically very close to him and his Dutch colleagues, equally friendly, expressed friendship by shaking hands while keeping an arm's length distance. This is also true of eye contact; in some cultures, avoidance of eye contact is a mark of showing respect rather than being regarded as evasive.

Stockton's thinking about counseling also has been informed by contact with a Ghanaian psychologist trained in Western theories and procedures. This psychologist spent several years working in an African mental hospital and talks about the importance of ancestors in some counseling settings. As S. Atindanbila (personal communication, February 15, 2006) related, when counselors in certain settings believe that progress is being made in the course of therapy, they have to understand that unless the client thinks that his or her ancestors will approve of their altered, presumably more therapeutic behavior, they will not change. Thus, it is incumbent on counselors and counseling psychologists to understand the local culture as well as counseling theory.

Levers (2006) who has conducted research with African traditional healers, underscores the importance of acknowledging local customs and indigenous practices when working in areas devastated by illness such as the treatment of HIV/AIDS. She noted that "at least 80% of all Africans throughout sub-Saharan Africa continue to seek health care services from traditional healers" (L. Levers, personal communication, January 19, 2009). The most enlightened Western programs have responded by providing information and training to the traditional healers.

Western counselors and counseling psychologists are sometimes surprised by the central role of religion in the lives of many other clients. When Stockton was first asked to provide training in Africa (Botswana) for human services personnel who worked with individuals who had HIV/AIDS, he made it a point to spend considerable time reading about African history and culture in general and Botswana in particular. Nevertheless, he was surprised when after beginning the training, a participant raised her hand and said, "Prof, don't you think we should begin with a prayer?" Although surprised, Stockton was able to say, "I need all the help I can get," and another participant then led a prayer. After this, a weeklong workshop proceeded with a prayer at the beginning of each day. Integration of prayer into the workshop content was appreciated by the participants and probably contributed to their positive response.

Wherever they work, counselors and counseling psychologists have to figure out how to conduct their activities in ways such as to reduce stigma. This is not only true with dreaded diseases such as HIV/AIDS, but even in more innocuous settings, this can be a major problem. A counselor from Mauritius who was trained in the United States related that she had to change her "mental health counselor" title to "counselor" once she started her private practice in her country so as to minimize stigma. This stigma is not restricted to Mauritius, but in either personal work or contacts with others, it seems to be a worldwide phenomenon (J. d'Argent, personal communication, January 21, 2009).

Some more traditional cultures place importance on storytelling and singing and dancing more so than is typical of the U.S. tradition. For example, in several African countries, when Stockton has provided training or consultation, participants who were either human service professionals or clients had almost always honored the occasion with a ceremonial dance and song. The meaning and intrinsic purpose of the ceremony can be very life affirming and may provide some solace in lives that, too often, are affected by poverty and disease.

Counseling in its broadest form, therefore, has been and is increasingly prevalent worldwide. However, beyond some fundamental values and common themes, it is expressed in ways that accommodate to various cultures and traditions. Above all else, it remains a means to formally provide help to those in need across a broad spectrum from vocational to mental health counseling services.

Trends and Challenges for Counseling Professionals Worldwide

Counseling principles may be enduring, but they are shaped by the needs of society, and we can expect that as the world is evolving, changes in both the profession of counseling and the provision of counseling services will also take place. People worldwide will continue, however, to be challenged by traditional counseling issues such as family and relationship problems, career choice, and finding employment, as well as stress, mood, anxiety, and other emotional concerns. With that being said, while it is obviously difficult to predict the future of counseling around the world, some developments can be anticipated with reasonable certainty. For example, we believe that the dire, potentially explosive nature of the world's urban slums will likely intensify. Additionally, there is also mounting evidence of the dramatic rise in addiction to the Internet, especially in Asian countries.

The number of individuals displaced and negatively affected by climate change will probably multiply as well. Individuals will continue to be traumatized by conflicts, civil wars, ethno-political conflicts, migration and immigration, and natural disasters. As long as the field of counseling remains supple, respectful of other cultures, research based, innovative, cooperative with other disciplines, and true to its core values, it should be in a position to play an important role in ameliorating some small fraction of our world's very significant ills.

As stated earlier and throughout this book, technology has made it possible for people to communicate in ways incomprehensible in prior generations. This technology and the emerging new technologies have great potential for training, practice, supervision, and networking in the field of counseling regardless where professionals are located. We do not know what will evolve or how technology will evolve (who would have predicted YouTube or FaceBook a generation ago?), but for certain, this rich and dynamic resource will produce momentous changes that will provide for challenges as well as opportunities.

The trend toward various national counseling organizations expanding their view to have a more international focus is likely to continue. It is hoped that this will be coupled with the increasing advancement of national and regional counseling organizations in countries where counseling is not as fully developed as is possible. While we cannot know with certainty the shape or disposition of counseling in the future, we can be sure that the need for this service and the need for counselors and counseling psychologists will only increase.

The need for other types of healers around the world will also be important in the years to come. It is critical, therefore, that counseling professionals either develop a respect for such individuals or remain appreciative of their work. However, there must be a clear recognition of what professional counseling is and who is qualified to provide such services. Perhaps, a concept often used in conducting research might help readers to better understand this challenge. Gelso (1979) introduced the *bubble hypothesis* as a way to think about balancing the importance of external and internal validity when formulating a research study. On one hand, it is essential to control the variables in a study (internal validity) in order to rule out confounding variables and competing hypotheses. On the other hand, it is important to capture the "real" environment connected to the variables of interest (external validity) in order to increase the likelihood of studying the rich context of interest and the "behavior" of interest in the natural environment. Achieving an acceptable balance between internal and external validity is frequently the best scenario to expect. In the context of the current discussion about the great diversity in how counseling is defined, how counseling is practiced, and who offers the service, a balance is also desirable. If the concepts of counseling, counselor, and counseling psychologist are broadened to include all forms of healing and all types of healers worldwide, the external validity of these concepts would be greatly increased. If this were the case, it would be challenging to identify a profession of counseling or a professional using the title counselor or counseling psychologist. Counseling professionals are not genetic counselors or financial counselors.

In contrast, if there was a much more specific and concrete definition of counseling, and greater quality control monitoring the practice of professional counseling and the use of the title counselor or counseling psychologist worldwide, the internal validity of these concepts would be greatly increased. As a result though, few people around the world would be able to practice counseling or use the title of counselor or counseling psychologist. Striking a balance between internal and external validity in the context just described is quite challenging given the diversity in the counseling profession and the diverse cultural context throughout the world. At the very least, it is important to establish an agreed on set of competencies and base of knowledge. Then, it would be possible to consider counseling as a profession in different countries instead of thinking that anyone who is involved in healing or helping is a counselor or a member of such a profession.

There is also a need for a very basic universal declaration of ethical principles in counseling and some common training paradigm to prepare counselors and counseling psychologists. While ethics are culture bound, it would seem possible for counseling professionals regardless of where they reside to agree on basic principles such as do no harm, provide competent services, act responsibly, and demonstrate respect to clients. Having a shared basic ethical framework throughout the world could instill greater hope in potential clients; serve to network counseling professionals around a common goal; and offer the profession a shared language for dialogue, discussion, and possible important competencies. Accomplishing these tasks will not be easy. The many professional associations discussed earlier in this chapter are key to the success of such an endeavor as they are often the gatekeepers and policymakers linked with the counseling fields around the world.

Another major challenge touched on very early in this chapter is the tension between the hegemony of the U.S. model of counseling and psychology and the indigenization of counseling and psychology elsewhere, especially in Asia (e.g., Japan, Taiwan, China) (see Leong, 2002). At this point, as stated earlier, there is a greater flow and exportation of U.S. models of counseling to other countries. One might say that there is a "McDonaldization" of counseling and psychology infiltrating countries worldwide. U.S. counseling professionals must seriously think about the consequences of continuing to uncritically export their models or accept the request of non-U.S. counseling professionals to import such models. U.S. counseling professionals must also contemplate this issue alongside the importance of respecting and embracing indigenous approaches to counseling found in other countries.

One other challenge must be mentioned, though it is discussed in much greater detail in Chapter 2 in this volume. There is a tension in the United States between counseling professionals who focus on domestic cultural issues and those who attend to international cultural topics. The reality of limited available resources to address the needs of both domestic and international populations is valid and critical to both meeting the needs of diverse clientele and securing the viability and prosperity of the counseling profession. At a recent meeting of the APA Educational Leadership Conference, one of the authors of this chapter observed that a majority of the participants informally surveyed through the use of DataMite software during a large group discussion indicated that international work would take away needed resources from the domestic U.S. population. Respondents also reported that focusing on international work would place limits on other coursework. Additionally, some respondents considered shifting the focus to international work another form of racism, where we treat "international work" as exotic and glamorous and yet ignore the same populations when they are in our own backyard (e.g., working in Mexico is positively viewed, while working with Mexican Americans is shunned).

There have been some anecdotal reports in the U.S. counseling profession of racial ethnic minorities not approving of the field's interest in international activities. From another perspective, some cross-cultural researchers outside the United States have commented that the U.S. multicultural counseling movement is about advocacy and justice, not scientific inquiry. Furthermore, some of these cross-cultural psychologists have stated that U.S. multicultural counseling professionals are preoccupied with race and ethnicity and more interested in social change than pursuing research for the sake of science.

It would seem, therefore, that the multicultural counseling movement and the cross-cultural and cross-national counseling movements might be on a collision course. As outlined in Chapter 2, however, all the movements can learn from each other, all can be enriched through respectful collaboration, and ultimately the science and practice of psychology and counseling will benefit from cross-fertilization. Some solutions focused on bringing the multicultural, cross-cultural, and cross-national counseling movements closer together are also discussed in Chapter 2. Regardless of the specific solution, what is required is the ability to think and act outside the self-serving box of each movement. In fact, the paradigms to resolve the conflicts between the movements are inside the box. It is fruitless and dangerous to believe that the counseling profession in the United States or elsewhere must choose between a domestic or international focus. Both foci are essential for the continued successful evolution of a vibrant and culturally rich and effective profession of counseling. Throughout the world, what is needed in the field of counseling is a new paradigm and a new way of thinking and acting. For as Heppner (2006) predicted, "In the future, the parameters of counseling psychology will cross many countries and many cultures" (p. 170). More specifically, the accumulative knowledge bases of the counseling profession will be grounded in the scientific and applied discoveries of counseling professionals from all corners of the world. As Leong and Blustein (2000) stated, "We need a global perspective that recognizes and is open to other cultures in other countries, whether on this continent or across the oceans, on the other side of the world" (p. 5).

Conclusion

It is rather apparent that the counseling profession is blossoming worldwide. This is good news as the rising number of psychological and other concerns experienced by people around the globe speaks of the importance of a highly effective profession that can function appropriately and successfully across borders and between cultures. There is increasing evidence that counseling professionals everywhere are waking up to the reality that they must embrace and enact both an insider or emic (culture specific) and outsider or etic (transcending culture) view about human behavior, culture, and a host of counseling theories, strategies, and methodologies. The available communication tools (e.g., e-mail, Skype) to many counseling professionals, including those located in remote regions of the world, have made it possible for a very large number of persons to actively and immediately connect and network with each other. The future success of a global integrated and collaborative counseling profession depends, in part, on maximizing the use of such tools. More important, it requires suspending biases, embracing differences and commonalities, and valuing and respecting multiple and diverse paradigms of conceptualizing human behavior, and also strategies to promote well-being and address problematic behaviors and situations. Additionally, it requires an extensive understanding of the philosophy and mechanics of cross-cultural validity to pursue valid, reliable, and useful indigenous and cross-cultural theories, strategies, and research methodologies (Ægisdóttir, Gerstein, & Çinarbaş, 2008).

We firmly believe that the counseling profession in the United States and elsewhere is at a crossroad, and there is no turning back. Instead, we fully expect to witness an exponential shift in how members of the counseling profession throughout the world interact with each other and work together to serve the needs of diverse populations. As was stated earlier in this chapter, international collaboration has a great deal of potential to strengthen the science and practice of the counseling profession, as well as greatly enhance our knowledge of the cultural context (see Heppner, 2008; Heppner, Leong, & Chiao, 2008; Leong & Blustein, 2000). Over time, such collaborative efforts will result in a tapestry of knowledge that will "put the puzzle together as an extraordinary picture of a worldwide psychology" (Heppner, Leong, & Chiao, 2008, p. 82) and counseling profession. Until that time, counseling professionals especially those in the United States must be diligent in their actions and clearly recognize that "as counseling psychology is transported to other cultures, we need to address the fundamental issues of counseling by whom, counseling for whom, and counseling for what" (Cheung, 2000, p. 130).

Chapter Questions

1. Consider this statement, "Counseling has been practiced for thousands of years and is not an invention of the last century or two."
   a. Identify and discuss the philosophy and role of a specific group of indigenous healers in one culture that has offered mental health services to their people for centuries.
   b. Focusing on a few specific types of services or interventions offered by a particular group of healers, compare and contrast them with services and interventions typically employed by U.S. counselors and counseling psychologists. Focus on both the process and outcome of services or interventions provided by these two types of professional groups (healers and counselors/ counseling psychologists) and use examples to clarify your points.

2. Brainstorm different ways international collaboration may increase the effectiveness of counseling across a wide range of diverse populations and explain why this may occur.

3. In order to become more culturally sensitive, should counselors or counseling psychologists embrace the roles of indigenous healers to be more effective with their clients or should they collaborate with or refer to indigenous healers? Support your argument and use examples to clarify your argument.

References

Arnett, J. J. (2008). The neglected 95%: Why American psychology needs to become less American. *American Psychologist, 63,* 602–614.

Berry, J. W. (1997). Lead article: Immigration, acculturation, and adaptation. *Applied Psychology: An International Review, 46*(1), 5–68.

Blocher, D. H. (2000). *The evolution of counseling psychology.* New York: Springer.

Borgen, F. H. (1984). Counseling psychology. *Annual Review of Psychology, 35,* 579–604.

Borgen, W. A. (2003). Remembering Hans: His ongoing legacy for guidance and counselling. *International Journal for the Advancement of Counselling, 25*(2/3), 83–88.

Bradley, G. (2000). Responding effectively to the mental health needs of international students. *Higher Education, 39,* 417–433.

Cheung, F. M. (2000). Deconstructing counseling in a cultural context. *The Counseling Psychologist, 28,* 123–132.

Emavardhana, T. (2005, December). *Counseling across borders: How to counsel within the Thai culture.* Keynote presentation at the 11th International Counseling Conference, Bangkok, Thailand.

Frank, J. D., & Frank, J. B. (1993). *Persuasion and healing: A comparative study of psychotherapy* (3rd ed.). Baltimore: Johns Hopkins University Press.

Gelso, C. J. (1979). Research in counseling: Methodological and professional issues. *The Counseling Psychologist, 8,* 7–35.

Gerstein, L. H. (2006). Counseling psychologists as international social architects. In R. L. Toporek, L. H. Gerstein, N. A. Fouad, G. Roysircar-Sodowsky, & T. Israel (Eds.), *Handbook for social justice in counseling psychology: Leadership, vision, and action* (pp. 377–387). Thousand Oaks, CA: Sage.

Gerstein, L. H., Heppner, P. P., Ægisdóttir, S., Leung, S. A., & Norsworthy, K. L. (2009). *International Handbook of Cross-Cultural Counseling: Cultural Assumptions and Practices Worldwide.* Thousand Oaks, CA: Sage.

Gerstein, L. H., & Ægisdóttir, S. (Guest Eds.). (2005a). Counseling around the world [Special issue]. *Journal of Mental Health Counseling, 27,* 95–184.

Gerstein, L. H., & Ægisdóttir, S. (Guest Eds.). (2005b). Counseling outside of the United States: Looking in and reaching out! [Special section]. *Journal of Mental Health Counseling, 27,* 221–281.

Gerstein, L. H., & Ægisdóttir, S. (2007). Training international social change agents: Transcending a U.S. counseling paradigm. *Counselor Education and Supervision, 47,* 123–139.

Heppner, P. P. (Ed.). (1990). *Pioneers in counseling and human development: Personal and professional perspectives.* Washington, DC: American Association of Counseling and Development.

Heppner, P. P. (2006). The benefits and challenges of becoming cross-culturally competent counseling psychologists. *The Counseling Psychologist, 34,* 147–172.

Heppner, P. P. (2007, September). *The role of culture in applied problem solving and coping: Overlooked and almost forgotten.* Keynote address presented at the IAEVG International Guidance Conference General Assembly, Padua, Italy.

Heppner, P. P. (2008). Expanding the conceptualization and measurement of applied problem solving and coping: From stages to dimensions to the almost forgotten cultural context. *American Psychologist, 63,* 803–816.

Heppner, P. P., Casas, J. M., Carter, J., & Stone, G. L. (2000). The maturation of counseling psychology: Multifaceted perspectives, 1978–1998. In S. D. Brown & R. W. Lent (Eds.), *Handbook of counseling psychology* (3rd ed., pp. 3–49). New York: Wiley.

Heppner, P. P., & Gerstein, L. H. (2008). International developments in counseling psychology. In F. T. L. Leong, E. M. Altmaier, & B. D. Johnson (Eds.), *The encyclopedia of counseling psychology: Changes and challenges for counseling in the 21st century* (Vol. 1, pp. 263–265). Thousand Oaks, CA: Sage.

Heppner, P. P., Leong, F. T. L., & Chiao, H. (2008). The growing internationalization of counseling psychology. In S. D. Brown & R. W. Lent (Eds.), *Handbook of counseling psychology* (4th ed., pp. 68–85). New York: Wiley.

Heppner, P. P., Leong, F. T. L., & Gerstein, L. H. (2008). Counseling within a changing world: Meeting the psychological needs of societies and the world. In W. B. Walsh (Ed.), *Biennial review in counseling psychology* (pp. 231–258). Thousand Oaks, CA: Sage.

Hoxter, H. (1998, August). *Counselling as a profession.* Paper presented at the meeting for the International Association for Counselling, Paris, France.

Ivey, A. E. (2003). Hans Zacharias Hoxter: Building counseling internationally. *International Journal for the Advancement of Counselling, 25*(2/3), 95–108.

Kwan, K.-L. K., & Gerstein, L. H. (2008). Envisioning a counseling psychology of the world: The mission of the international forum. *The Counseling Psychologist, 36,* 182–187.

Leong, F. T. L. (2002). Challenges for career counseling in Asia: Variations in cultural accommodation [Special issue]. *Career Development Quarterly, 50,* 277–284.

Leong, F. T. L., & Blustein, D. L. (2000). Toward a global vision of counseling psychology. *The Counseling Psychologist, 28,* 5–9.

Leong, F. T. L., & Leach, M. M. (2007). Internalizing counseling psychology in the United States: ASWOT analysis. *Applied Psychology: An International Review, 56,* 165–181.

Leong, F. T. L., & Ponterotto, J. G. (2003). A proposal for internationalizing counseling psychology in the United States: Rationale, recommendations, and challenges. *The Counseling Psychologist, 31,* 381–395.

Leong, F. T. L., & Savickas, M. L. (2007). Introduction to special issue on international perspectives on counseling psychology. *Applied Psychology: An International Review, 56,* 1–6.

Leung, S. A. (2003). A journey worth traveling: Globalization of counseling psychology. *The Counseling Psychologist, 31,* 412–419.

Levers, L. L. (2006). Identifying psychoeducational HIV/AIDS interventions in Botswana: Focus groups and related rapid assessment methods. In C. Fischer (Ed.),

Qualitative research methods for the psychological professions (pp. 377–410). New York: Elsevier Press.

Marsella, A. J. (1998). Toward a global-community psychology: Meeting the needs of a changing world. *American Psychologist, 53,* 1282–1291.

Marsella, A. J., & Pedersen, P. B. (2004). Internationalizing the counseling psychology curriculum: Toward new values, competencies, and directions. *Counseling Psychology Quarterly, 17,* 413—423.

McWhirter, J. J. (1988). The Fulbright program in counseling psychology. *The Counseling Psychologist, 16,* 279–281.

McWhirter, J. J. (2000). And now, up go the walls: Constructing an international room for counseling psychology. *The Counseling Psychologist, 28,* 117–122.

Meara, N. M., & Myers, R. A. (1999). A history of Division 17 (Counseling Psychology): Establishing stability amid change. In D. A. Dewsbury (Ed.), *Unification through division: Histories of divisions of the American Psychological Association* (Vol. 3, pp. 9–41). Washington, DC: American Psychological Association.

National Board of Certified Counselors. (2009). *NBCC international history.* Retrieved March 30, 2009, from http://www.nbccinternational.org/home/about-nbcc-i/about-history

Norsworthy, K. L. (2006). Bringing social justice to international practices of counseling psychology. In R. L. Toporek, L. R. Gerstein, N. A. Fouad, G. Roysircar-Sodowsky, & T. Israel (Eds.), *Handbook for social justice in counseling psychology: Leadership, vision, and action* (pp. 421—441). Thousand Oaks, CA: Sage.

Pedersen, P. (2005). Series editor's foreword. In R. Moodley & W. West (Eds.), *Integrating traditional healing practices into counseling and psychotherapy* (pp. xi–xii). Thousand Oaks, CA: Sage.

Pedersen, P., & Leong, F. (1997). Counseling in an international context. *The Counseling Psychologist, 25,* 117–122.

Scott, C. W. (1980). History of the division of counseling psychology: 1945–1963. In J. M. Whiteley (Ed.), *The history of counseling psychology* (pp. 25–40). Monterey, CA: Brooks/Cole.

Segall, M. H., Lonner, W. J., & Berry, J. W. (1998). Cross-cultural psychology as a scholarly discipline: On a flowering of culture in behavioral research. *American Psychologist, 53,* 1101–1110.

Stockton, R., Garbelman, J., Kaladow, J., & Terry, L. (2007). The international development of counseling as a profession. In W. K. Schweiger, D. A. Henderson, T. W. Clawson, D. R. Collins, & M. W. Nucholls (Ed.), *Counselor preparation: Programs, faculty, trends* (12th ed., pp. 75–97). New York: Taylor & Francis Group and National Board for Certified Counselors.

Torrey, E. F. (1972). *The mind game: Witchdoctors and psychiatrists.* New York: Emerson Hall.

Tyler, F. B., Brome, D. R., & Williams, J. E. (1991). *Ethnic validity, ecology, and psychotherapy: A psychosocial competence model.* New York: Plenum Press.

Whiteley, J. M. (1980). *Counseling psychology: A historical perspective.* Schenectady, NY: Character Research Press.

Whiteley, J. M. (1984). A historical perspective on the development of counseling psychology as a profession. In S. D. Brown & R. W. Lent (Eds.), *Handbook of counseling psychology* (pp. 3–55). New York: Wiley.

Wrenn, C. G. (1962). *The counselor in a changing world.* Alexandria, VA: American Personnel and Guidance Association.

Ægisdóttir, S., & Gerstein, L. H. (2010). International counseling competencies: A new frontier in multicultural training. In J. C. Ponterotto, J. M. Casas, L. A. Suzuki, & C. A. Alexander (Eds.), *Handbook of multicultural counseling* (3rd ed., pp. 175–188). Thousand Oaks, CA: Sage.

Ægisdóttir, S., Gerstein, L. H., & Çinarbaş, D. C. (2008). Methodological issues in cross-cultural counseling research: Equivalence, bias, and translations. *The Counseling Psychologist, 36,* 188–219.

Chapter Four

Exportation of U.S.-Based Models of Counseling and Counseling Psychology

A Critical Analysis

Kathryn L. Norsworthy, P. Paul Heppner, Stefanía Ægisdóttir, Lawrence H. Gerstein, and Paul B. Pedersen

Collaboration and partnerships across cultures are increasingly important in this age of global connection. What happens in one part of the world now affects people, economies, and governments on the other side of the globe. How a problem is solved in one culture or region can be a valuable source of learning for people facing a similar challenge in another part of the world. Counseling and counseling psychology are certainly part of this interconnected process, as evidenced by the increasing numbers of professionals traveling to other parts of the world to teach, research, and consult, and by the thousands of international students enrolled in Western university counseling and psychology training programs. Yet, we are faced with the sobering reality that Western, and particularly U.S., corporations, governments, and even organized counseling and psychology exert tremendous influence and power globally. Fortunately, conversations are emerging in our professions regarding how to internationalize in ways that support indigenous development of the professions within each country or culture rather than fostering uncritical exportation of Western models (Leung, 2003; Norsworthy, 2006; Pedersen, 2003; Yang, Hwang, Pedersen, & Daibo, 2003).

Several scholars have indicated that U.S. counselors and psychologists within the American Counseling Association and the American Psychological Association (APA) are becoming more aware of the importance of cultivating cross-cultural and international partnerships of mutuality rather than operating from a hegemonic, potentially colonizing, stance in the global arena (Chung, 2005; Gerstein, 2006; Pedersen, 2003; Rice & Ballou, 2002). As we acknowledge that we all have much to learn from one another, noting the importance of bi- and multidirectional learning, we move closer to a more relevant global counseling profession, one that truly centers culture, context, and identities in the theory, practice, and research of counseling. Cross-national collaboration and partnering that supports the interests and understanding of all people is increasingly critical in this age of globalization and the attendant pressures toward global "homogenization" and "assimilation" (Bochner, 1999).

This chapter explores the issues associated with the transportation of Western counseling models to cultures and countries outside the West. Inherent in this discussion is an examination of the efforts of U.S.-based counseling and psychology researchers in conducting research aimed at informing multicultural, cross-cultural, and transnational work. To this end, we begin this chapter by exploring efforts in the counseling field to understand the role of culture in the counseling profession and in the often blurred distinction between cross-cultural and cultural counseling and psychologies, their research methodologies, their assumptions, and their goals. Attention is given to how to bring this understanding to cross-cultural counseling. With this foundation, we move to an exploration of the context and variables setting the stage for the uncritical transportation of counseling knowledge and skills, particularly from the United States to other countries and regions of the world. Conceptualizing this process as potentially colonizing, we offer an explanation of psychological colonization and imperialism, the dynamics and effects of this process, and how these global power arrangements contextualize the inherent problems connected to the uncritical exportation of U.S. counseling models. We close the chapter with a call for decolonizing and support for indigenizing counseling and counseling psychology around the globe, setting the stage for upcoming chapters that offer more detailed explorations of these topics.

As Paul Pedersen (2003) pointed out regarding U.S. counseling psychology, "We have been all too ready to 'teach' and to 'lead' other countries but perhaps not nearly ready enough to 'learn' and to 'follow'" (p. 397). He goes on to remark, "Counseling psychology does not 'belong' to any single cultural, national, or social group," (p. 398) and wisely acknowledges that the goal is not so much the internationalization of counseling psychology "but more properly about the reinvention of counseling psychology as a profession in a global context" (p. 402).

Cross-Cultural and Cultural Counseling and Psychology: Understanding the Background

With the increased interest in culture as an important fourth force in counseling (e.g., Pedersen, 1999), one logically assumes that U.S. counseling professionals working with culturally diverse clientele across one or more countries would possess awareness and knowledge about cultural influences on behavior and psychological processes and about the limitations of uncritically applying U.S. theories outside their cultural context. Counseling professionals need to demonstrate cultural competence and be tentative in their approaches. This points to the importance of understanding the centrality of culture in how humans grow, develop, and manifest distress and psychological problems and disorders. As the world gets smaller, counseling and psychology are in greater need of research and theoretical frameworks for understanding and counseling clients across the spectrum of lived human experience. This section offers a discussion of the contributions and conundrums of cultural and cross-cultural research and psychology in our somewhat fledgling attempts at research and practice within and across cultures.

An interest in studying and understanding contextual influences on behavior is not new. In fact, this interest can be traced all the way back to Wilhelm Wundt's extensive writings on *Volkerpsychologie* in 1900 (Adamopoulos & Lonner, 2001). In particular, during the past 40 years we have witnessed more systematic and increasingly methodologically sophisticated (van de Vijver, 2001) cross-cultural and cultural research in psychology (especially social psychology). Attention to issues of cross-cultural international research and practice has a shorter history in counseling and counseling psychology. It is only in the past decade that there has been an increase in the number of publications including international topics and samples of counseling outside the Unites States (e.g., Gerstein & Ægisdóttir, 2005a, 2005b, 2005c, 2007; Heppner, 2006; Heppner & Gerstein, 2008; Heppner, Leong, & Gerstein, 2008; Kwan & Gerstein, 2008; Leong & Blustein, 2000; Leong & Ponterotto, 2003; Leong & Savickas, 2007; Pedersen, Draguns, Lonner, & Trimble, 2008; Ægisdóttir & Gerstein, 2005). Even though the counseling field has seen an increased interest in international topics, publications in contemporary journals appear at an alarmingly low rate. For instance, Gerstein and Ægisdóttir (2007) found that international topics only accounted for about 6% of publications between the years 2000 and 2004 in four U.S. counseling journals.

Most scholars within Western psychology and counseling treat culture as an important factor influencing persons' thoughts, feelings, and behaviors (e.g., feminist, multicultural, cross-cultural, and cultural movements within counseling and counseling psychology) rather than as a confounding or nuisance variable. Pike (1966) first introduced the emic/etic framework (from linguistics), positing that both aspects were the same single and unified reality seen from two different vantage points. A dualistic perspective has emerged regarding etic (universal) and emic (relativistic) approaches in studying culture. Indeed, the interpretation that divides emic and etic into polarized alternatives may indicate one of the most obvious cultural biases in Western psychology, a point argued convincingly by Pedersen, Crethar, and Carlson (2008) in their discussion of cultural empathy and the Western categorization into a quantitative framework. This is perhaps a clear illustration that, indeed, we can learn from the more holistic, non-dualistic contributions of indigenous psychology, where there is more credit given to qualitative interpretations in a balance of quality and quantity rather than a one-sided approach.

Currently, the status of culture in psychological theory and the methods used to study culture remain under debate as does the definition of culture (Gerstein, Rountree, & Ordonez, 2007), and it is useful to understand the current debate in Western psychology. Those approaching culture emphasizing an emic or relativistic stance aim to achieve the best possible description of psychological processes in a culture, employing concepts used in that particular culture. In contrast, within the etic approach, psychological phenomena are conceptualized and investigated using universal concepts (Triandis, 2000). Thus, *emic* represents the insider view, whereas the *etic* approach is the outsider view, using concepts that are considered common across cultures. By employing concepts common across cultures (etic), cross-cultural/national comparisons are possible (Lonner, 1999; Triandis, 2000; Ægisdóttir, Gerstein, & Çinarbaş, 2008).

The contrasting emphases of cultural and cross-cultural psychology are somewhat in line with the emic/etic debate. Cross-cultural psychology is a section of psychology mainly focused on how culture affects behavior, and the aim is to develop an inclusive universal psychology (Adamopoulos & Lonner, 2001). Most of the research is comparative, whereby culture or cultural variables are treated as independent variables affecting individuals' behaviors and psychological processes. Culture is treated as independent of the person's psychological makeup, as either moderating or mediating behavior. Scholars identifying with cross-cultural psychology employ varied types of methodologies, and their main challenges are resolving issues of equivalence of constructs, methods, and bias (Adamopoulos & Lonner, 2001; Brislin, 1986; Brislin, Lonner, & Thorndike, 1973; van de Vijver & Leung, 1997; Ægisdóttir et al., 2008). A major challenge within cross-cultural psychology is the lack of causative and explanatory power of cultural variables and culture as a construct (independent variable), which limits theory building. Most often, etic, or derived etic (Berry, 1999), approaches are employed within cross-cultural psychology and counseling research.

The basic purpose of cultural psychology is enhancing the understanding of people in a historical and socio-cultural context (Adamopoulos & Lonner, 2001). Studies within cultural psychology see culture as central to the understanding of human processes and behavior. With this approach, the culture and the person or psyche are seen as inseparable (Miller, 1997); thus, culture cannot be treated as an independent variable, and cross-cultural comparisons are seen as inappropriate. Rather, individuals are understood in their cultural contexts—a relative, ontological stance best suited for qualitative means of inquiry. With this approach, the primary challenge is translating subjectively defined phenomena into a theoretical context within the constraints of relativism (Adamopoulos & Lonner, 2001). Those advocating for indigenous psychology (e.g., Kim, 2001) seem to share this conceptualization with cultural psychologists.

In short, there has been a debate and controversy between cross-cultural psychologists and universalists on the one hand and cultural psychologists and relativists on the other. Both approaches to investigating and conceptualizing culture have their merits and challenges and can potentially provide the proverbial "two sides to the coin" for a more complete, holistic picture. This debate is akin to the ideographic versus nomothetic controversy in personality psychology (e.g., Lonner, 1999) as well as the objective-subjective (statistical-clinical) debate in clinical psychology (e.g., Meehl, 1954; Ægisdóttir et al., 2006). The main questions revolve around how one can use group data and empirical results in understanding a unique individual. Many counseling professionals are aware of the value of both nomothetic (e.g., use of standardized test data) and idiographic (clinical interview) data, and they are able to operate from a more holistic framework by integrating these sources of information to be of assistance to an individual client, a family, a couple, a group, or a community. Similarly, scholars studying cultural influences on behavior often bridge emic and etic approaches by using both quantitative and qualitative types of inquiry to obtain a better understanding of cultural influences of behavior and psychological processes. The issue of where to place culture in psychological theory (outside of or as an integral part of the human mind) remains unresolved, though U.S. multicultural counseling scholars emphasize the importance of viewing cultures and identities as central in understanding human functioning (Sue & Sue, 2008). Other counseling professionals have suggested that we should look to anthropology when attempting to examine the relationship between culture and human behavior (Gerstein et al., 2007).

How do the issues connected with the concepts of etic/emic and cross-cultural/cultural psychology perspectives translate into counseling practice? And what are the implications of exporting theories developed in one country or culture to another? Kim (2001), a supporter of indigenous psychology, argued that mainstream psychological theories are emic and culture bound; in essence, they are deeply rooted in Euro-American values of rationalism, freedom, and individualism. Thus, many, if not most, counseling and psychotherapy approaches are founded on an individualistic philosophy that emphasizes individual freedom, self-reliance, autonomy, and uniqueness. These values, however, are often inconsistent with collectivistic values that emphasize social responsibility and the preservation and well-being of the group (Lee & Sue, 2001). Thus, there are serious questions about whether dominant U.S. models of psychotherapy and counseling, especially individual approaches, and the attendant professional roles of the counselor or psychotherapist generalize to individuals from cultural backgrounds who do not share these values and worldviews. The role of the counseling professional as advisor, social change agent, or facilitator of indigenous support or healing systems might, for instance, be more fitting in some cultural contexts than in others (e.g., Atkinson, Thompson, & Grant, 1993).

By using a more holistic approach that values both perspectives as part of a broader perspective, we find that many psychological constructs are universal or etic (e.g., well-being, coping, dysphoria, anxiety). But their expressions may differ significantly across cultures (e.g., Heppner, 2008; Lee & Sue, 2001; Tanaka-Matsumi, 2001). For example, cross-cultural and cultural research on psychopathology has demonstrated that "culture has a major influence on identification, labeling, course, and outcome of maladaptive behavior" (Tanaka-Matsumi, 2001, p. 280). The effectiveness of various counseling approaches may vary by culture as well. However, studies testing the effectiveness of empirically supported treatments across cultures and nations are scarce (Draguns, 2004), but they are greatly needed to help discern cultural effects. Both the science and practice of the counseling profession would greatly benefit from research that focused on understanding indigenous healing approaches as well as their efficacy (e.g., Jaipal, 2004; Lei, Askeroth, Lee, 2004; Lei, Lee, Askeroth, Bursteyn, & Einhorn, 2004; Tanaka-Matsumi, 2004). Furthermore, investigations exploring the possible integration of traditional U.S. Western counseling approaches with indigenous cultural healing systems are also long overdue.

One general criterion to evaluate the appropriateness of a theory to a new cultural context is the cultural distance between the culture/country in which a theory was developed versus applied (Triandis, 1994, 2001). The greater the distance, in terms of cultural values, language, politics, and so forth, the less congruence or applicability the theory might have. Cultural syndromes, or recognizable characteristics and patterns (Triandis, 1993, 1996, 2001), offer useful ways to assist in evaluating such applicability, as well as adapting and bridging counseling theories to other cultural contexts. Triandis (1993) noted that cultural syndromes can be identified when shared elements of subjective culture (e.g., attitudes, beliefs, norms) "(a) are organized around a theme, (b) there is evidence that the within-culture variance of these constructs is small relative to the between-cultures variance, and (c) there is a link between these patterns of subjective culture and geography" (p. 155). Triandis (2002, chap. 1) also suggested that cultural syndromes promote a focus on constructs that we can measure and get beyond the more general notions of "culture." Examples of cultural syndromes include collectivism-individualism, which can be either vertical (subordination to authority) or horizontal (equity orientation), tightness-looseness (many-few social norms/rules), and complexity-simplicity (information societies-hunters, gatherers). The belief is that the closer the target culture is to the culture in which the theory was developed, the more applicable the theory might be to the new cultural context, in part or total or with modification.

A deeper look at the questions and issues in cross-cultural research and theory application must be accompanied by an analysis of the larger global context in which the professions of counseling and counseling psychology are emerging, particularly through the lens of power, privilege, and influence. Where we currently stand as a "profession in a global context" (Pedersen, 2003, p. 402) involves seeing as clearly as possible the global politics of counseling and psychology and identifying what it will take to reinvent the profession so that it is relevant for the 21st century and beyond.

Exportation of U.S. Counseling Models: Issues and Challenges

The U.S.-based counseling profession, as well as psychology in general, has had a dramatic influence on the practice and science of psychology and counseling outside the United States (Blowers, 1996; Cheung, 2000; Gergen, Gulerce, Lock, & Misra, 1996; Gerstein & Ægisdóttir, 2005b; Jing, 2000; Leong & Ponterotto, 2003; Leung, 2003). Professionals around the world have embraced many of the theories, methods, and strategies developed and employed in the United States. This trend began in the middle of the 20th century, accelerated toward the end of that century, and continues in this current century. Whereas there are no data to substantiate why this happened or how widespread this influence might be, it seems to us that there may be several reasons. First, professionals from outside the United States were drawn to the apparent "scientific" sophistication and merit of psychology and counseling in the United States. Second, many of these professionals were able to easily access the scholarly U.S. literature published. Psychologists in the United States have dominated this literature, with international colleagues having little or no success publishing in U.S. (and other Western) counseling and psychology journals (Gerstein & Ægisdóttir, 2005a, 2005b, 2005c). Third, a large number of international students have studied counseling and/or psychology in the United States and later secured employment in their home country armed with U.S.-based knowledge bases. Finally, a sizable number of U.S. psychologists and counselor educators have traveled abroad (e.g., exchange programs, Fulbright, consultation) and have disseminated their knowledge and skills through service, teaching, and research.

Cross-national collaboration in the counseling profession goes back at least half a century or more. As discussed in Chapter 2 of this book, some of the earliest cross-national collaboration occurred in the 1950s and 1960s as U.S. counseling psychologists (W. Lloyd, E. G. Williamson, D. Super, H. Barrow, and L. Brammer) were asked to consult with the Japanese government to help establish a counseling profession similar to that in the United States (Heppner, Leong & Chiao, 2008). In the 1960s, again U.S. counseling psychologists (C. G. Wrenn, F. Robinson) provided international consultation to establish a counseling profession modeled on the U.S. system. In essence, the goal seemed to be to transport counseling models that were achieving some success in the United States to other countries. In doing so, however, it was not simply transporting a model of counseling but also the dominant U.S. cultural norms, practices, and values underlying the counseling model. As discussed earlier, the transportation of counseling models based on the U.S. cultural context can become problematic when the values of the recipient's culture differ substantially from those of the United States.

For example, when Heppner first visited Taiwan in 1989, several of the Taiwanese counseling faculty indicated they were experiencing difficulties in applying the well-known U.S.-based Rogerian counseling model with Taiwanese clients. In Taiwan, the word for counselor is synonymous with teacher, and students were accustomed to seeking help from elders, including teachers (and later counselors), to receive advice. But the Rogerian approach does not typically engage in advice-giving but rather provides therapeutic conditions through unconditional positive regard to facilitate the development of the person (Rogers, 1951). However, the counseling techniques related to reflection and unconditional positive regard did not provide the direct advice the Taiwanese clients expected, which created significant problems, such as premature client termination. In short, the uncritical exportation of the widely accepted U.S.-based Rogerian counseling theory and methods did not achieve the same level of success within the different Taiwanese cultural context, which emphasized filial piety, respect, and seeking advice from elders.

Unfortunately, the Taiwan example is not an isolated incident. Around the turn of the 21st century, several scholars articulated concerns about transporting U.S.-based counseling models to other countries. For example, Cheung (2000) aptly noted as follows:

> The meaning of counseling may seem obvious to American psychologists. The understanding of its meaning by American clients is assumed. In another cultural context, however, counseling may imply a different nature of relationship to both the provider and the recipient. Counseling needs to be deconstructed in the context of the culture in which it is offered. (p. 124)

Cheung indicated that culture defines what constitutes clients' problems, the cause of the problems (see Cheung, 1988), and the solutions and therapeutic interventions (see Sue & Sue, 1990). In essence, Cheung argued that it is problematic and thus inappropriate to simply transport a counseling theory and methods from one culture to another without examining the culturally encapsulated assumptions of the model's congruence with the recipient's cultural context.

Several scholars have discussed the need to examine the culturally encapsulated assumptions within prevailing U.S.-based counseling theories and research methods (e.g., Gerstein, 2006; Heppner, 2006; Heppner, Casas, Carter, & Stone, 2000; Heppner, Leong, & Gerstein, 2008; Heppner, Wampold, & Kivlighan, 2008; Leong & Blustein, 2000; Leong & Ponterotto, 2003; McWhirter, 2000; Norsworthy, 2006; Pedersen 2003; Pedersen & Leong, 1997).

Cheung (2000) highlighted several of these assumptions in U. S. counseling psychology:

> Counseling psychology has been encapsulated in ethnocentric assumptions that are taken to be universal. The theories, research, and practice of counseling psychology, as a specialized profession, originate in the United States but are assumed to be universally applicable. When transported to another culture where the field of psychology in general and counseling psychology in particular is fledging, it is simply transported. There has often been little regard as to the applicability of the theories and practices. (p. 123)

In short, the rather wholesale transportation of U.S.-based counseling theories and research models has not only resulted in inappropriate generalizations of U.S.-based models but also led to another instance of Western Eurocentric domination, or Western psychological hegemony. Such neocolonialism can not only deepen inequities but also be destructive of indigenous cultures.

As previously discussed, until quite recently, U.S. counseling and psychology have been imported and exported worldwide almost without restrictions, oversight, or careful attention to the consequences or implications. It would seem that, in general, U.S. professionals have uncritically transported, promoted, and shared U.S. models of counseling and psychology with persons in other countries. Concurrently, a number of U.S. scholars (Douce, 2004; Leung, 2003; Marsella, 1998; Pedersen, 2003) have noted that the U.S. counseling profession itself is still facing the challenge of ethnocentrism, isolation, cultural encapsulation, and hegemony. Very early in the history of the U.S. counseling profession, Wrenn (1962) also spoke of a similar challenge, characterizing U.S. counselors as culturally encapsulated. In part, he suggested that counselors protect themselves against the uncomfortable reality of change by maintaining an encapsulation within their subculture. Pedersen and Leong (1997) expanded on this observation by urging the counseling psychology profession to examine the culturally encapsulated assumptions of its theories, models, and practices.

Apparently, cultural encapsulation has not prevented U.S. mental health professionals from exporting their models and strategies around the world. Some writers have even suggested that Western experts in psychology and Western volunteers engaged in activities outside of the West were prone to practicing a form of psychological colonization, neocolonialism (Lugones & Spelmann, 1983) and cultural imperialism. Leong and Ponterotto (2003) further argued that "the belief that American psychology is in some ways more advanced or superior to other national psychologies is U.S.-centric and isolationist" (p. 383). Again, although no formal research has been conducted on this topic, substantial ethnographic, anecdotal, and case study evidence exists based on the experiences of both U.S. and non-U.S. professionals.

Typically, *colonialism* refers to nations exploring new areas, occupying the territory, controlling its inhabitants, and creating colonies ruled by the colonizing nation's government (Said, 1993). *Colonization* has been defined as "a system of domination characterized by social patterns or mechanisms of control which maintain oppression and which vary from context to context" (Moane, 1994, p. 252). Imperialism (Said, 1993), where a more powerful nation or society enforces its stance of superiority through domination and control, reinforces colonization through exertion of "dominant values, practices, and meanings within the colonized context. This renders the perspectives of the colonized invisible while simultaneously negatively stereotyping and 'othering' (objectifying) the colonized group" (Norsworthy, 2006, p. 424). From this perspective, a country or culture may undergo psychological colonization even if the colonizing nations have no significant physical presence. According to Norsworthy (2006),

> Due to the overwhelming power differential and the exertion of control by the colonizers over the minds, bodies, and spirits of those colonized, many

colonized individuals internalize these negative qualities. . . . According to Memmi (1965) those who are colonized may develop attitudes of dependency and ambivalence toward the colonizers, including feelings of hate, fear, admiration, affection, and sometimes, identification. At the same time, the colonizers depend on the colonized for their status and identity, survival and comfort while simultaneously projecting their disowned aspects on to the colonized group. Thus, there is interdependency between the colonizers and the colonized that leads to ambivalence for each group with regard to the other. Enforced by the colonizers, a kind of social and psychological complementarity develops that can become deeply entrenched and difficult to change (Kenny, 1985). (pp. 424–425)

Thus, it is critical to understand the dynamics and intricacies of psychological colonization and imperialism, including how each of us has learned and internalized the attitudes and behaviors connected with positions of privilege and oppression. Our experience has been that the deeper the levels of understanding, the more we can avoid perpetuating domination-subordination dynamics. Furthermore, we are able to act differently and engage in collaboration, genuine power sharing (Cheung, 2000; Norsworthy, 2006; van Strien, 1997; Wang & Heppner, Chapter 8, this volume), and mutuality in our international collaborations and partnerships. The mutual respect and attitude of "learning from one another" also fosters a valuing and appreciation of the indigenous values, beliefs, and behaviors of diverse cultures and countries. Moreover, the collaboration and mutual respect promotes a deeper understanding that professionals around the world have the knowledge and skills to create indigenous counseling models that are relevant to their contexts. Our experience has been that authentic cross-national collaboration and power-sharing, along with ongoing reflection about the relationship dynamics among the members of the team, can lessen the potential for psychological colonization (Norsworthy, 2006). Such discussions and reflection are important because everyone has been enculturated into these systems, dynamics, and structures of power, privilege, domination, and subordination; subsequently, we often unconsciously enact our part in the dynamic when we have not done our own personal "decolonization" work of "conscientization" (Freire, 1972). Conscientization involves becoming aware of and understanding the dynamics of colonization, domination, and subordination and one's own associated attitudes, thoughts, feelings, and behaviors. Furthermore, real conscientization demands taking action to change the oppressive conditions, including learning how to liberate ourselves from the colonized mentality and associated behaviors to engage in creative collaboration and partnership.

It is important to note that endorsing and implementing these principles cannot insure that U.S. mental health professionals will not continue to promote or maintain psychological colonization and cultural imperialism outside the United States or that colleagues outside the United States will not collude with this process. Nonetheless, such principles can serve as a framework to help guide our culturally sensitive professional work. As Pedersen (2003) so cogently stated,

> Given the difficulty of conducting psychological research, it is essential that the presence of cultural bias be acknowledged in a global context so that we do not confuse the discipline of psychology with the more narrowly defined boundaries of "American" psychology. (p. 403)

This same warning and recommendation can apply to various practices of the counseling profession. When practicing different forms of counselor interventions (e.g., individual or group counseling, consultation, prevention), mental health professionals can be aware of the cultural bias inherent in models developed in the United States and then proceed in developing indigenous counseling models in their own cultures and countries.

Applying counseling theories and research models from one culture to another requires considerable cross-cultural competencies to understand how and why they work in one cultural context, as well as how they may or may not work in another cultural context. Scholars have identified a wide array of obstacles and challenges confronting the U.S. counseling profession to becoming cross-culturally competent. Heppner, Leong, and Chiao (2008) summarized some of these obstacles as (a) short and superficial contacts with international colleagues; (b) a limited number of major U.S. institutions to support the internationalizing of the profession; (c) a tendency to believe one's own behaviors are typical of others; (d) feelings of superiority as a profession relative to other countries; (e) lack of exposure to and knowledge of the work of international colleagues; (f) xenophobia; (g) difficulty in understanding and accepting others' worldviews; (h) inability to accept differences across cultures as simply differences; (i) an overemphasis on internal validity; and (j) psychological reactance, defensiveness, and other personality styles that contribute to the obstacles above (e.g., Gerstein & Ægisdóttir, 2005a, 2005c; Heppner, 2006; Leong & Ponterotto, 2003; Leong & Santiago-Rivera, 1999; Leung, 2003; Marsella, 1998; Segall, Lonner, & Berry, 1998).

Problems emerging from a lack of cross-cultural competence may be two-sided. On the one hand, U.S. scholars and practitioners in our counseling and psychology training programs can lack cultural sensitivity and hold encapsulated attitudes such as "U.S. professionals are the experts." U.S. scholars steeped in an individualistic, personal agency, and assertiveness paradigm, coupled with the lack of cultural competencies, may be particularly prone to cultural insensitivity and be oblivious to differences and thus feel superior. The other side pertains to internalized racism and/or the colonized mentality of some international colleagues who have been led to believe that "even the moon is bigger in the United States" and that in some way one comes to believe their ideas are inferior or even that they are inferior beings. Internalized racism, coupled with a lack of cultural competence, may lead one to be prone to wholesale adoption of U.S.-based counseling theories and research methods. Moreover, as discussed earlier, sometimes, these two dynamics can promote a comfortable or ambivalent collusion. Another set of consequences may be the adoption of counseling theories and research models that are culturally inappropriate and most likely less effective for the recipient's culture. Such theories and models might also continue the colonizer-colonized cycle, and they could potentially be a waste of time in the therapeutic process.

Another dimension of the wholesale exportation of U.S.-based counseling theories pertains to graduate students from other countries studying counseling and counseling psychology in the United States. During the course of studying for a master's or doctoral degree, international students are typically taught almost exclusively about Western, U.S.-based counseling models. Even when students are warned about adopting these Western models uncritically, the Western-based assumptions frequently become instilled in the thinking processes of international students, often unknowingly. When this happens, these students are frequently unaware of assumptions, based on a Western cultural context; subsequently, when they return to their home country to practice, the Western-based assumptions can create obstacles in responding appropriately in their home cultures. For example, when one international graduate student returned to her home country from the United States to practice counseling for a few months, it took some time to recognize that some of her assumptions and ways of behaving, the norm in the United States, were incongruent with her home culture; a turning point was when she realized that even though both she and her supervisor were Taiwanese, their interaction was nonetheless cross-cultural. This realization then sparked additional reflection and awareness of the different cultural dynamics affecting her thinking and behavior.

In short, although there are many benefits to sharing information across cultures, there are also some challenges that require additional awareness, discussion, and examination. Understanding the dynamics of colonization and imperialism in relation to the transportation of counseling and psychology outside the United States and bringing a reflective stance to our international partnerships, counseling training, and cross-cultural/intracultural research will increase the likelihood of culturally sensitive and effective collaboration with our cross-national colleagues.

Conclusion

This chapter underscores the importance of understanding the major questions and conundrums in contemporary cultural and cross-cultural research as they relate to the cross-national movement in the counseling profession. The chapter also illustrates the need for an awareness of more emic, indigenous research to contribute to a complex counseling and psychology capable of responding to the myriad of challenging contemporary global mental health problems through "culture-centered perspectives on human behavior" (Pedersen, 2003, p. 402).

We have maintained that the exportation of U.S. psychology and counseling can become an instrument of psychological colonization, particularly in relation to the exportation of U.S. counseling models to non-Western contexts. Based on their research with groups from Southeast Asia (e.g., Thailand), Khuankaew and Norsworthy (2005) observed, "When we work with groups to analyze their suffering, globalization emerges as a root cause of the structural inequities encountered in the Global South" (p. 3). Furthermore, local activists and grassroots communities in Thailand (where Khuankaew and Norsworthy engage in collaborative projects focusing on issues of violence against women, HIV/AIDS, and other social problems) consistently express the view that "globalization, by definition, is a destructive force in the region" partially because "at the global level, countries of the Global North define the rules and standards regarding how globalization should work and who should benefit" (p. 3). The same themes emerge when discussing the impact of the unaware Western "expert" or researcher who enters their spaces to provide "help" or to study without a real understanding of the culture, context, desires, concerns, and priorities of local people.

In addition, it is important to highlight how international students deal with the cross-cultural challenges while studying in the United States and then on returning to their home countries, and how such challenges are also intertwined with U.S. values, worldviews, and models of counseling. Few programs include sufficient examination of these complex cultural issues in the curriculum (Heppner, Leong, & Chiao, 2008; Leong & Ponterotto, 2003), including the conscientization of students so that they do not internalize U.S. counseling models as universal and the standard of practice globally.

In 2004, the APA, noting the current issues related to exportation of U.S. psychology, passed a resolution focusing on bringing culture and gender awareness to international psychology in an effort to offer guidance in the internationalization movement (see Appendix, end of chapter). Steps such as these signal a recognition by organized U.S. psychology that it is time to seriously attend to how we interact at the global level and how psychology can contribute to the common good of all citizens of the world, not just those in the West.

The analysis presented in this chapter allows us to understand the problems and challenges associated with the cross-national movements in counseling and counseling psychology around the globe. From here, it is important to explore examples of decolonization, conscientization, partnership, and collaboration in cross-cultural, cross-national, and international research, training, and practice. In a few upcoming chapters, the benefits and challenges of cross-national collaboration and partnerships in research and practice are highlighted. Additionally, several international scholars describe their experiences of completing their counseling training in the United States and their discoveries on returning to their home countries to work and practice. Through these narratives, models of creative collaboration emerge, and we can learn more about how to create an interconnected mosaic among mental health professionals around the globe.

Chapter Questions

1. Taking into account the dominance of western psychology globally and issues related to the uncritical exportation discussed in this chapter, choose one western theory of counseling and discuss the specific problems with its uncritical exportation to a culture or country outside the West. What might be ways to address these problems so that the counselor/counseling psychologist operates in a culturally/contextually relevant way?

2. In working with immigrant and refugee communities within the U.S., discuss how we would want to incorporate the emic and etic perspectives into counseling members of these communities. Give several concrete examples of bringing this two-sided coin to the counseling process.

3. What next steps might the professions of counseling and counseling psychology take to incorporate the guidelines outlined in the APA Resolution on Culture and Gender Awareness in Psychology?

References

Adamopoulos, J., & Lonner, W. J. (2001). Culture and psychology at a crossroad: Historical perspective and theoretical analysis. In D. Matsumoto (Ed.), *Handbook of culture and psychology* (pp. 11–34). New York: Oxford University Press.

American Psychological Association. (2004). *Resolution on culture and gender awareness in international psychology.* Washington, DC: Author.

Atkinson, D. R., Thompson, C. E., & Grant, S. K. (1993). A three dimensional model for counseling racial/Ethnic minorities. *The Counseling Psychologist, 21,* 257–277.

Berry, J. W. (1999). Emics and etics: A symbiotic conception. *Culture and Psychology, 5,* 165–171.

Blowers, G. H. (1996). The prospects for a Chinese psychology. In M. H. Bond (Ed.), *The handbook of Chinese psychology* (pp. 1–14). Hong Kong: Oxford University Press.

Bochner, S. (1999). Cultural diversity within and between societies: Implications for multicultural social systems. In P. B. Pedersen (Ed.), *Multiculturalism as a fourth force* (pp. 19–60). Washington, DC: Taylor & Francis.

Brislin, R. W. (1986). The wording and translation of research instruments. In W. J. Lonner & J. W. Berry (Eds.), *Field methods in cross-cultural research* (pp. 137–164). Beverly Hills, CA: Sage.

Brislin, R. W., Lonner, W. J., & Thorndike, R. M. (1973). *Cross-cultural research methods.* New York: Wiley.

Cheung, F. M. (1988). Surveys of community attitude toward mental health facilities: Reflections or provocations? *American Journal of Community Psychology, 16*(4), 877–882.

Cheung, F. M. (2000). Deconstructing counseling in a cultural context. *The Counseling Psychologist, 28,* 123–132.

Chung, R. C-Y. (2005). Women, human rights, and counseling: Crossing international boundaries. *Journal of Counseling and Development, 83*(3), 262–268.

Douce, L. A. (2004). Globalization of counseling psychology. *The Counseling Psychologist, 32,* 142–152.

Draguns, J. (2004). From speculation through description toward investigation: A prospective glimpse at cultural research in psychotherapy. In U. P. Gielen, J. M. Fish, & J. G. Draguns (Eds.), *Handbook of culture, therapy, and healing* (pp. 369–387). Mahwah, NJ: Lawrence Erlbaum.

Freire, P. (1972). *Pedagogy of the oppressed.* New York: Herder & Herder.

Gergen, K. J., Gulerce, A., Lock, A., & Misra, G. (1996). Psychological science in cultural context. *American Psychologist, 51,* 496–503.

Gerstein, L. H. (2006). Counseling psychologists as international social architects. In R. L. Toporek, L. H. Gerstein, N. A. Fouad, G. Roysircar-Sodowsky, & T. Israel (Eds.), *Handbook for social justice in counseling psychology: Leadership, vision, and action* (pp. 377–387). Thousand Oaks, CA: Sage.

Gerstein, L. H., Rountree, C., & Ordonez, M. A. (2007). An anthropological perspective on multicultural counselling. *Counselling Psychology Quarterly, 20,* 375–400.

Gerstein, L. H., & Ægisdóttir, S. (2005a). Counseling around the world. *Journal of Mental Health Counseling, 27,* 95–184.

Gerstein, L. H., & Ægisdóttir, S. (Guest Eds.). (2005b). Counseling outside of the United States: Looking in and reaching out [Special issue]. *Journal of Mental Health Counseling, 27,* 221–281.

Gerstein, L. H., & Ægisdóttir, S. (2005c). A trip around the world: A counseling travelogue! *Journal of Mental Health Counseling, 27,* 95–103.

Gerstein, L. H., & Ægisdóttir, S. (2007). Training international social change agents: Transcending a U.S. counseling paradigm. *Counselor Education and Supervision, 47,* 123–139.

Heppner, P. P. (2006). The benefits and challenges of becoming cross-culturally competent counseling psychologists. *The Counseling Psychologist, 34,* 147–172.

Heppner, P. P. (2008). Expanding the conceptualization and measurement of applied problem solving and coping: From stages to dimensions to the almost forgotten cultural context. *American Psychologist, 63,* 803–816.

Heppner, P. P., Casas, J. M., Carter, J., & Stone, G. L. (2000). The maturation of counseling psychology: Multifaceted perspectives from 1978 to 1998. In S. D. Brown & R. W. Lent (Eds.), *Handbook of counseling psychology* (3rd ed., pp. 3–49). Thousand Oaks, CA: Sage.

Heppner, P. P., & Gerstein, L. H. (2008). International developments in counseling psychology. In E. Altmaier & B. D. Johnson (Eds.), *Encyclopedia of counseling: Changes and challenges for counseling in the 21st century* (Vol. 1, pp. 260–266). Thousand Oaks, CA: Sage.

Heppner, P. P., Leong, F. T. L., & Chiao, H. (2008). A growing internationalization of counseling psychology. In S. D. Brown & R. W. Lent (Eds.), *Handbook of counseling psychology* (4th ed., pp. 68–85). Hoboken, NJ: Wiley.

Heppner, P. P., Leong, F. T. L., & Gerstein, L. H. (2008). Counseling within a changing world: Meeting the psychological needs of societies and the world. In W. B. Walsh (Ed.), *Biennial review of counseling psychology* (1st ed., pp. 231–258). New York: Taylor & Francis.

Heppner, P. P., Wampold, B. E., & Kivlighan, D. M. (2008). *Research design in counseling* (3rd ed.). Belmont, CA: Thompson Brooks/Cole.

Jaipal, R. (2004). Indian conceptions of mental health, healing, and the individual. In U. P. Gielen, J. M. Fish, & J. G. Draguns (Eds.), *Handbook of culture, therapy, and healing* (pp. 293–308). Mahwah, NJ: Lawrence Erlbaum.

Jing, Q. (2000). International psychology. In K. Pawlik & M. R. Rosenzweig (Eds.), *International handbook of psychology* (pp. 570–584). London: Sage.

Kenny, V. (1985). The post-colonial personality. *The Crane Bag, 9,* 70–78.

Khuankaew, O., & Norsworthy, K. L. (2005). Crossing borders: Activist responses to globalization by women of the Global South. *Globalization Research Center, University of South Florida, Occasional Papers on Globalization, 2*(2), 1–12.

Kim, U. (2001). Culture, science, and indigenous psychology: An integrated analysis. In D. Matsumoto (Ed.), *The handbook of culture and psychology* (pp. 51–75). New York: Oxford University Press.

Kwan, K.-L. K., & Gerstein, L. H. (2008). Envisioning a counseling psychology of the world: The mission of the international forum. *The Counseling Psychologist, 36,* 182–187.

Lee, J., & Sue, S. (2001). Clinical psychology and culture. In D. Matsumoto (Ed.), *The handbook of culture and psychology* (pp. 287–305). New York: Oxford University Press.

Lei, T., Askeroth, C., & Lee, C. (2004). Indigenous Chinese healing: Theories and methods. In U. P. Gielen, J. M. Fish, & J. G. Draguns (Eds.), *Handbook of culture, therapy, and healing* (pp. 191–212). Mahwah, NJ: Lawrence Erlbaum.

Lei, T., Lee, C., Askeroth, C., Bursteyn, D., & Einhorn, A. (2004). Indigenous Chinese healing: A criteria-based meta-analysis of outcomes research. In U. P. Gielen, J. M. Fish, & J. G. Draguns (Eds.), *Handbook of culture, therapy, and healing* (pp. 213–251). Mahwah, NJ: Lawrence Erlbaum.

Leong, F. T. L., & Blustein, D. L. (2000). Toward a global vision of counseling psychology. *The Counseling Psychologist, 28,* 5–9.

Leong, F. T. L., & Ponterotto, J. G. (2003). A proposal for internationalizing counseling psychology in the United States: Rationale, recommendations, and challenges. *The Counseling Psychologist, 31,* 381–395.

Leong, F. T. L., & Santiago-Rivera, A. L. (1999). Climbing the multiculturalism summit: Challenges and pitfalls. In P. Pedersen (Ed.), *Multiculturalism as a fourth force* (pp. 61–74). Philadelphia: Brunner/Mazel.

Leong, F. T. L., & Savickas, M. (2007). Introduction to special issue on international perspectives on counseling psychology. *Applied Psychology: An International Review, 56,* 1–6.

Leung, S. A. (2003). A journey worth traveling: Globalization of counseling psychology. *The Counseling Psychologist, 31,* 412–419.

Lonner, W. J. (1999). Helfrich's "Principle of Triarchic Resonance": A commentary on yet another perspective on the ongoing and tenacious etic-emic debate. *Culture and Psychology, 5,* 173–181.

Lugones, M. C., & Spelmann, E. V. (1983). Have we got a theory for you! Feminist theory, cultural imperialism, and the demand for "the woman's voice." *Women's Studies International Forum, 6,* 573–581.

Marsella, A. J. (1998). Toward a "global-community psychology": Meeting the needs of a changing world. *American Psychologist, 53,* 1282–1291.

McWhirter, J. J. (2000). And now, up go the walls: Constructing an international room for counseling psychology. *The Counseling Psychologist, 28,* 117–122.

Meehl, P. E. (1954). *Clinical versus statistical prediction.* Minneapolis: University of Minnesota Press.

Memmi, A. (1965). *The colonizer and the colonized.* Boston: Beacon Press.

Miller, J. G. (1997). Theoretical issues in cultural psychology. In J. W. Berry, Y. H. Poortinga, & J. Pandey (Eds.), *Handbook of cross-cultural psychology: Theory and method* (Vol. 1, 2nd ed., pp. 85–128). Boston: Allyn & Bacon.

Moane, G. (1994). A psychological analysis of colonialism in an Irish context. *The Irish Journal of Psychology, 15*(2/3), 250–265.

Norsworthy, K. L. (2006). Bringing social justice to international practices of counseling psychology. In R. L. Toporek, L. H. Gerstein, N. A. Fouad, G. Roysircar-Sodowsky, & T. Israel (Eds.), *Handbook for social justice in counseling psychology: Leadership, vision, and action* (pp. 421–441). Thousand Oaks, CA: Sage.

Pedersen, P. (1999). Culture-centered interventions as a fourth dimension in psychology. In P. Pedersen (Ed.), *Multiculturalism as a fourth force* (pp. 3–18). Philadelphia: Brunner/Mazel.

Pedersen, P. B. (2003). Culturally biased assumptions in counseling psychology. *The Counseling Psychologist, 31,* 396–403.

Pedersen, P. B., Crethar, H. C., & Carlson, J. (2008). *Inclusive cultural empathy: Making relationships central in counseling and psychotherapy*. Washington, DC: American Psychological Association.

Pedersen, P. B., Draguns, J. G., Lonner, W. J., & Trimble, J. E. (2008). *Counseling across cultures* (6th ed.). Thousand Oaks, CA: Sage.

Pedersen, P. B., & Leong, F. (1997). Counseling in an international context. *The Counseling Psychologist, 25*, 117–122.

Pike, K. L. (1966). *Language in relation to a unified theory of the structure of human behavior*. The Hague, the Netherlands: Mouton.

Rice, J., & Ballou, M. (2002). *Cultural and gender awareness in international psychology*. Washington, DC: American Psychological Association, Division 52, International Psychology, International Committee for Women.

Rogers, C. (1951). *Client-centered therapy*. Boston: Houghton Mifflin.

Said, E. W. (1993). *Culture and imperialism*. New York: Knopf.

Segall, M. H., Lonner, W. J., & Berry, J. W. (1998). Cross-cultural psychology as a scholarly discipline: On a flowering of culture in behavioral research. *American Psychologist, 53*, 1101–1110.

Sue, D. W., & Sue, D. (1990). *Counseling the culturally different: Theory and practice* (2nd ed.). New York: Wiley.

Sue, D. W., & Sue, D. (2008). *Counseling the culturally diverse: Theory and practice* (5th ed.). New York: Wiley.

Tanaka-Matsumi, J. (2001). Abnormal psychology and culture. In D. Matsumoto (Ed.), *The handbook of culture and psychology* (pp. 265–286). New York: Oxford University Press.

Tanaka-Matsumi, J. (2004). Japanese forms of psychotherapy: Naikan therapy and Morita therapy. In U. P. Gielen, J. M. Fish, & J. G. Draguns (Eds.), *Handbook of culture, therapy, and healing* (pp. 277–292). Mahwah, NJ: Lawrence Erlbaum.

Triandis, H. C. (1993). Collectivism and individualism as cultural syndromes. *Cross-Cultural Research, 27*, 155–180.

Triandis, H. C. (1994). *Culture and social behavior*. New York: McGraw-Hill.

Triandis, H. C. (1996). The psychological measurement of cultural syndromes. *American Psychologist, 51*, 407–415.

Triandis, H. C. (2000). Dialectics between cultural and cross-cultural psychology. *Asian Journal of Social Psychology, 3*, 185–195.

Triandis, H. C. (2001). Individualism and collectivism: Past, present, and future. In D. Matsumoto (Ed.), *The handbook of culture and psychology* (pp. 35–50). New York: Oxford University Press.

Triandis, H. C. (2002). Odysseus wandered for 10, I wondered for 50 years. In W. J. Lonner, D. L. Dinnel, S. A. Hayes, & D. N. Sattler (Eds.), *Online readings in psychology and culture* (Unit 2). Bellingham, WA: Center for Cross-Cultural Research, Western Washington University. Retrieved January 26, 2009, from http://www.ac.wwu.edu/~culture/triandis2.htm

van de Vijver, F. (2001). The evolution of cross-cultural research methods. In D. Matsumoto (Ed.), *The handbook of culture and psychology* (pp. 77–97). New York: Oxford University Press.

van de Vijver, F., & Leung, K. (1997). *Methods and data analysis for cross-cultural research*. Thousand Oaks, CA: Sage.

van Strien, P. J. (1997). The American "colonization" of northwest European social psychology after World War II. *Journal of the History of the Behavioral Sciences, 33*, 349–363.

Wrenn, C. G. (1962). The culturally encapsulated counselor. *Harvard Educational Review, 32*(4), 444–449.

Yang, K. S., Hwang, K. K., Pedersen, P. B., & Daibo, I. (Eds.). (2003). *Progress in Asian social psychology: Conceptual and empirical contributions*. Westport, CT: Praeger.

Ægisdóttir, S., & Gerstein, L. H. (2005). Reaching out: Mental health delivery outside the box. *Journal of Mental Health Counseling, 27*, 221–224.

Ægisdóttir, S., Gerstein, L. H., & Çinarbaş, D. C. (2008). Methodological issues in cross-cultural counseling research: Equivalence, bias, and translations. *The Counseling Psychologist, 36*, 188–219.

Ægisdóttir, S., White, M. J., Spengler, P. M., Maugherman, A. S., Anderson, L. A., Cook, R. S. et al. (2006). The meta-analysis of clinical judgment project: Fifty-six years of accumulated research on clinical versus statistical prediction. *The Counseling Psychologist, 34*, 341–382.

Appendix: APA Resolution on Culture and Gender Awareness in International Psychology

Adopted by the APA Council of Representatives July 28, 2004

WHEREAS an estimated 60 percent (or more) of the world's psychologists now live outside the US (Hogan, 1995);

WHEREAS psychologists outside of the US have generated perspectives, methods, and practices that correspond to the needs of the people in their societies and data that are relevant to the development of a more complete psychology of people (Bhopal, 2001; Espin & Gaweleck, 1992; Martin-Baro, 1994; Weiss, Whelan, & Gupta, 2000; Winslow, Honein, & Elzubeir, 2002);

WHEREAS US leadership in world psychology is sometimes perceived as disproportionately influential, partly because of access to research funds, an abundance of US publication outlets and the wide acceptance of the English language (Kagitçibasi in Sunar, 1996; Sloan 2000);

WHEREAS US psychology needs to more fully consider the ramifications of national and cultural perspectives and indigenous psychologies (Castillo, 2001; Frank & Frank, 1991; Sue & Zane 1987) in its research, practice, and educational efforts (Best & Williams, 1997; Draguns, 2001; Segall, Lonner, & Berry, 1998);

WHEREAS US grounded, normed, and structured measures dominate US empirical psychology, while internationally based, qualitative methods such as community action research are less known or valued in the US (Denzin & Lincoln, 2001; Murray & Chamberlain, 1999; Robson, 1993);

WHEREAS US assessment procedures, tests and normative data have been used extensively in other countries, sometimes without consideration of cultural differences that affect reliability and validity (Dana, 2000);

WHEREAS people of other cultures have adopted US methods of clinical diagnosis and intervention and US psychology has also exported these methods based on US norms and values to other cultures (Foa, Keane, & Friedman, 2000; Mezzich, 2002; Nakane & Nakane, 2002; Thorne & Lambers, 1998);

WHEREAS there is a need to develop and disseminate materials that will facilitate the training of psychologists to conduct culturally-appropriate research and practice around the world as well as within the culturally diverse United States (diMauro, Gilbert, & Parker, 2003; Friedman, 1997; Hays, 2001);

WHEREAS universities and colleges have called upon faculty and departments to internationalize their courses and curriculum, given the increasing number of international students at North American institutions (Marsella & Pedersen, 2002; Woolf, Hulsizer, & McCarthy, 2002);

WHEREAS most individuals from the United States, including psychologists, do not speak a second language or read journals or books in another language other than English, and therefore are unlikely to be familiar with firsthand sources of international research in other countries other than English speaking countries;

WHEREAS research focused on immigration and discrimination against immigrants and undocumented immigrants is sparse (Esses, Dovidio, Jackson, & Armstrong, 2001; Evans, 2002; Martin, 1994);

WHEREAS decades of psychological studies have demonstrated that scientifically sound practice requires taking into account issues of gender and culture at all stages of the research process (Bem, 1993; Brodsky & Hare-Mustin; 1980; Harding, 1987; Schmitz, Stakeman, & Sisneros, 1996; Sherif, 1979; Spence, 1987; White, Russo, & Travis, 2001);

WHEREAS psychologists have demonstrated how privilege and oppression affect the lives of women and men across sexual orientations, disabilities, social class, age, ethnic, and religious memberships (APA Guidelines for Psychological Practice with Older Adults, 2003; Banks, 2003; Eberhardt & Fiske, 1998; Gershick, 2000; Sidanius, Levin, Federico, & Pratto, 2001; Sidanius & Pratto, 1999);

WHEREAS women worldwide experience discrimination in terms of resources and access to food, health care, inheritance, credit, education, vocational training, hiring, fair compensation for paid work, family and public rights, individual mobility and travel, and religious education and participation, and they also may face legal, societal, cultural, and religious practices which justify and endorse this discrimination (Bianchi, Casper & Peltola, 1999; Goode, 1993; Hauchler & Kennedy, 1994; Smeeding & Ross, 1999; United Nations, 2000; United Nations Population Fund, 2000), and psychology could address these global problems internationally (United Nations, 2000; United Nations Population Fund, 2000);

WHEREAS, as a result of gender discrimination, women internationally constitute a majority of the poor, and female headed families are the lowest income groups in many countries around the world (Blossfield, 1995; Duncan & Edwards, 1997; Goldberg & Kremen, 1990; McLanahan & Kelly, 1998); moreover, educational achievements and opportunities and literacy rates for women are significantly less than for men (United Nations Department of Public Information, 1995; UNESCO, 2002);

WHEREAS, as a result of gender discrimination, women experience violations of their body integrity, interpersonal violence, and physical abuse (Center for Policy Alternatives, 1998; European Women's Lobby, 2000; Nylen & Heimer, 2000); and under repressive systems, in wars, and in postwar conditions, women are targeted for violence (Comas-Diaz & Jansen, 1995);

WHEREAS, as a result of gender discrimination individuals with differently gendered identity and gender expression experience violence and discrimination within many societies from both the populace and from those in authority (Dworkin & Yi, 2003);

WHEREAS psychologists strive to promote international peace and understanding and to decrease ethnic and gender violence;

WHEREAS, in contrast to the United States where professional practices and policies generally are in concert with and support governmental structures, in many other countries, psychologists must advocate for social justice and oppose unjust governmental structures and policies (Fox & Prilleltensky, 2001; Martin-Baro, 1994; Moane, 1999; Moler & Catley, 2000; Nandy, 1987);

WHEREAS knowledge management, production and dissemination of information are also affected by global politics and economics in ways that maintain social inequality (Capra, 1996; Fox & Prilleltensky, 2001; Giddens, 2000; Harding, 1993; Wallerstein, 1992);

WHEREAS the field of psychology could benefit significantly from the expansion of its knowledge base through international perspectives, conclusions, and practices (Bronstein & Quina, 1988; Gielen & Pagan, 1993; Marsella, 1998; Nandy, 1983; Pareek, 1990);

WHEREAS the opportunity for mutual benefit and greater effectiveness in solving global problems is at hand in research partnerships across nations and cultures if psychologists proceed with critical awareness and a commitment to gender, cultural, social, economic and religious justice (Sloan, 1996);

WHEREAS psychologists have a responsibility to better understand the values, mores, history, and social policies of other nations and cultures that affect generalizations and recommendations about best practices (Schmitz, Stakeman, & Sisneros, 1996);

WHEREAS psychologists are committed to culture fair and gender fair competent unbiased practice (APA Guidelines on Cross Cultural Education and Training, Research, Organizational Change and Practice for Psychologists, 2002; APA Guidelines for Practice with Girls and Women (Draft), 2002; APA Guidelines for Psychotherapy with Lesbian, Gay, and Bisexual Clients, 2000; American Psychological Association, A New Model of Disability, 2003);

WHEREAS psychologists are ethically guided to "recognize that fairness and justice entitle all persons to access to and benefit from the contributions of psychology" and to "respect the rights, dignity, and worth of all people" (American Psychological Association, Ethical Principles of Psychologists and Code of Conduct, 2002);

WHEREAS the International Committee for Women Task Force of Division 52, International Psychology, has developed an important position paper on "Cultural and Gender Awareness in International Psychology" that identifies critical areas of consideration for psychologists to consider in cross-cultural research (Rice & Ballou, 2002);

THEREFORE LET IT BE RESOLVED that the American Psychological Association will:

(1) advocate for more research on the role that cultural ideologies have in the experience of women and men across and within countries on the basis of sex, gender identity, gender expression, ethnicity, social class, age, disabilities, and religion.

(2) advocate for more collaborative research partnerships with colleagues from diverse cultures and countries leading to mutually beneficial dialogues and learning opportunities.

(3) advocate for critical research that analyzes how cultural, economic, and geopolitical perspectives may be embedded within US psychological research and practice.

(4) encourage more attention to a critical examination of international cultural, gender, gender identity, age, and disability perspectives in psychological theory, practice, and research at all levels of psychological education and training curricula.

(5) encourage psychologists to gain an understanding of the experiences of individuals in diverse cultures, and their points of view and to value pluralistic worldviews, ways of knowing, organizing, functioning, and standpoints.

(6) encourage psychologists to become aware of and understand how systems of power hierarchies may influence the privileges, advantages, and rewards that usually accrue by virtue of placement and power.

(7) encourage psychologists to understand how power hierarchies may influence the production and dissemination of knowledge in psychology internationally and to alter their practices according to the ethical insights that emerge from this understanding.

(8) encourage psychologists to appreciate the multiple dilemmas and contradictions inherent in valuing culture and actual cultural practices when they are oppressive to women, but congruent with the practices of diverse ethnic groups.

(9) advocate for cross-national research that analyzes and supports the elimination of cultural, gender, gender identity, age, and disability discrimination in all arenas—economic, social, educational, and political.

(10) support public policy that supports global change toward egalitarian relationships and the elimination of practices and conditions oppressive to women.

BE IT FURTHER RESOLVED that the American Psychological Association (1) recommend that Boards and Committees consider the impact of the globalization of psychology and the incorporation of international perspectives into their activities, and (2) charge the Committee on International Relations in Psychology, in collaboration appropriate APA Boards and Committees, to implement any directives from the Council of Representatives that result from the adoption of the resolution.

SOURCE: Copyright © 2005 by the American Psychological Association. Reproduced with permission. The official citation that should be used in referencing this material is: Paige, R. U. (2005). Proceedings of the American

Psychological Association for the Legislative Year 2004: Minutes of the Annual Meeting of the Council of Representatives, February 20–22, 2004, Washington, D.C., and July 28 and 30, 2004, Honolulu, Hawaii; and Minutes of the February, April, June, August, October, and December 2004 Meetings of the Board of Directors. *American Psychologist, 60*(5), 436–511. Reproduced with permission of the American Psychological Association. The use of this information does not imply endorsement by the publisher.

References

American Psychological Association. (2000). *Guidelines for psychotherapy with lesbian, gay, and bisexual clients.* Washington, DC: Author.

American Psychological Association. (2002). Ethical principles of psychologists and code of conduct. *American Psychologist, 57* (12).

American Psychological Association. (2002). *Guidelines for psychological practice with girls and women (Draft).* Joint Task Force of APA Divisions 17 and 35, American Psychological Association.

American Psychological Association. (2002). *Guidelines on cross cultural education and training, research, organizational change, and practice for psychologists.* Washington, DC: Joint Task Force of APA Divisions 17 and 45.

American Psychological Association. (2003*). Guidelines for psychological practice with older adults.* Washington, DC: Division 12-Section II and Division 20 Interdivisional Force on Practice in Clinical Geropsychology.

American Psychological Association. (April, 2003). Special Issue. A new model of disability. *American Psychologist, 58,* 279–311.

Banks, M. E. (2003). Disability in the family: A life span perspective. *Cultural Diversity and Ethnic Minority Psychology, 9,* 367–384.

Bem, S. L. (1993). *The lenses of gender.* New Haven: Yale University Press.

Best, D., & Williams, J. (1997). Sex, gender, and culture. In J. W. Berry, M. H. Segall, & C. Kagitçibasi (Eds.), *Handbook of cross-cultural psychology: Social behavior and applications* (V.3, pp. 163–212). Needham Heights, MA: Allyn & Bacon.

Bhopal, K. (2001). Researching South Asian women: Issues of sameness and difference in the research process. *Journal of Gender Studies, 10,* 279–286.

Bianchi, S. M., Casper, L. M., & Peltola, P. K. (1999). A cross-national look at married women's earnings dependency. *Gender Issues, 17*(3), Summer, 3–33.

Blossfield, H. P. (Ed.). (1995). *The new role of women: Family formation in modern societies.* Boulder, CO: Westview Press.

Brodsky, A., & Hare-Mustin, R. (1980). Part one: The influence of gender on research. In A. Brodsky & R. Hare-Mustin (Eds.), *Women and psychotherapy* (pp. 3–34). New York: Guilford Press.

Bronstein, P., & Quina, K. (Eds.). (1988). *Teaching a psychology of people.* Washington, DC: American Psychological Association.

Capra, F. (1996). *The web of life.* New York: Anchor Books.

Castillo, R. (2001) Lessons from folk healing practices. In WSA. Tseng & J. Streltzer (Eds.), *Culture and psychotherapy: A guide to clinical practice* (pp. 81–101). Washington, DC: American Psychiatric Association.

Center for Policy Alternatives. (1988). *America's economic agenda: Women's voices for solutions. Health care and security.* Women's Economic Leadership Summit, Washington, DC, White House and Center for Policy Alternatives, April 3–5, 1997.

Comas-Diaz, L., & Jansen, M. A. (1995). Global conflict and violence against women. *Peace and Conflict: Journal of Peace Psychology, 1*(4), 315–331.

Dana, R. H. (2000). An assessment intervention model for research and practice with multicultural populations. In R. H. Dana (Ed.), *Handbook of cross-cultural and multicultural personality assessment* (pp. 5–16). Mahwah, NJ: Lawrence Erlbaum.

Denzin, N., & Lincoln, Y. (Eds.). (2001). *Handbook of qualitative research.* Thousand Oaks, CA: Sage.

di Mauro, D., Gilbert, H., & Parker, R. (Eds.). (2003). *Handbook of sexuality research training initiatives.* London: Carfax.

Draguns, J. G. (2001). Toward a truly international psychology: Beyond English only. *American Psychologist, 56,* 1019–1030.

Duncan, S., & Edwards, R. (Eds.). (1997). *Single mothers in an international context: Mothers or workers?* London: University College London Press.

Dworkin, S. H., & Yi, H. (2003). LGBT identity, violence, and social justice: The psychological is political. *International Journal for the Advancement of Counseling, 25,* 269–279.

Eberhardt, J. L., & Fiske, S. T. (Eds.). (1998). *Confronting racism: The problem and the response.* Thousand Oaks, CA: Sage.

Espin, O., & Gaweleck, M. A. (1992). Women's diversity: Ethnicity, race, class, and gender in theories of feminist psychology. In L. Brown and M. Ballou, *Personality and psychopathology, feminist reappraisals.* New York: Guilford Press.

Esses, V. M., Dovidio, J. F., Jackson, L. M., & Armstrong, T. L. (2001). The immigration dilemma: The role of perceived group competition, ethnic prejudice, and national identity. *The Journal of Social Issues, 57*(3), 389–412.

European Women's Lobby. (January, 2000). *Unveiling the hidden data on domestic violence in the European Union.* Brussels: European Women's Union Studies.

Evans, C. (2002). At war with diversity: U.S. language policy in an age of anxiety. *Bilingual Research Journal, 26*(2), 485–491.

Fernando, S., Ndwgwa, D., Wilson, M. (Eds.). (1998). *Forensic psychiatry, race, and culture.* New York: Routledge.

Foa, E. B., Keane, T. M., & Friedman, M. J. (Eds.). (2000). *Effective treatments for PTSD: Practice guidelines from the International Society for Traumatic Stress Studies.* New York: Guilford Press.

Fox, D., & Prilleltensky, I. (2001). *Critical psychology.* London: Sage.

Frank, J. D., & Frank, J. B. (1991). *Persuasion and healing: A comparative study of psychotherapy.* Baltimore, MD: Johns Hopkins.

Friedman, S. (Ed.). (1997). *Cultural issues in the treatment of anxiety.* New York: Guilford.

Gershick, T. (2000). Towards a theory of disability and gender. *Signs, 24,* 1263–1269.

Giddens, A. (2000). Runaway world: How globalization is reshaping our lives. New York: Routledge.

Gielen, U. P., & Pagan, M. (1993). International psychology and American mainstream psychology. *The International Psychologist, 34*(1), 16–19.

Goldberg, G. S., & Kremen, E. (1990). *The feminization of poverty: Only in America?* New York: Praeger.

Goode, W. J. (1993). *World changes in divorce patterns.* New Haven, CT: Yale University Press.

Harding, S. (Ed.). (1987). *Feminism and methodology.* Bloomington: Indiana University Press.

Harding, S. (1993). *The radical economy of science toward a democratic future.* Bloomington, IN: Indiana University Press.

Hauchler, I., & Kennedy, P. M. (Eds.). (1994). *Global trends: The world almanac of development and peace.* New York: Continuum Publishing.

Hays, P. A. (2001). *Addressing cultural complexities in practice: A framework for clinicians and counselors.* Washington, DC: American Psychological Association Books.

Hogan, J. D. (1995). International psychology in the next century: Comment and speculation from a U.S. perspective. *World Psychology, 1,* 9–25.

Marsella, A. J. (1998). Toward a global psychology: Meeting the needs of a changing world. *American Psychologist, 53,* 1282–1291.

Marsella, A. J., & Pedersen, P. B. (2002). Fifty ways to internationalize the curriculum of Western psychology. *APA Continuing Education Workshop.* Chicago: American Psychological Association.

Martin, S. F. (1994). A policy perspective on the mental health and psychosocial needs of refugees. In A. J. Marsella, T. Bornemann, S. Ekblad, & J. Orley, *Amidst peril and pain: The mental health and well-being of the world's refugees* (pp. 69–80). Washington, DC: American Psychological Association.

Martin-Baro, I. (1994). *Writings for a liberation psychology.* Cambridge, MA: Harvard University Press.

McLanahan, S. S., & Kelly, E. L. (1998). *The feminization of poverty: Past and future.* Princeton, NJ: Office of Population Research.

Mezzich, J. E. (2002). International surveys on the use of ICD10 and related diagnostic systems. *Psychopathology, 35*(2–3), 72–75.

Moane, G. (1999). *Gender and colonialism: The psychological analysis of oppression and liberation.* New York: St. Martin's Press.

Moler, D., & Catley, B. (2000). *Global America: Imposing liberalism on a recalcitrant world.* Westport, CT: Praeger.

Murray, M., & Chamberlain, K. (Eds.). (1999). *Qualitative health psychology theories and methods.* London: Sage.

Nakane, Y., & Nakane, H. (2002). Classification systems for psychiatric diseases currently used in Japan. *Psychopathology, 35*(2–3), 191–194.

Nandy, A. (1983). Towards an alternative politics of psychology. *International Social Science Journal, 25*(2), 323–338.

Nandy, A. (1987). *Traditions, tyranny, and utopia.* Delhi: Oxford University Press.

Nylen, L., & Heimer, G. (April, 2000). *Sweden's response to domestic violence.* Stockholm: The Swedish Institute.

Pareek, U. (1990). Culture-relevant and culture-modifying action research for development. *Journal of Social Issues, 45,* 110–131.

Rice, J. K., & Ballou, M. (2002). *Cultural and gender awareness in international psychology.* Washington, DC: American Psychological Association, Division 52, International Psychology, International Committee for Women.

Robson, C. (1993). *Real world research.* Oxford, UK: Blackwell.

Schmitz, C. L., Stakeman, C., & Sisneros, J. (1996). Educating professionals for practice in a multicultural society: Understanding oppression and valuing diversity. *Families in Society, 82*(6), 612–622.

Segall, M. H., Lonner, W. J., & Berry, J. W. (1998). Cross cultural psychology as a scholarly discipline: On the flowering of culture in behavioral research. *American Psychologist, 53,* 1101–1110.

Sherif, C. W. (1979). Bias in psychology. In J. A. Sherman & E. T. Beck (Eds.), *The prism of sex: Essays in the sociology of knowledge.* Madison, WI: The University of Wisconsin Press.

Sidanius, J., Levin, S., Federico, C. M., & Patto, F. (2001). Legitimizing ideologies: The social dominance approach. In J. T. Jost & B. Major (Eds.), *The psychology of legitimacy: Emerging perspectives on ideology, justice, and intergroup relations.* New York: Cambridge University Press, pp. 307–331.

Sidanius, J., & Pratto, F. (1999). *Social dominance: An intergroup theory of social hierarchy and oppression.* New York: Cambridge University Press.

Sloan, T. S. (1996). Psychological research methods in developing countries. In S. Carr & J. Schumaker (Eds.), *Psychology in the developing world* (pp. 38–45). London: Praeger.

Sloan, T. (Ed.). (2000). *Critical psychology: Voices for change.* Hampshire, England: Plagrave.

Smeeding, T. M., & Ross, K. (1999). *Social protection for the poor in the developed world: The evidence from LIS.* Washington, DC: Inter-American Development Bank.

Spence, J. (1987). Masculinity, femininity, and gender-related traits: A conceptual analysis and critique of current research. In B. A. Maher & W. B. Maher (Eds.), *Progress in experimental research in personality,* (V. 13, pp. 1–97). New York: Academic Press.

Sue, S., & Zane, N. (1987). The role of culture and cultural techniques in psychotherapy: A critique and reformulation. *American Psychologist, 42,* 37–45.

Sunar, D. (1998). An interview with Cigdem Kagitçibasi. *World Psychology, 2,* 139–152.

Thorne, B., & Lambers, E. (Eds.). (1998). *Person-centered therapy: A European perspective.* London: Sage.

UNESCO. (2002). *Literacy rates.* New York: United Nations Educational, Scientific, and Cultural Organization. United Nations. (2000). *The world's women 2000: Trends and statistics.* New York: Author.

United Nations Department of Public Information. (1995). *Beijing platform for action.* New York: United Nations.

United Nations Population Fund. (2000). *Lives together, worlds apart: Men and women in a time of change.* New York: Author.

Wallerstein, I. (1992). America and the world today, yesterday, and tomorrow. *Theory and Society, 21,* 1–28.

Weiss, E., Whelan, D., Gupta, G. (2000). Gender, sexuality, and HIV: Making a difference in the lives of young women in developing countries. *Sexual and Relationship Therapy, 15,* 234–245.

White, J. W., Russo, N. F., & Travis, C. B. (2001). Feminism and the decade of behavior. *Psychology of Women Quarterly, 25,* 267–279.

Winslow, W., Honein, G., Elzubeir, M. (2002). Seeking Emirati women's voices: The use of focus groups with an Arab population. *Qualitative Health Research, 12,* 566–576.

Woolf, L. M., Hulsizer, M. R., & McCarthy, T. (2002). *Internationalization of introductory psychology: Challenges, benefits, and resources.* Twenty-Fifth annual National Institute on the Teaching of Psychology, St. Petersburg Beach, FL, January 2–5, 2002.

Chapter Five

Theoretical and Methodological Issues When Studying Culture

Stefanía Ægisdóttir, Lawrence H. Gerstein, Seung-Ming Alvin Leung, Kwong-Liem Karl Kwan, and Walter J. Lonner

M ost scholars today agree that engaging in and disseminating results from cross-cultural and cultural research is an important component of the advancement of the science and practice of counseling and counseling psychology. However, issues and debates surrounding the construct of culture are often complicated and controversial. The issues of the importance of emic (culture-specific) and etic (transcending culture) constructs in advancing knowledge in psychology and the value of universality (discovering universal laws; i.e., cross-cultural comparative studies, hypothetico-deductive positivistic or post-positivistic framework) versus cultural relativism (all "laws" are emic, constructivism) continue to plague those engaged in cross-cultural and cultural research. In this chapter, we examine the two often "opposing forces" of universalism and cultural relativism in the study of cultural influences on behavior and discuss methodological and conceptual challenges and issues facing each approach. The benefits of each approach for enhancing psychological and counseling knowledge are discussed as well. Finally, we provide some examples from anthropology that may benefit counseling scholars interested in cross-cultural research and in bridging the gap between cultural relativism (emics) and universalism (etics) to further enhance the science of counseling and psychology.

Why Do Phenomena Have to Be Either This or That? or, Do They?

Throughout the history of psychology, there have been complications and debates similar and related to the debates about emics and etics, and cultural relativism and universalism. These debates can be traced to ontological concerns (the nature of being, existence, and reality: What exists?) and epistemological questions (the nature, scope, and limitations of knowledge: What is knowledge? How is it acquired?). Some examples include the validity of subjective as compared with objective realities; the nomothetic (e.g., psychological tests and other quantitative methods) versus idiosyncratic (e.g., interview and other qualitative techniques) debate in the assessment and understanding of an individual's functioning; and the statistical versus clinical controversy surrounding clinical judgment. All these debates and dilemmas can be tied to the same issues: What is an appropriate and valid source of knowledge? And what is the nature of existence and reality? Moreover, with these diverse points of view come different methods and approaches to seeking knowledge and gaining an understanding of human psychological functioning.

When exploring how these divergent views have been resolved, scholars have usually concluded that both debated polarities have something to offer and that one does not exclude the other. For instance, those involved in clinical assessment have concluded that both idiosyncratic and clinical (e.g., clinical interview) data and nomothetic and statistical (e.g., results from psychological tests, decision rules) data complement one another and can be combined to gain a more holistic and perhaps more accurate assessment of a person (e.g., Strohmer & Arm, 2006; Ægisdóttir et al., 2006). Furthermore, counseling professionals in the United States are trained to attend both to the subjective realities of their clients (e.g., asking clients about their phenomenological experiences with diagnostic labels such as depression) and to the objective, observable diagnostic signs clients may be displaying (e.g., comparing signs against a diagnostic rubric) and to consult the outcome literature on empirically supported interventions. Thus, ideally, counseling professionals consult two sources of knowledge and realities (the subjective and the objective) and bridge these two to be of the best help to their clients. In short, the complexity of human existence is acknowledged. This also involves abandoning philosophical purism and a polar opposite mentality for a functionalist view with the belief that it offers a more comprehensive understanding of the individual.

Whereas in counseling practice, this pragmatic functionalist philosophical stance of seeking knowledge from both idiographic and nomothetic sources is considered acceptable and, in fact, best practice, in counseling and psychology *research*, the issue becomes more complicated. This is because psychology and counseling are heavily influenced by the positivistic framework and the scientific method, which can be traced back to the time when psychology was branching off from philosophy and struggling to be considered a scientific discipline in line with the natural sciences. This struggle between the subjective world and the objective world becomes extremely salient in studies involving the construct of culture. The struggle is exemplified in the emic-etic debate, the controversy concerning universalism versus cultural relativism, and the issues revolving around the merits of quantitative and qualitative research methodologies.

It is not surprising, therefore, that scholars interested in culture and cultural influences on behavior conceptualize and approach their investigation from different frameworks and methodologies. For instance, one can group, compare, and contrast how different disciplines approach the study of culture (e.g., psychology and anthropology). One can further group scholars within these disciplines into subcategories based on their conceptualization of culture and their methods, aims, and goals. These subcategories span cross-cultural psychology, cultural psychology, indigenous psychology, cultural anthropology, social anthropology, and psychological anthropology (e.g., Adamopoulos & Lonner, 2001; Triandis, 2000). Furthermore, and to some degree regardless of the discipline (psychology, anthropology), one can categorize cultural studies based on ontological and epistemological schools of thought. Therefore, one can adhere to the thought of cultural relativism and take an emic epistemological stance in which one can understand individuals' psychological functioning only in the context of their culture, using culture-specific concepts that are meaningful and deemed appropriate by natives within that culture (e.g., Lett, 1996). This relativistic stance is constructivist in that meaning and knowledge are considered a human construction and therefore leads one to qualitative research. Or one can adhere to the universalistic school of thought. Here, one operates from the assumption that there are core human characteristics shared across cultures (e.g., aggression; Bond & Tedeschi, 2001) that can be studied using scientific methods. Etic constructs (or derived etics, e.g., Berry, 1999) that are regarded meaningful and appropriate by the community of scientific observers are the main focus within this school of thought (Lett, 1996).

Lonner (2011), when speaking for the universalist position, identified seven levels of universals in terms of the feasibility and importance of each for psychological science. The levels range from simple universals (e.g., human sexuality) that are invariant across cultures to cocktail party universals (e.g., phenomenological experiences of psychological pain; meaning hermeneutics) that are difficult to categorize and compare.

Universalists operate from the hypothetico-deductive framework of positivism. Absolutism has also been mentioned within this context. The absolutist view is that there is one absolute truth about human behavior that can be studied and understood using etic concepts and the scientific experiment (positivism). Within absolutism, culture and cultural influence on behavior are not considered of value but are considered to be masking and standing in the way for absolute laws to be identified (Adamopoulos & Lonner, 2001, Hwang, 2005). Within the absolutist view, theories and approaches should be equally effective and appropriate regardless of culture. Some say (e.g., Shweder, 1990) that absolutism and therefore ethnocentrism characterize mainstream scientific psychology (U.S. psychology)—a viewpoint shared by both cultural and cross-cultural psychologists, who place culture at the core of their inquiries, even though they approach the construct of culture differently.

Studying Culture

Although culture has been of some interest to psychology scholars and researchers in the United States since World War II or even earlier (Adamopoulos & Lonner, 2001; Marsella, Dubanoski, Hamada, & Morse, 2000; Segall, Lonner, & Berry, 1998), it was not until the mid- to late 1960s that systematic cross-cultural and cultural research began to emerge. Up to that time period or even later, an absolutist Eurocentric/ethnocentric framework mostly guided the research agenda, namely translating and indiscriminately testing U.S- (or Western-) developed psychological inventories (e.g., personality and intelligence tests) and theories in countries outside the United States. This was done without much consideration given to cultural bias in the constructs and theories being tested and the methodology employed (Adamopoulos & Lonner, 2001; Marsella et al., 2000). In the 1970s, however, more attention was paid to the conceptual challenges with this absolutist stance and the methodological problems in cross-cultural comparative research using Euro-American tools. During this time, for instance, the first book was published on psychology on methodological issues and problems in cross-cultural research: *Cross-Cultural Research Methods*, by Brislin, Lonner, and Thorndike (1973). Since that time, additional publications have followed (e.g., Lonner & Berry, 1986; van de Vijver & Leung, 1997a) introducing scholars to the unique challenges of cross-cultural and cultural research. Additionally, during this time the controversy between universalist and relativist, and emic versus etic approaches to understanding and studying cultural influences on behavior began to emerge.

In psychology, scholars have aligned with different schools of thought and methodologies when studying culture, depending on the fundamental goals of their efforts. These schools include indigenous psychology, cultural psychology, and cross-cultural psychology. According to Adamopoulos and Lonner (2001), in the indigenous approach, psychological phenomena are studied in their specific cultural context by scholars indigenous to that culture. The main goal is to develop an indigenous psychology that has meaning and that benefits people within a specific culture (e.g., Kim, Park, & Park, 2000). The indigenous approach advocates the perspectives of both "insiders" (emic) and "outsiders" (etic), which necessitates multiple methodologies (qualitative, quantitative) (Kim, Yang, & Hwang, 2006). The primary theoretical challenge for this approach is avoiding existing conceptualization of behavior and psychological processes and therefore determining what is indigenous (Adamopoulos & Lonner, 2001).

As with the indigenous approach, the basic purpose of the cultural approach is to advance the understanding of individuals in their cultural context. In contrast to the indigenous approach, however, those who identify as cultural psychologists often study cultures other than their own (Triandis, 2000), many times employing ethnographic methods originating in cultural anthropology. Quantitative methods are also sometimes applied. The meaning of constructs within a culture is of greatest interest (emic), and those adhering to this perspective refute treating culture and cultural variables as independent of the person. Instead, culture is viewed as an integral, important, and inseparable part of the human mind (Adamopoulos & Lonner, 2001). Cultural psychologists espouse a relativistic framework, and explicit comparison between cultural groups is not of interest and does not make sense to these professionals. Often, the epistemological framework guiding this type of approach is constructivist, in which meaning and knowledge is considered a construction of the mind. The main theoretical challenge for the relativistic stance is conceptualizing culture to fit the idea of it being an integral and inseparable part of the human mind. Thus, it appears that the theorization of culture could be so inclusive that it becomes useless. Additionally, Adamopoulos and Lonner noted inconsistencies in how cultural psychologists have conceptualized culture. Furthermore, they questioned if meaning can be a scientific object of explanation.

Those adhering to the cross-cultural approach generally obtain data from many cultures with the aim of studying their similarities and differences in psychological functioning. Constructs shared across cultures are investigated, and the primary purpose is the development of an inclusive universal psychology (etics/derived etics, e.g., Berry, 1999) and discerning how and why contextual factors affect the universal core of human functioning (Adamopoulos & Lonner, 2001; Triandis, 2000). In cross-cultural studies, culture and cultural variables are often treated as quasi-independent variables either moderating or mediating behavior. Therefore, cultural variables can be separated from the individual and approximated by tests and inventories (e.g., demographic variables, psychological variables, societal variables). A positivistic ontological stance is usually taken within this framework. The main methodological challenges of this comparative framework are issues of equivalence of constructs and observations, bias, and levels of analysis (Adamopoulos & Lonner; Smith, 2002, Chapter 7). Theoretical challenges of the universalist comparative framework have to do with the status of culture within it as an intervening variable that has no explanatory or causative power. As Adamopoulos and Lonner (2001) stated, "This results in the degradation of the status of culture and makes it much easier to ignore in theory construction" (p. 24).

The approaches to studying culture just mentioned have different aims, challenges, and merits; yet they can also complement one another. In the following sections, we discuss in more detail the cross-cultural, cultural, and anthropological frameworks and approaches with connotation to the emic-etic and the relativist-universalist distinctions. Even though commonalities can be derived from cultural psychology and anthropology, we submit that counseling scholars interested in international counseling psychology performing cross-cultural and cultural research might draw some important lessons from anthropology in studying cultures.

Methodological Issues

Etics, Universalism, and the Cross-Cultural Approach

The term *etic* is derived from the word *phonetics*, which in linguistics refers to universal sounds used in human language regardless of their meaning in a particular language (Pike, 1967). In psychology and anthropology, therefore, the etic perspective relies on extrinsic concepts and categories that have meaning to scientific observers. Etic concepts transcend culture, and the etic approach relies on a descriptive system (taxonomy, categorization) that is equally valid for all cultures so that similarities and differences between cultures can be found (Helfrich, 1999). Etic perspectives to studying and understanding culture are closely linked to cross-cultural approaches, even though emic constructs may also be of interest to cross-cultural psychologists. *Cross-cultural psychology* and *cross-cultural strategies* refer to collecting data in two or more cultures. Within this comparative framework, the generalizability of psychological theories and approaches is examined to see how culture affects theories and approaches, and to offer suggestions about adaptations to a new cultural context (Helfrich, 1999). More specifically, *cross-cultural etic approaches* refer to the "study of similarities and differences in individual functioning in various cultural and ethnic groups; of the relationship between psychological variables and socio-cultural, ecological, and biological variables; and of changes in these variables (Berry, Poortinga, Segall, & Dasen, 1992, p. 2). With cross-cultural and etic strategies to studying human functioning, therefore, concepts (e.g., counseling expectations) that exist in the cultures of interests are the subject of focus. With this approach, culture is "elevated" to the status of a quasi-independent variable that may either mediate or moderate behavior (Adamopoulos & Lonner, 2001). Since with this approach cultural groups are compared on a particular variable, teasing out measurement artifacts (e.g., different meaning attached to the constructs under study: counseling expectations) as potential explanations of cultural differences becomes the main challenge. These artifacts or confounds are issues of bias and equivalence.

Bias

In cross-cultural comparison, between-group differences found in test scores could be viewed as evidence of cultural differences on underlying traits or characteristics. However, cross-cultural scholars have identified a number of possible biases that could cause researchers to misattribute observed similarities and differences to culture. Unfortunately, many cross-cultural research studies have been published that did not pay sufficient attention to bias (e.g., Berry, Poortinga, Segall, & Dasen, 2002; Ægisdóttir, Gerstein, & Çinarbaş, 2008). Furthermore, van de Vijver and Tanzer (2004) commented that "the history of psychology has shown various examples of sweeping generalizations about differences in abilities and traits of cultural populations which, upon close scrutiny, were based on psychometrically poor measures" (p. 264). Thus, one important consideration to increase the rigor in cross-cultural research is controlling for bias. According to van de Vijver and Leung (1997a), *bias* is "a generic term for all nuisance factors threatening the validity of cross-cultural comparison" (p. 10). They identified three main types of bias: construct bias, method bias, and item bias.

Construct bias occurs when the construct measured (e.g., coping) is not the same across cultural groups (van de Vijver & Leung, 1997a, 1997b). Construct bias is a concern in cross-cultural comparisons when (a) there is only partial overlap in the definition of the target construct across cultures (e.g., how coping is defined might be different across cultures), (b) the behaviors associated with a particular construct vary in appropriateness across culture (e.g., coping strategies prized in one culture might not be cherished in another), and (c) there is insufficient sampling of relevant behaviors associated with a construct (e.g., a measure of coping does not comprehensively include major coping strategies in the target cultures) (van de Vijver & Poortinga, 1997; van de Vijver & Tanzer, 2004). To minimize the impact of construct bias, researchers should examine if the definition and expression of a construct is the same across cultural groups in the instrument development or selection process. Van de Vijver and Tanzer (2004) identified two strategies that could effectively deal with construct bias. The first method is called *decentering*, where the measures used are developed or adapted simultaneously in the cultures in which they are to be administered. In this process, researchers eliminate and modify words, ideas, and concepts that are not shared across these cultural groups. The resulting instruments consist of items and samples of behavior that have more or less identical meaning and relevance to all participants. The second method to eliminate construct bias is the *convergence approach*. Here the researchers either develop or use culture-specific instruments relevant to each of the target cultures that are administered to participants from all the target cultures. Similarities of findings across instruments (e.g., same patterns of cross-cultural differences on all instruments) support the validity of the cross-cultural results, whereas discrepancies across measures suggest biases (van de Vijver & Leung, 1997a). Ægisdóttir et al. (2008) also suggested that if an instrument developed in only one of the cultures under study is to be used for cross-cultural comparison, new culture-specific emic items relevant to the construct could be constructed in the other culture and added to the instrument to decrease construct bias. While only identical items can be compared cross-culturally, the inclusion of culture-specific items may indicate cultural differences that the original instrument would not have detected. Instead of developing new items, researchers could also include open-ended response options on the measures prompting respondents for additional thoughts regarding the construct. These responses might indicate additional cross-cultural differences and similarities regarding the construct.

When construct bias is properly managed, observed cross-cultural differences might still be compounded by method bias. Method bias occurs when aspects or characteristics of an instrument or its administration elicit diverse responses from members of a different culture, resulting in "unwanted inter-group differences" (van de Vijver & Leung, 1997b). Van de Vijver and Tanzer (2004) identified three sources of method bias: (1) there is sample bias when the characteristics of the samples compared are different (e.g., education, age), (2) there is administration bias when the data collection procedures and processes vary across cultural groups (e.g., in-person versus web-based methods of data collection, test administrators with different levels of expertise), and (3) there is instrument bias when differences in response styles exist among the cultural groups (e.g., social desirability, stimulus familiarity, extreme scoring).

To control for method bias, researchers should use designs (e.g., scales, interviews) that make sense to the cultures under study. They should also use samples that are equivalent in socio-demographic characteristics (e.g., age, gender, education, socio-economic status). Furthermore, they should standardize data collection procedures through developing detailed protocols for test administration, scoring, and interpretation. Additionally, test administrators should receive training such that they have the necessary cultural sensitivity and technical knowledge required for cross-cultural data collection. Moreover, methodological procedures should be used (e.g., test-retest method, structural equation modeling) to assess and discern response styles that might jeopardize cross-cultural comparisons (e.g., Cheung & Rensvold, 2000).

The third kind of bias challenging valid cross-cultural comparisons is item bias, also referred to as *differential item functioning* (van de Vijver & Leung, 1997b). This is a bias at the item level of an instrument caused by erroneous or inaccurate item translation or the use of test items that are inappropriate or irrelevant (e.g., items describing experiences or activities that are unfamiliar) to some of the cultural groups under study. Item bias is present if participants who have the same standing on an underlying trait (e.g., have equal math ability and skill) do not have the same probability of getting a correct answer on a target item.

Item bias can be managed through the use of a range of item bias analysis techniques, including Item Response Theory (IRT), analysis of variance (ANOVA) procedures, structural equation methods (SEM), and logistic regression, to determine if the distribution of item scores for individuals who have equivalent standing on a latent trait is the same across cultural groups (van de Vijver & Leung, 1997b; Ægisdóttir et al., 2008). In addition to using psychometric strategies to detect possible item bias, researchers using multiple language versions of instruments should follow a rigorous language translation procedure to eliminate bias. Prior to translating an instrument, though, investigators should be careful when selecting and adapting an instrument so as to minimize construct, method, and item bias and to ensure that its content and structure are consistent with the cultural context where the instrument is to be administered. A number of authors have written about translation methods (e.g., Brislin, 1976, 1986; Hambleton & de Jong, 2003; Shiraev & Levy, 2006; van de Vijver & Hambleton, 1996; van de Vijver & Leung, 1997a; Ægisdóttir et al., 2008) that are reflected in the standards of the International Test Commission (ITC). In brief, the following procedures have been recommended: (a) Employ bilingual persons speaking the original and target languages to conduct the translation. They need to be familiar with test construction, the construct under study, and the cultures of interest. (b) Use a committee of persons rather than a single person at different stages of the translation process to reduce biases of an individual person. This is done by comparing the individual translations and developing a single translated version of the instrument based on consensus agreement among the translation committee. (c) Perform a back-translation using either a committee of persons or a single individual, where the translated version is converted back to its original-language version. (d) Compare the back-translated version of the measure to the original version and make corresponding modifications to increase equivalence. (e) Pretest the translated version by, for instance, administering both language versions of the instrument to bilingual individuals (in the two target languages) to determine language equivalence. (f) Assess the translated instruments' reliability and validity and potential bias, and compare this with psychometric properties of the original language version. (g) Document and report in published articles the translation procedures, the challenges involved, and the evidence of the translated versions' equivalence.

It is important to note that method bias and item bias might not be exhibited uniformly on different levels of scores (or scales) or an item of an instrument (van de Vijver & Leung, 1997a; Ægisdóttir et al., 2008). A bias is considered uniform when its effect is more or less the same across all levels of the scores. It is considered non-uniform if the effects of bias are not the same for all score levels.

In sum, bias is a major threat to validity in cross-cultural comparisons. The greater the cultural distance (e.g., language, social structure, political structure, climate, human development index) between the cultures under investigation, the greater the potential bias is (Triandis, 2001; Ægisdóttir et al., 2008). Counseling researchers need to identify the types of biases that are likely to exert an influence on their studies and make deliberate efforts to minimize their potential impact on their designs and findings. If at all possible and appropriate, structured tests administered in standardized conditions are less likely to be influenced by bias than are open-ended question formats (e.g., Ægisdóttir et al., 2008). While it is impossible to rule out bias entirely, the documentation of steps taken to reduce, rule out, and assess bias allows researchers to interpret cultural differences in psychological and counseling constructs more accurately.

Equivalence

Equivalence is closely related to bias such that the less the bias, the greater the equivalence. Direct cross-cultural comparisons are greatly challenged and cannot be accurately performed unless the equivalence of the measures that are used has been ensured. Equivalence has been conceptualized in at least two complementary ways. Lonner (1985) discussed four types: functional, conceptual, metric, and linguistic. Functional equivalence refers to the various functions tied to constructs across cultures. For instance, if different functions are connected to behaviors or activities across cultures, their parameters cannot be used for cross-cultural comparison. One example of a nonequivalent habit or phrase salient for the first author is the common U.S. greeting, "Hi, how are you?" While in the United States this greeting is basically met with a simple "Hello" response, in some other cultures this greeting may elicit long accounts of how the person receiving the greeting is actually doing and feeling at that time. Thus, in this example the greeting does not have functional equivalence. Another classic example is pet ownership. In the United States, dogs and cats are often treated as family members, whereas in other cultures they are annoyances and, at best, food. Issues of functional equivalence can often be resolved in the translation of measures.

Conceptual equivalence is closely related to *functional equivalence* and refers to the meaning associated with a concept. Psychological help seeking may, for instance, mean seeking help from a professional mental health provider in one culture, whereas it could mean seeking advice from a shaman or a family member in another. *Metric equivalence* according to Lonner (1985) refers to the psychometric properties (validity, reliability, item distribution) of the tools (e.g., scales) used in cross-cultural research, whereas *linguistic equivalence* refers to the form, structure, reading difficulty, and naturalness of the items used to elicit information about the construct under study (Lonner, 1985; van de Vijver & Leung, 1997a; Ægisdóttir et al., 2008).

A complementary conceptualization of equivalence was introduced by van de Vijver and Leung (1997a). They distinguished between four levels of equivalence that have a hierarchical order: construct nonequivalence, construct or structural equivalence, measurement unit equivalence, and scalar equivalence. At the lowest end, representing a total lack of equivalence, is *construct nonequivalence,* referring to constructs being so dissimilar or nonexistent across cultures (e.g., culture-bound syndromes) that they cannot be compared. This conceptualization incorporates Lonner's (1985) lack of functional equivalence. The second level of equivalence in van de Vijver and Leung's conceptualization is *construct* or *structural equivalence.* It refers to the meaning attached to a construct and the construct's nomological network (convergent and divergent validity) (e.g., Ægisdóttir et al., 2008). At this level, a construct might have the same definition and meaning (e.g., career interests) across cultures, yet the operational definitions may differ. For example, the meaning and conceptual structure of *career interests* might be the same across cultures and may predict similar outcomes, but the operational definitions could differ (i.e., activities to express the same interest type vary across cultures).

The third level of equivalence is *measurement unit equivalence* (van de Vijver, 2001; van de Vijver & Leung, 1997a). Here, the scales used to measure the concept are equivalent, but their origins are different across groups. In some instances, there is a known constant that can be applied to one measure to make the measures equivalent. The most commonly used example to illustrate measurement unit equivalence is the measurement of temperature using Kelvin and Celsius scales (e.g., van de Vijver & Leung, 1997a). Even though both scales are at the interval level of measurement, they cannot be directly compared because they have different origins. To make them comparable, a constant of 273 (their origins differ by 273) needs to be added to the Kelvin scale. Only then do the temperatures measured by these two scales have the same meaning. Counseling scholars are familiar with measurement unit equivalence in their practice. For instance, in some cases different cut-scores on psychological inventories are used to identify psychological characteristics (e.g., personality traits) of individuals from different groups (Ægisdóttir et al., 2008), and thus different scores on a measure represent the same quality (meaning) based on group memberships. Biases affecting the origins of scale scores render valid cross-cultural comparisons difficult.

The last and highest level of equivalence is scalar equivalence. *Scalar equivalence* refers to complete score comparability. It is achieved if the same instrument is employed as a measure across cultures, using an equivalent unit of measurement, and bias has been ruled out (van de Vijver & Leung, 1997a). When this level of equivalence has been reached, scale scores using mean score comparisons can be performed between cultural groups. Establishing scalar equivalence involves the use of psychometric procedures. Van de Vijver and Leung (1997b) maintained that statistical techniques employed to demonstrate structural equivalence of instruments across cultures (e.g., correlation matrices and factor structures) are insufficient in assessing scalar equivalence—a similar factor structure of a construct does not assure scalar equivalence. Van de Vijver and Leung recommended the use of internal validation procedures such as intracultural techniques to examine if empirical data are consistent with theoretical expectations for each of the cultures that are compared (e.g., to examine if the order of item difficulty of an intelligence test is the same in different cultures). Differential item functioning techniques (e.g., IRT) could also be used to check for item bias and uniformity of item bias. Therefore, various techniques used to assess for bias (e.g., van de Vijver & Leung, 1997b; Ægisdóttir et al., 2008) should be applied before measures are compared across cultures.

Merits of the Etic, Universalistic, Cross-Cultural Approach

Despite the challenges involved in valid cross-cultural comparisons, the cross-cultural approach has informed psychological theory and practice in important ways. For instance, in personality psychology, extensive research worldwide has been performed on the NEO Personality Inventory (NEO-PI-R; McCrae & Costa, 1997). This research has measured the "Big Five" personality factors that have been found to be somewhat robust across cultures, even though their robustness does not preclude other culturally specific personality factors (e.g., Ho, 1996). We refer the reader to Church and Lonner (1998) and Smith, Bond, and Kagitçibasi (2006), who provided comprehensive overviews of the cross-cultural research on personality. Likewise, extensive cross-cultural research has been performed on the "abnormal" personality (e.g., Tanaka-Matsumi, 2001; Tanaka-Matsumi & Draguns, 1997). This research has, for example, indicated that for schizophrenia, some universal core symptoms have been reported even though the prognosis and course of the symptoms vary by sociocultural context. Furthermore, extensive cross-cultural research has been performed on emotions and emotional display rules (e.g., Matsumoto, 2001, in press), human development (e.g., Kagitçibasi, 1996; Smith et al., 2006), values (Hofstede, 1980), and cultural syndromes and the self (Triandis, 2001) that have greatly influenced psychological theory, research, and practice.

In addition to the accumulation of knowledge regarding cultural similarities and differences in psychological variables across cultures, it cannot be denied that these and other efforts to examine and identify universals in psychology have made many scholars aware of the dangers of indiscriminately exporting theories developed within individualistic Anglo-American frameworks to cultures founded on different values and philosophies. Over the years, there has been increased sophistication in the research methodologies employed (attention to bias and equivalence) and more demands made on researchers to document the validity of their methodologies and findings (e.g., van de Vijver, 2001).

The crux of cross-cultural and etic approaches is comparative research using quasi-experimental methods, wherein culture and cultural variables are treated as independent variables either mediating or moderating behavior. What remains unresolved, though, is the status of culture and cultural variables in explaining observed differences among cultural groups. It stands to reason that culture (e.g., nationality) and cultural variables (individualism, collectivism) are never more than *descriptions* of observed differences. Designating them an explanatory power is highly suspect. Therefore, within the often positivistic hypothetico-deductive approach espoused within cross-cultural psychology, a serious limitation is placed on the type of theoretical development possible and the usefulness of the construct of culture (e.g., Adamopoulos & Lonner, 2001; Kim, 2001).

Emics, Cultural Relativism, and the Cultural Approach

Another school of thought within psychology focusing on cultural influences on behavior is cultural psychology. The main purpose of this framework is to increase the knowledge and understanding of the person in a cultural context (Adamopoulos & Lonner, 2001). As mentioned earlier, cross-cultural comparisons are not of interest within this approach but rather investigation of the meaning constructs have within a specific culture. This approach to cultural studies espouses emic constructs that are unique to a culture. *Emic* is extracted from the word *phonemics,* which is a linguistic concept that focuses on the meaning and context of words (Pike, 1967). In anthropological linguistics, regardless of variations, an emic unit of data or an emic construct remains the same entity and means the same thing for insiders of a culture (Pike, 1967). For example, a *strike* means "emically" one thing within the sports of U.S. baseball; yet, within the world of English speakers, a strike "etically" comprises many different types of events. Thus, an emic construct is derived and operationalized through the eyes of natives in a particular cultural system. It reflects the insiders' reported beliefs, thoughts, attitudes, and behavioral practices (Harris, 1968). For instance, in Chinese culture, filial piety is a normative familial concept that defines intergenerational relationships in terms of the reverence and obedience the junior generation (i.e., children) is morally obliged to reciprocate for the beneficence afforded by the senior generation (i.e., parents, grandparents) within a family. The moral mandate, in turn, prescribes normative behaviors the junior generations are expected to follow such that the senior generation and the family name are graced with honor and face (Kwan, 2000). When adult children defer their life decisions (e.g., career, mate selection) to the expectations of parents or live with parents and grandparents after marriage, for example, these behaviors follow certain rules and serve a functional purpose within the cultural context that may not be explicitly observable or understood by an (outside) investigator. An emic construct, therefore, points to a rule-system in a culture that needs to be teased out by the investigator through an intracultural analysis (Price-Williams, 1975). In this case, an understanding of filial piety cautions scholars not to label these filial behaviors as "dependent," "indecisive," or "immature" (Kwan, 2000), which may be the meaning attached to the values and behaviors in another culture such as in the United States.

In anthropology and within cultural psychology, an emic focus refers to studying a culture ipso facto (i.e., as it is). It is a locality-specific perspective from which descriptions (e.g., how a certain pattern of behaviors is labeled) and meanings (e.g., function or purpose of a certain pattern of behaviors) of observed phenomena are derived and understood in the context of the local culture rather than interpreted with reference to external criteria or a priori assumptions ascribed to or imposed by the investigators. Therefore, it is a relativistic framework in contrast to a universalistic one. The goal is to gain an insider's perspective of the phenomena of interest within a given culture and to adopt the local language or even create a new term to best capture and explain the observations (e.g., filial piety).

Methods

Cultural psychologists operating from the relativistic (constructivist) framework tend to rely on qualitative methods. They focus on raw data and seek to understand the constructs on the basis of the meanings and functions they serve within the cultural context. This is a discovery-oriented approach, in contrast to the positivistic cross-cultural approach, in which one tests or compares observed material against a priori assumptions or theory. In fact, the positivistic cross-cultural approach has been criticized by cultural researchers (relativists) for imposing a Euro-American structure, meaning, and values on other cultures and thus psychologically colonizing them (Kim, 1995, 2001; Kim & Berry, 1993). Therefore, along with immersing oneself (geographically or psychologically) in the unfamiliar culture to acquire or develop the "insider's" lens, the cultural researcher is to refrain from imposing an external set of cognitive or phenomenological references (e.g., an existing construct, a hypothesis) in the data-analytic, labeling, and explanatory process. Direct comparison across cultures is not of interest in this approach and may, in some cases, not make sense, given that emic constructs might not exist outside the cultures in which they were conceived. For this reason, some scholars have even voiced the concern that the cultural relativistic approach rejects the possibility of scientific knowledge and that the insights gained from this stance are no more than historical accounts (Helfrich, 1999; Hunt, 2007). Triandis (1976), however, indicated that indirect comparison of a given phenomenon between cultures is possible.

Bias

As with the cross-cultural approach, there are some methodological challenges that cultural (relativist) researchers focusing on emics need to confront and solve. One common critical question asked by positivists (universalists) relates to whose construction of reality is being reported in books and articles on results of cultural studies (e.g., Adamopoulos & Lonner,

2001; Helfrich, 1999). Is it the participants' construction, the observers', or the readers'? This criticism points to the ontological and epistemological framework of the relativist, which is in contrast with the traditional scientific viewpoint of the positivists.

Regardless of the ontological and epistemological debate, though, engaging in qualitative research—the research methodology most often applied to understand how individuals construct meaning—has methodological challenges that need to be confronted and resolved. There are, for instance, various types of biases that may confound qualitative data collection, analyses, and interpretations. These can be grossly categorized into method bias and interpretive bias. In terms of method bias, one critical issue that needs to be attended to is the selection of participants in a study. To increase the validity of the information obtained about a cultural group, participants need to be representative of the cultural group to increase the generalizability of the conceptual analysis. Good representation is considered more important than the size of the sample (Bernard, 1995), and frequently purposive or dimensional sampling strategies are used (Miles & Huberman, 1994). That is, the sample is selected so as to best answer the research question (e.g., to ensure all viewpoints are represented).

Another type of method bias has to do with a study's internal validity. To enhance rigor of qualitative research, triangulation has been suggested (e.g., Devers, 1999; Kuzel, 1998). This technique refers to using multiple data sources (e.g., people, events), multiple investigators, and/or methods (e.g., interviews, observations). Triangulation, then, will elucidate different aspects of experiences and context and reduce bias tied with any one method, investigator, and data source. Furthermore, transparency in data collection and analysis (Fossey, Harvey, McDermott, & Davidson, 2002) is suggested so that consumers of the research can see if and how competing accounts and disconfirming evidence within the data were explored and interpreted, and how the researcher's own values and thinking process contributed to the analysis. Moreover, this also involves demonstrating the extent to which the participants' views and knowledge were honored (Fossey et al., 2002).

There is also potential for bias in interpretation. To reduce this type of bias, it is extremely important that the participants' views be presented in their own voices (e.g., verbatim quotes in reports) (Fossey et al., 2002). In addition, to decrease this type of bias, a validation process needs to be implemented in which the research participants themselves are involved in the data analysis and interpretation process such that they provide their view of the credibility of interpretations and findings. Moreover, investigators need to keep a reflective journal of notes on how their own personal characteristics, feelings, values, and biases may be influencing their work.

This may help researchers manage and to some degree separate their own experiences and interpretations from their observations. In terms of the external validity of the study and to provide a richer interpretation and understanding of the data, it is extremely important that the investigator provide detailed descriptions of the cultural context in which the research takes place (Devers, 1999; Fossey et al., 2002).

In sum, the cultural relativistic approach to studying culture espouses the use of qualitative methods to best capture the phenomenological world of people in their cultural context. Meaningfulness in a specific cultural context at a specific point in time is a central focus. The main methodological challenge with this approach is making sure that the voices of participants are heard and that accurate recording and interpretations are offered. To ensure the accuracy of such studies while recognizing the subjectivity involved in them, qualitative researchers have incorporated in their methodology means to increase the rigor of their projects by confronting and resolving bias in their methods and interpretation. Lonner and Hayes (2007), in discussing the life and contributions of the cultural psychologist Ernest E. Boesch, give examples of how a cultural psychologist deals with the concept of "culture."

Merits of the Relativistic, Emic, Cultural Approach

The cultural relativistic approach to studying culture and the focus on emic constructs have informed psychology and counseling in important ways. An important development, for instance, is the attempt in the *DSM* diagnostic system (American Psychiatric Association [APA], 2000) to recognize culture-bound syndromes as valid and meaningful constructs. These culture-bound syndromes (emic constructs) refer to recurrent, locality-specific patterns of aberrant behavior and troubling experiences that are indigenously considered an illness, or an affliction. These syndromes represent "localized, folk, diagnostic categories that frame coherent meanings for repetitive or patterned sets of troubling experiences and observations" (APA, 2000, p. 898) that may or may not be linked to a particular *DSM* diagnostic category. A number of the culture-bound syndromes discussed in the *DSM-IV-TR* are actually formal psychiatric diagnoses in their culture of origin. For example, *qi gong psychotic reaction, shenjung-shuairuo,* and *koro* are diagnosable mental disorders in the Chinese Classification of Mental Disorders. These culture-bound syndromes are linked to common practice (e.g., *qi gong)* and etiological beliefs of diseases that are specific to the (Chinese) cultural context.

In addition to the discovery of culture-bound syndromes, numerous studies have been performed on culture, context, and human development.

We recommend Gardiner's (2001) and Gardiner, Mutter, and Kosmitzki's (1998) comprehensive reviews of this topic. There are also many studies on justice and morality (e.g., Leung & Stephan, 2001) that examined these concepts from both a cultural relativistic point of view and a universalistic framework. Additionally, Berry (e.g., 1976) suggested an ecological framework in studying persons in their cultural context and highlighted how the ecological context constructs culture, which in turn affects one's cognitive style.

It is clear that the cultural approach has informed psychology. The most important contribution in our mind is its (as in the contemporary cross-cultural approach) emphasis on cultural context and the danger and limitations of imposed etics. The emphasis on cultural relativism as an opposing force to absolutism has resulted in scholars searching for emic variables to fully comprehend individuals in their cultural context. An example is the Chinese personality. Ho (1996), for instance suggested filial piety to be an important personality variable in Chinese culture. Similarly, in constructing the Chinese Personality Assessment Inventory (CPAI), which was developed using a combined emic-etic approach (Cheung et al., 1996), it was discovered that in addition to universal personality constructs also found in Western personality theories (e.g., Leadership, Optimism vs. Pessimism, Emotionality), indigenous personality constructs derived from the local context were needed to accurately depict the Chinese personality. These included filial piety, trust, persuasion tactics, and group communication styles (Cheung et al., 2001).

Despite the positive developments that have emerged as a result of the cultural relativistic stance, and despite the quality control strategies implemented in qualitative research geared toward enhancing internal and external validity, the issue of the value of meaning and interpretation as explanations still remains unresolved in the scientific community (Adampoulos & Lonner, 2001).

Lessons From Anthropology: Enhancing Cultural Validity in Counseling Research

Anthropology as a discipline is at the core of the cultural sciences (Adamapoulos & Lonner, 2001). Anthropology is the study of humans, their origins, and their variations. This discipline has been around for at least as long as psychology. There are a number of differences in how psychologists and anthropologists approach studying cultural influences on behavior. In general, anthropologists strive to understand phenomena such as culture by looking at shared patterns of thought and action among people within a culture (emics), whereas psychologists (especially those who identify as cross-cultural psychologists) may be more prone to focusing on behavior and psychological processes as universal features of all humans (etics) (Ross, 2004). Both these approaches are important as they can inform each other. This has not often been the case, though.

One important reason for this disconnect is the difference in the onto-logical and epistemological frameworks employed, as previously discussed. Few psychologists have built on the foundation of anthropology (perhaps considering their approach unscientific), and few anthropologists have pursued projects grounded in psychology (perhaps seeing their approach as too mechanical and lacking construct, functional, and conceptual valid-ity). Ross (2004) even claimed that "it often seems as if psychologists are reinventing the wheel, rather than building on the foundation provided by some of anthropology's work" (p. 9). Similarly, Ross argued that there is limited research in anthropology that has employed clear methods, and fewer projects that considered the results generated in psychology. The two groups of professionals also differ in the formulation of a priori hypotheses when conducting research. Psychologists tend to stipulate hypotheses a priori to connect predictions to theory, establish and implement methodol-ogy, possibly reduce experimenter bias, and potentially increase the validity and generalizability of findings. Anthropologists, however, infrequently generate hypotheses a priori, believing that such predictions can bias the methodology, threaten researcher objectivity, and influence the results (Gerstein, Rountree, & Ordonez, 2007).

Many anthropologists question, as do cultural psychologists affili-ated with the cultural relativist view presented earlier, the use of the construct of culture as a quasi-independent variable affecting behavior and whether members of a culture act and think in a similar way (Ross, 2004). Some have even argued that cultures should only be investigated "within their own unique framework" (Laungani, 2007, p. 33). It is our opinion, though, and this is also espoused by others (e.g., Adamopoulos & Lonner, 2001; Helfrich, 1999; Hunt, 2007), that such extreme views do nothing to enhance the science of psychology. Efforts are needed to bridge the two polar-opposite dichotomous viewpoints (i.e., etic-emic; universal-ism-cultural relativism; positivism-constructivism) (see also Helfrich, 1999) and to take a more pragmatic stance in conceptualizing and studying cul-tural influences on behavior and psychological processes. An anthropologi-cal view to cultural research might be a step in that direction in that it may enhance the methodological repertoire of counseling researchers.

In anthropology, as in psychology, theory is very important and closely con-nected to practice. In anthropology, theory informs ethnography (the prac-tice of researching and writing about the culture of local communities) and the results of ethnography inform larger theories of culture (Barnard, 2000).

There are four basic elements of theory in social anthropology (questions, assumptions, methods, and evidence) along with two other specific aspects of investigation:

(a) observing a society as a whole, to see how each element of that society fits together with, or is meaningful in terms of, other such elements; [and]
(b) examining each society in relation to others, to find similarities and differences and account for them. (Barnard, 2000, p. 6)

The first aspect of investigation, "observing society as a whole," involves understanding how variables are related, for example, how attitudes about help-seeking are linked to collectivism. The second aspect, "examining each society in relation to others," deals with gathering information on the similarities and differences, for instance, between the help-seeking behaviors of individuals from European and Asian societies. When engaged in such comparisons, it is essential that researchers have a deep understanding of each culture and a strong theoretical framework to guide the effort (Markus & Kitayama, 1991; Ross, 2004).

Anthropological theory can also help frame the research questions or topics of interest, the design methodology and data collection strategy, the analyses, the interpretation of the findings, and the feedback process to the stakeholders. Anthropologists often first immerse themselves in a culture to formulate research questions and topics for investigation. As participant observers, they may interact with a host of stakeholders and they may gather information, for instance, on human behavior (e.g., affect, cognition, behavior), the environment, and cultural, social, economic, and physical structures in targeted locations. Through the use of participatory mapping (an ethnographic technique), they can also collect additional information from key informants about these structures and the interactions of individuals connected to a specific locale. Basically, mapping involves touring an area with key informants and asking these individuals to share their observations and experiences about particular topics and/or life in general in this location (Agar, 1996; Bernard, 2002; Crane & Angrosino, 1984).

The data collected from participant observation and mapping help familiarize and educate the anthropologist about the unique and common norms, values, attitudes, expectations, behaviors, structures, and environment of the culture under investigation. Possessing this information contributes to the formulation of research questions, topics for investigation, and the appropriate methodology and analyses to be employed. Frequently, anthropologists engage relevant stakeholders in the entire research process from conceptualization to implementation to data analyses to interpretation of the findings.

Selecting a research design is also "influenced by the social, political, technological conditions and particularly by the existing states of knowledge within the culture at a given period of time" (Laungani, 2007, p. 99).

Anthropology has much to offer counseling professionals interested in conducting research in a foreign culture (Gerstein et al., 2007). One anthropologist (Varenne, 2003) also reported that anthropological concepts could assist counseling professionals involved in applied international work. Anthropology has a long history of studying specific cultures (Geertz, 1973; Shweder & Sullivan, 1993) not only by comparing the similarities and differences within and between cultures but also by understanding them within a geographical, historical, and social context (Ross, 2004). Interestingly, very little has been written about the application of anthropological methods to the study of counseling in general and of multicultural counseling specifically (Gerstein et al., 2007). Even less has been written on integrating such methods when performing cross-cultural counseling research. Counseling professionals have adapted, however, a number of anthropological research methods without attributing these strategies to anthropology. Many of the qualitative methodologies employed within the counseling profession can be traced to anthropology, sociology, and linguistics. For instance, such strategies as in vivo observation, participant observation, interviewing, and ethnography have their roots in these disciplines.

Gerstein et al. (2007) contended it was an oversight of the U.S. multicultural counseling movement to not draw from anthropology in the development of multicultural theories, applied strategies, and training paradigms. We contend that the cross-cultural/international counseling movement must not make this same mistake. The implications of doing this and also ignoring the literature accumulated by cultural, cross-cultural, and indigenous psychology can be quite serious and can result in conducting invalid and irrelevant studies, drawing erroneous and inappropriate conclusions from such research, providing poor and ineffective client services, violating cultural norms, attitudes, and behaviors, and even threatening the existence of a culture itself.

Not all cultures can be studied and assessed in terms of numbers. In some cultures, individuals cannot relate to numbers as a way to capture their thoughts, feelings, and/or experiences. Therefore, it might be inappropriate to use self-report instruments containing a reductionistic item response format (e.g., Likert-type scale) with individuals living in cultures that value storytelling and oral tradition (e.g., Gerstein et al., 2007; van de Vijver & Leung, 1997a; Ægisdóttir & Gerstein, 2010; Ægisdóttir et al., 2008). Employing such a numeric instrument with this population may substantially decrease the richness, utility, validity, and heuristic value of the obtained data. For members of cultures that are not used to this type of self-presentation, a more effective method to collect information about them would be studying their use of symbols, artifacts, and storytelling or observing their behavior. When investigators employ methodologies that are more congruent with the targeted cultures, there is a greater probability that the acquired responses from participants will be much more descriptive, accurate, and revealing and richer. Obviously, there are tremendous challenges involved in conducting cross-culturally valid comparative studies of cultures where individuals differ in how they gather, process, and interpret information and experiences.

There are a number of anthropological methods that can be used to address such challenges effectively. Ethnography is a valuable methodological tool used to capture the unique and shared aspects of a particular culture. Ethnography is descriptive in nature, and it provides the interested party with a detailed understanding of cultural phenomena and nuances. Ethnography can target a couple of specific cultural variables or focus on a broader examination of general lifeways or daily traditions in a culture (Bernard, 1995; Gerstein et al., 2007). Most often, anthropologists employ qualitative methods when performing ethnography, but quantitative methods can be used as well, depending on the nature of the research (Bernard, 1995). Critical to the validity of the obtained results is the method of thick description. This strategy takes into consideration the behavior of interest, the context, and the interaction between the two. An effective thick description conveys to an outsider the meaning of the behavior(s) under investigation.

Not surprisingly, anthropologists acquire much more revealing and valid information through extended periods of time in the field. This is in sharp contrast to cross-cultural counseling researchers, who often spend a limited time in the field and instead rely on interviews and survey methodology to collect data. Anthropologists believe that to investigate and more fully comprehend diverse cultures, it is critical to understand the ways of living and collective cognitive schemas of the targeted population. This can be accomplished only by spending long periods of time in the culture. In lieu of this, it is imperative that those engaged in cross-cultural comparative research or international research collaborate and consult with natives about appropriate and culturally congruent methodologies.

Anthropologists rely heavily on participant observation to collect data during all phases of a study. This strategy is thought to decrease the potential of participant reactivity (Ross, 2004). The goal of this strategy is to live in a culture for an extended period of time to gather valid and rich "insider" information and to blend in with the population or become somewhat unnoticeable (Gerstein et al., 2007). Through this strategy, the investigator can develop a deep rapport with the population and, at times, the needed language skills (Ross, 2004). One must be cautious, however, about becoming enmeshed in the target culture or "going native," as this has the potential of decreasing an investigator's objectivity (DeLoria, 1969). Knowing the native language greatly enhances the validity and outcome of participant observation.

Information generated through participant observation can assist in shaping culturally relevant research questions and methodologies. The strategy is also helpful when quantitative methods might be inappropriate to investigate certain phenomena (Bernard, 1995). There are a number of participant observation strategies that anthropologists may employ, for example, field notes and interviewing. Sanjek (1990) reported that it is critical in participant observation research for the anthropological investigator to generate extensive, descriptive, and detailed field notes through the use of, for instance, a diary, a journal, a log, and/or jottings. Such notes allow the researcher to document biases and observations, and they represent one source of data to be analyzed in the later stages of a study. Qualitative strategies are frequently used to code the notes and to capture common themes to describe and evaluate the cultural variable of interest (Gerstein et al., 2007).

Interviewing is another important participant observation strategy employed by anthropologists. In fact, anthropologists rely heavily on this strategy to understand members of a culture, the context of the culture, and the environment connected to the culture (Gerstein et al., 2007). By listening to the voices of members of the targeted cultures, anthropologists obtain rich data and reduce the potential error of drawing inferences based on invalid methods and/or sources. Of course, this assumes selecting a sufficient number of appropriate informants. A sample is representative when all relevant persons and groups have an equal opportunity in the selection process.

Anthropologists prefer to conduct unstructured or semi-structured interviews since interviewees have a greater chance to openly and freely share their responses through these formats as compared with structured interviews. Bernard (1995) claimed that anthropologists most often conduct unstructured interviews because this approach encourages a wide range of responses from the interviewees. Regardless of the interviewing strategy employed, the information that is gathered can be assessed through qualitative procedures, and the results can help increase the investigator's understanding of the targeted cultures (Gerstein et al., 2007).

Free listing is yet another method used by anthropologists to gather data. The goal of this strategy is to acquire "a list of culturally relevant items on which most of the informants agree" (Ross, 2004, p. 90). There are various techniques used to generate these lists, ranging from asking participants to simply name the elements to using computer-generated, weighted lists that are presented to the participants. The listing process can also range from being unrestricted and unconditioned (generate as many elements as possible related to a construct) to restricted (name a limited number of elements) and conditioned (e.g., generate all the causes leading to . . .). The results obtained can offer some understanding of the items that are most culturally salient and relevant to the targeted population.

While the aforementioned anthropological methods appear useful when studying the cultural influence on behavior and psychological processes, some (Ross, 2004) have suggested that anthropology lacks conceptual and methodological clarity and that, as a result, there are limitations to the obtained findings, theories, and the heuristic value of building a valid knowledge base. Ross further stated that for anthropology to possess sound predictions, it must have "fine-tuned methodologies that allow for formal comparisons of the individual results" (p. 23).

To increase cultural validity, generalizability, relevance, and the appropriateness of findings obtained from international and cross-cultural counseling research and to reduce the potential for bias, it is critical that counseling researchers employ mixed designs (e.g., quantitative and qualitative) drawn from both anthropology and psychology. As Whiting (1968) has argued, there are many different types of data that can be studied in cross-cultural comparisons. Predictive models based on empirical data are highly valued by anthropologists interested in sound cultural descriptions (Ross, 2004). These models may permit comparing data across tasks, methods, and theories.

There are also many different strategies that anthropologists use to analyze data. A few will be discussed here. Content or thematic analysis is often employed to examine patterns and themes generated by qualitative methods. Trained raters and/or computer programs are employed to assess and categorize the descriptive data. Frequently, the researcher is intimately involved in this process as well. The results generated by this type of analysis can offer a deep understanding of the cultural variables under investigation.

Another common analytic technique used by anthropologists is informant agreement/disagreement. Numeric data are well suited for this technique, though at times qualitative data can also be transformed into numbers. Analyzing agreement data first involves setting up an informant-by-response matrix and then assessing differences and similarities between the participants (Ross, 2004). There are a number of strategies that can be used to conduct this assessment, including a weighted and unweighted agreement calculation, and much more sophisticated approaches known as correlational agreement analysis and weighted similarity measures.

Multidimensional scaling based on the informant's level of agreement is another sound technique to assess agreement/disagreement. Ultimately, the results of an agreement/disagreement analysis can crystallize "the underlying dynamics within a given domain in a given culture" (p. 22).

The cultural consensus model (Romney, Weller, & Batchelder, 1986) in anthropology addresses how many informants are needed to draw sound conclusions about a cultural domain and how to recognize culturally correct responses. This is critical to determining whether the obtained data and interpretations can represent a consensus among the informants and any identifiable deviations. The consensus model uses agreement/disagreement data in the analysis of participants' responses. Frequently, statistical procedures are employed to analyze the data. It should be mentioned that a cultural consensus model must be tied to a theory to choose the participants and to interpret the obtained data (Ross, 2004).

Clearly, cross-cultural and international counseling researchers can enhance their research methodologies by adopting some of the anthropological strategies that we have discussed. Our profession is in the very early stages of conducting international research, and employing these strategies can strengthen studies and bolster the validity of the results. Furthermore, we have very few cross-cultural findings reported in the counseling literature. There are cross-cultural studies on problem solving (e.g., Heppner, Witty, & Dixon, 2004), coping (e.g., Heppner, 2008), and psychological help-seeking and counseling expectations (e.g., Surgenor, 1985; Todd & Shapira, 1974; Ægisdóttir & Gerstein, 2000, 2004). Some questions can be raised, however, about the cross-cultural validity (e.g., construct equivalence and bias, measurement equivalence and bias) of these studies, questions that could be addressed by also employing anthropological methods. As a result of the shortcomings in the cross-cultural and international counseling literature, it would appear that description and observation would represent a good first step when conducting research. The anthropological strategies discussed earlier are useful in this regard. Employing them can help capture the unique meaning and importance of various counseling constructs and intervention strategies relevant to diverse cultures and societies.

Emic data can be considered building blocks for cross-cultural counseling researchers to tease out what is truly (or entirely) indigenous and what aspects may be shared by other cultures toward the delineation of universal constructs or etic. Price-Williams (1975) noted that within a framework of the sociology of knowledge, all etic systems become emic. Descriptive methods adapted from anthropology enable and challenge researchers to examine the cultural lens through which observed data from a different culture are organized and interpreted (i.e., with reference to the local context or to an existing framework). Furthermore, Draguns (1996) cautioned that neither the emic perspective nor the etic one should be considered inherently superior or inferior. Moreover, Draguns offered the analogy that the etic approach "provides an unsurpassed panoramic view. . . . of Paris from the top of the Eiffel Tower, but offers no substitute for the immersion into the hustle and bustle of street life, normal or disturbed, within a specific milieu" (p. 49).

Conclusion

Despite our call and that of others (see also Adamopoulos & Lonner, 2001; Ægisdóttir et al., 2008) for combined etic-emic approaches and methodologies when studying culture, the status of culture in psychological theory and the methods used to study culture remain under debate. The etic-emic debate continues to be dualistic even though Pike (1967) introduced the emic-etic framework such that both aspects were the same single and unified reality seen from two different points of view—the insider and the outsider views.

Today, most contemporary scholars would probably agree that the study of culture and the influence of culture on behavior and psychological processes could contribute tremendously to the science and practice of psychology and counseling. Whereas the field of counseling in the United States is in its infancy in appreciating the value of a more global knowledge base and studying cultural variations (within and between ethnic groups and nationalities) in psychological functioning, the history of this focus is much longer in anthropology and various disciplines in psychology (e.g., social psychology). It is our belief that counseling researchers have much to learn from these efforts. In this chapter, we described some of these efforts. Cultural context is and continues to be an important construct in describing and understanding human functioning. Despite the importance of this construct, how one conceptualizes and investigates culture and culture's role in theories remains an important challenge for the future of both counseling and psychology.

In this chapter, we outlined the conceptual and methodological challenges involving the construct of culture, which is characterized by a dualistic, either-or mentality. We also suggested that this dualistic framework be abandoned and replaced by a more holistic functionalistic framework. In particular, we recommended combining etic and emic approaches and methodologies and placing a greater importance on the centrality of culture in theory development and application. It would deeply enrich counseling scholars to know how culture influences behavior, to know how culture and personality interact, and to know how culture is constructed (e.g., Adamopoulos & Lonner, 2001). Acquiring this understanding would substantially contribute to our knowledge base in psychology and counseling. We urge counseling and psychology professionals to continue to tackle the challenge of conceptualizing and investigating culture. Such a sustained effort can only enhance our ability to be a profession concerned with the well-being of *all* human beings.

Chapter Questions

1. Scholars have increasingly been emphasizing the importance of equivalence of constructs and measures in cross-cultural comparisons. Given the complexity of translation and adaptation of instruments between languages and the potential for bias (construct, method, item) should counseling researchers give up cross-cultural comparative research? Support your argument and use examples to clarify your argument.

2. For many counselors or counseling psychologists providing counseling services the construct of "meaning" plays an important role (e.g., "what does your depression mean to you?"). Yet, for counseling researchers this construct often becomes problematic. Discuss some ways that this schism between the science and practice of counseling can be resolved?

3. Discuss why treating culture/nationality as an independent variable with causative qualities is problematic. Discuss some solutions to this problem and provide examples to support your argument.

References

Adamopoulos, J., & Lonner, W. J. (2001). Culture and psychology at a crossroad: Historical perspective and theoretical analysis. In D. Matsumoto (Ed.), *Handbook of culture and psychology* (pp. 11–34). New York: Oxford University Press.

Agar, M. H. (1996). *The professional stranger: An informal introduction to ethnography.* New York: Academic Press.

American Psychiatric Association. (2000). *Diagnostic and statistical manual of mental disorders* (4th ed., Text rev.). Washington, DC: Author.

Barnard, A. (2000). *History and theory in anthropology.* Cambridge, UK: University Press.

Bernard, H. R. (1995). *Research methods in anthropology.* New York: AltaMira Press.

Bernard, H. R. (2002). *Research methods in anthropology: Qualitative and quantitative methods* (3rd ed.). Walnut Creek, CA: AltaMira Press.

Berry, J. W. (1976). *Human ecology and cognitive style: Comparative studies in cultural and psychological adaptation.* New York: Wiley.

Berry, J. W. (1999). Emics and etics: A symbiotic conception. *Culture and Psychology, 5,* 165–171.

Berry, J. W., Poortinga, Y. H., Segall, M. H., & Dasen, P. R. (1992). *Cross-cultural psychology: Research and applications.* Cambridge, UK: Cambridge University Press.

Berry, J. W., Poortinga, Y. H., Segall, M. H., & Dasen, P. R. (2002). *Cross-cultural psychology: Research and applications* (2nd ed.). Cambridge, UK: Cambridge University Press.

Bond, M. H., & Tedeschi, J. T. (2001). Polishing the jade: A modest proposal for improving the study of social psychology across cultures. In D. Matsumoto (Ed.), *Handbook of culture and psychology* (pp. 309–324). New York: Oxford University Press.

Brislin, R. W. (1976). Comparative research methodology: Cross cultural studies. *International Journal of Psychology, 11,* 213–229.

Brislin, R. W. (1986). The wording and translation of research instruments. In W. J. Lonner & J. W. Berry (Eds.), *Field methods in cross-cultural research* (pp. 137–164). Beverly Hills, CA: Sage.

Brislin, R. W., Lonner, W. J., & Thorndike, R. M. (1973). *Cross-cultural research methods.* New York: Wiley.

Cheung, F. M., Leung, K., Fan, R., Song, W. Z., Zhang, J. X., & Zhang, J. P. (1996). Development of the Chinese Personality Assessment Inventory (CPAI). *Journal of Cross-Cultural Psychology, 27,* 181–199.

Cheung, F. M., Leung, K., Zhang, J. X., Sun, H. F., Gan, Y. G., Song, W. Z., et al. (2001). Indigenous Chinese personality constructs: Is the Five-Factor Model complete? *Journal of Cross-Cultural Psychology, 32,* 407–433.

Cheung, G. W., & Rensvold, R. B. (2000). Assessing extreme and acquiescence response sets in cross-cultural research using structural equation modeling. *Journal of Cross-Cultural Psychology, 31,* 188–213.

Church, A. T., & Lonner, W. J. (1998). The cross-cultural perspective in the study of personality: Rationale and current research. *Journal of Cross-Cultural Psychology, 29,* 32–62.

Crane, J. G., & Angrosino, M. V. (1984). *Field projects in anthropology: A student handbook* (2nd ed.). Prospect Heights, IL: Waveland Press.

DeLoria, V. (1969). *Custer died for your sins: An Indian manifesto.* New York: MacMillan.

Devers, K. J. (1999). How will we know "good" qualitative research when we see it? Beginning the dialogue in health service research. *HRS: Health Service Research, 34,* 1153–1188.

Draguns, J. G. (1996). Multicultural and cross-cultural assessment: Dilemmas and decisions. In G. R. Sodowsky & J. C. Impara (Eds.), *Multicultural assessment in counseling and clinical psychology* (pp. 37–84). Lincoln, NE: Buros Institute of Mental Measurements.

Fossey, E., Harvey, C., McDermott, F., & Davidson, L. (2002). Understanding and evaluating qualitative research. *Australian and New Zealand Journal of Psychiatry, 36,* 717–732.

Gardiner, H. W. (2001). Culture, context, and development. In D. Matsumoto (Ed.), *Handbook of culture and psychology* (pp. 101–117). New York: Oxford University Press.

Gardiner, H. W., Mutter, J. D., & Kosmitzki, C. (1998). *Lives across cultures: Cross-cultural human development.* Boston: Allyn & Bacon.

Geertz, C. (1973). *The interpretation of cultures.* New York: Jossey-Bass.

Gerstein, L. H., Rountree, C., & Ordonez, M. A. (2007). An anthropological perspective on multicultural counselling. *Counselling Psychology Quarterly, 20,* 375–400.

Hambleton, R. K., & de Jong, J. H. A. L. (2003). Advances in translating and adapting educational and psychological tests. *Language Testing, 20,* 127–134.

Harris, M. (1968). *The rise of anthropological theory: A history of theories of culture.* New York: Thomas Y. Crowell.

Helfrich, H. (1999). Beyond the dilemma of cross-cultural psychology: Resolving the tension between etic and emic approaches. *Culture and Psychology, 5,* 131–153.

Heppner, P. P. (2008). Award for distinguished contributions to the international advancement of psychology. *American Psychologist, 63,* 803–816.

Heppner, P. P., Witty, T. E., & Dixon, W. A. (2004). Problem-solving appraisal and human adjustment: A review of 20 years of research utilizing the Problem Solving Inventory. *The Counseling Psychologist, 32,* 344–428.

Ho, D. Y. F. (1996). Filial piety and its psychological consequences. In M. H. Bond (Ed.), *Handbook of Chinese psychology* (pp. 155–165). Hong Kong: Oxford University Press.

Hofstede, G. (1980). *Culture's consequences: International differences in work-related values.* Beverly Hills, CA: Sage.

Hunt, R. C. (2007). *Beyond relativism: Rethinking comparability in cultural anthropology.* New York: AltaMira Press.

Hwang, K. K. (2005). From anticolonialism to postcolonialism: The emergence of Chinese indigenous psychology in Taiwan. *International Journal of Psychology, 40,* 228–238.

Kagitçibasi, C. (1996). *Family and human development across cultures.* Mahwah, NJ: Erlbaum.

Kim, U. (1995). Psychology, science, and culture: Cross-cultural analysis of national psychologies in developing countries. *International Journal of Psychology, 30,* 663–679.

Kim, U. (2001). Culture, science, and indigenous psychologies. In D. Matsumoto (Ed.), *Handbook of culture and psychology* (pp. 51–75). New York: Oxford University Press.

Kim, U., & Berry, J. W. (1993). *Indigenous psychologies: Research and experience in cultural context.* Thousand Oaks, CA: Sage.

Kim, U., Park, Y. S., & Park, D. H. (2000). The challenge of cross-cultural psychology: The role of indigenous psychologies. *Journal of Cross-Cultural Psychology, 31,* 63–75.

Kim, U., Yang, K. S., & Hwang, K. K. (2006). *Indigenous and cultural psychology: Understanding people in context.* New York: Springer.

Kuzel, A. J. (1998). Naturalistic inquiry: An appropriate model for family medicine. *Family Medicine, 18,* 369–374.

Kwan, K.-L. K. (2000). Counseling Chinese peoples: Perspectives of filial piety. *Asian Journal of Counselling, 7,* 23–42.

Laungani, P. D. (2007). *Understanding cross-cultural psychology.* Thousand Oaks, CA: Sage.

Lett, J. W. (1996). Emic/etic distinctions. In D. Levinson & M. Ember (Eds.), *Encyclopedia of cultural anthropology* (pp. 382–383). New York: Henry Holt.

Leung, K., & Stephan, W. G. (2001). Social justice from a cultural perspective. In D. Matsumoto (Ed.), *Handbook of culture and psychology* (pp. 375–410). New York: Oxford University Press.

Lonner, W. J. (1985). Issues in testing and assessment in cross-cultural counseling. *Counseling Psychologist, 13,* 599–614.

Lonner, W. J. (2011). The continuing challenge of discovering psychological "order" across cultures. In A. Chastiosis, S. Breugelmans, & F. van de Vijver (Eds.), *Fundamental questions in cross-cultural psychology* (pp. 64–94). Cambridge, UK: Cambridge University Press.

Lonner, W. J., & Berry, J. W. (Eds.). (1986). *Field methods in cross-cultural research.* Beverly Hills, CA: Sage.

Lonner, W. J., & Hayes, S. H. (2007). *Discovering cultural psychology: A profile and selected readings of Ernest E. Boesch.* Charlotte, NC: Information Age.

Markus, H. R., & Kitayama, S. (1991). Culture and the self: Implications for cognition, emotion, and motivation. *Psychological Review, 98,* 224–253.

Marsella, A. J., Dubanoski, J., Hamada, W. C., & Morse, H. (2000). The measurement of personality across cultures. Historical, conceptual, and methodological issues and considerations. *American Behavioral Scientist, 44,* 41–62.

Matsumoto, D. (2001). Culture and emotion. In D. Matsumoto (Ed.), *Handbook of culture and psychology* (pp. 171–194). New York: Oxford University Press.

Matsumoto, D. (in press). Culture and emotional expression. In C. Y. Chiu, Y. Y. Hong, S. Shavitt, & R. S. Wyer (Eds.), *Problems and solutions in cross-cultural theory, research, and application.* New York: Psychology Press.

McCrae, R. R., & Costa, P. T. (1997). Personality trait structure as a human universal. *American Psychologist, 52,* 509–516.

Miles, M. B., & Huberman, A. M. (1994). *Qualitative data analysis: An expanded sourcebook* (2nd ed.). Thousand Oaks, CA: Sage.

Pike, K. L. (1967). *Language in relation to a unified theory of structure of human behavior* (2nd ed.). The Hague, the Netherlands: Mouton.

Price-Williams, D. R. (1975). *Explorations in cross-cultural psychology.* San Francisco: Chandler & Sharp.

Romney, A. K., Weller, S. C., & Batchelder, W. H. (1986). Culture as consensus: A theory of culture and informant accuracy. *American Anthropologist, 88,* 313–338.

Ross, N. (2004). *Culture and cognition: Implications for theory and method.* Thousand Oaks, CA: Sage.

Sanjek, P. (1990). *Fieldnotes.* Ithaca, NY: Cornell University Press.

Segall, M. H., Lonner, W. J., & Berry, J. W. (1998). Cross-cultural psychology as a scholarly discipline: On the flowering of culture in behavioral research. *American Psychologist, 53,* 1101–1110.

Shiraev, E., & Levy, D. (2006). *Cross-cultural psychology: Critical thinking and contemporary applications* (3rd ed.). Boston: Allyn & Bacon.

Shweder, R. A. (1990). Cultural psychology: What is it? In J. W. Stigler, R. A. Shweder, & G. Herdt (Eds.), *Cultural psychology: Essays on human cognitive development* (pp. 1–43). New York: Cambridge University Press.

Shweder, R. A., & Sullivan, M. A. (1993). Cultural psychology: Who needs it? *Annual Review of Psychology, 44,* 497–523.

Smith, P. B. (2002). Levels of analysis in cross-cultural psychology. In W. J. Lonner, D. L. Dinnel, S. A. Hayes, & D. N. Sattler (Eds.), *Online readings in psychology and culture* (Unit 2). Bellingham, WA: Center for Cross-Cultural Research, Western Washington University. Retrieved March 28, 2009, from http://www.ac.wwu.edu/~culture

Smith, P. B., Bond, M. H., & Kagitçibasi, C. (2006). *Understanding social psychology across cultures: Living and working in a changing world.* Thousand Oaks, CA: Sage.

Strohmer, D. C., & Arm, J. R. (2006). The more things change, the more they stay the same. *The Counseling Psychologist, 34,* 383–390.

Surgenor, L. J. (1985). Attitudes toward seeking professional psychological help. *New Zealand Journal of Psychology, 14,* 27–33.

Tanaka-Matsumi, J. (2001). Abnormal psychology and culture. In D. Matsumoto (Ed.), *Handbook of culture and psychology* (pp. 265–286). New York: Oxford University Press.

Tanaka-Matsumi, J., & Draguns, J. G. (1997). Culture and psychopathology. In J. W. Berry, M. H. Segall, & C. Kagitçibasi (Eds.), *Handbook of cross-cultural psychology: Social behavior and applications* (Vol. 3, 2nd ed., pp. 449–492). Boston: Allyn & Bacon.

Todd, J. L., & Shapira, A. (1974). US and British self-disclosure, anxiety, empathy, and attitudes to psychotherapy. *Journal of Cross-Cultural Psychology, 5,* 364–369.

Triandis, H. C. (1976). Approaches toward minimizing translation. In R. Brislin (Ed.), *Translation: Applications and research* (pp. 229–243). New York: Wiley.

Triandis, H. C. (2000). Dialectics between cultural and cross-cultural psychology. *Asian Journal of Social Psychology, 3,* 185–195.

Triandis, H. C. (2001). Individualism and collectivism: Past, present, and future. In D. Matsumoto (Ed.), *Handbook of culture and psychology* (pp. 35–50). New York: Oxford University Press.

van de Vijver, F. J. R. (2001). The evolution of cross-cultural research methods. In D. Matsumoto (Ed.), *Handbook of culture and psychology* (pp. 77–97). New York: Oxford University Press.

van de Vijver, F. J. R., & Hambleton, R. K. (1996). Translating tests: Some practical guidelines. *European Psychologist, 1,* 89–99.

van de Vijver, F. J. R., & Leung, K. (1997a). *Methods and data analysis for cross-cultural research.* Thousand Oaks, CA: Sage.

van de Vijver, F. J. R., & Leung, K. (1997b). Methods and data analysis of comparative research. In J. W. Berry, Y. H. Poortinga, & J. Pandey (Eds.), *Handbook of cross-cultural psychology: Vol. 1: Theory and method* (pp. 257–300). Boston: Allyn & Bacon.

van de Vijver, F. J. R., & Poortinga, Y. H. (1997). Towards an integrated analysis of bias in cross-cultural assessment. *European Journal of Psychological Assessment, 13,* 29–37.

van de Vijver, F. J. R., & Tanzer, N. K. (2004). Bias and equivalence in cross-cultural assessment: An overview. *European Review of Applied Psychology, 47,* 263–279.

Varenne, H. (2003). On internationalizing counseling psychology: A view from cultural anthropology. *The Counseling Psychologist, 31,* 404–411.

Whiting, J. W. M. (1968). Methods and problems in cross-cultural research. In G. Lindzey & E. Aronson (Eds.), *Handbook of social psychology* (Vol. 2, pp. 693–728). Cambridge, MA: Addison-Wesley.

Ægisdóttir, S., & Gerstein, L. H. (2000). Icelandic and American students' expectations about counseling. *Journal of Counseling and Development, 78,* 44–53.

Ægisdóttir, S., & Gerstein, L. H. (2004). Icelanders' and U.S. nationals' expectations about counseling: The role of nationality, sex, and Holland's Typology. *Journal of Cross-Cultural Psychology, 35,* 734–748.

Ægisdóttir, S., & Gerstein, L. H. (2010). International counseling competencies: A new frontier in multi-cultural training. In J. C. Ponterotto, J. M. Casas, L. A. Suzuki, & C. A. Alexander (Eds.), *Handbook of multicultural counseling* (3rd ed., pp. 175–188). Thousand Oaks, CA: Sage.

Ægisdóttir, S., Gerstein, L. H., & Çinarbaş, D. C. (2008). Methodological issues in cross-cultural counseling research: Equivalence, bias, and translations. *The Counseling Psychologist, 36,* 188–219.

Ægisdóttir, S., White, M. J., Spengler, P. M., Maugherman, A. S., Anderson, L. A., Cook, R. S. et al. (2006). The meta-analysis of clinical judgment project: Fifty-six years of accumulated research on clinical versus statistical prediction. *The Counseling Psychologist, 34,* 341–382.

Chapter Six

Internationalization of the Counseling Profession

An Indigenous Perspective

Seung-Ming Alvin Leung, Thomas Clawson, Kathryn L.
Norsworthy, Antonio Tena, Andreea Szilagyi, and Jennifer Rogers

In ways and magnitude unseen in previous generations, the forces of glo-balization and internationalization have altered the spectrum and nature of economic, business, and financial activities and transformed the lives of individuals around the globe. Notable authors on the subject of economic globalization observed that globalization has substantially accelerated the flow of capital and human resources around the world, diminished national and geographic boundaries, and leveled the competitive playing field among nations varying in resources and status of development (e.g., Friedman, 2006; Greenwald & Kahn, 2009). The counseling profession, as a human service discipline, has also been involved in a movement of internationalization in the past decade. Internationalization is a move-ment initiated and led by scholars in the United States aiming to capture the immense possibilities for collaboration among counseling and psycho-logical professionals worldwide, made possible by advances in technologies and communication tools that have greatly reduced the distance that has separated regions and countries (e.g., Douce, 2004; Gerstein & Ægisdóttir, 2005; Heppner, 2006; Leong & Blustein, 2000; Leong & Ponterotto, 2003; Savickas, 2007). Internationalization is also prompted by the awareness that counseling professionals can no longer afford to be ethnocentric and unilateral (Leong & Ponterotto, 2003), that a linear and mono-cultural perspective of psychology and counseling cannot adequately respond to mental health challenges, such as poverty, migration, natural disasters, over-population and urbanization, and international war and violence, which are global in size and impact (Marsella, 1998; Marsella & Pedersen, 2004). Outside the United States, internationalization is broadly seen as an important and positive move that will strengthen the counseling profession worldwide (Savickas, 2007).

We would like to accomplish several goals through this chapter. First, we explore the special meaning of internationalization to the counseling profession, and the role that internationalization can play in facilitating the development of the counseling profession. Second, we conceptualize indigenization as an important concurrent step to internationalization, drawing from the rich literature on indigenous psychology to identify broad strategies to indigenize the counseling profession. Third, we discuss the interface between internationalization and indigenization, and highlight initiatives from the U.S.-based National Board for Certified Counselors Inc. & Affiliates (NBCC) as examples of how internationalization efforts can enhance mental health delivery and capacity building at the local, indigenous level. We hope these examples illustrate how internationalization and indigenization can coexist and complement each other. In this chapter, we argue that "internationalization" and "indigenization" are not dichotomous processes with incompatible goals. Ideally, they are actually mutually informing processes that enhance the substance and relevance of the counseling profession in local settings and around the globe.

The Meaning of Internationalization to the Counseling Profession

At this point, the discipline has not reached a consensus on what constitutes "internationalization," yet a number of key themes can be extracted from the literature (also see Chapter 1, this volume). First, internationalization refers to the nurturance of a global perspective in counseling scholarship, through our teaching, research, and service. Coming from a U.S. counseling psychology perspective, Leong and Ponterotto (2003) proposed that internationalization should be carried out at multiple levels, including (a) methods of psychological science (e.g., through diversifying research design and methodology to accommodate research in diverse cultural contexts), (b) profession-based initiatives (e.g., facilitate international connection and cooperation at the level of corresponding psychological associations),

(c) initiatives from the Division of Counseling Psychology (e.g., formalizing international goals, objectives, and action plans into the counseling psychology agenda), and (d) counseling program-specific activities (e.g., enhancing students' exposure to international events and internship opportunities at the program training level to facilitate international perspectives and competence). Leung and Hoshmand (2007) suggested that an international perspective should be centrally reflected in the counseling literature. They asserted that internationalization requires counseling scholars and students to anchor their scholarly work on what has been done around the world by (a) integrating and synthesizing relevant studies from around the world into the review of literature and/or research conceptualization, (b) diversifying the cross-cultural composition of research samples, and (c) extrapolating research findings in light of the global literature and the counseling community.

Second, internationalization refers to the facilitation of collaboration among counseling professionals globally, in practice, research, and training (Gerstein & Ægisdóttir, 2007; Heppner, 2006). This mutual support and the aggregation of strengths could elevate the substance and standing of the counseling profession locally and internationally. As discussed in Chapter 4 of this volume, Heppner (2006) suggested that cross-cultural competence is a prerequisite to effective cross-border collaborations.

Some authors have cautioned against the assumption that internationalization and international collaboration should be led by U.S. professionals. Pedersen (2003) suggested that the United States might have a longer history and experience in the development of psychology (and counseling), yet internationalization "is not a contest or a competition to see who is superior or more advanced" (p. 397). Similarly, Leung (2003) maintained that the concept of equal partnerships is important to international collaboration, emphasizing that "collaboration should be structured as between equal partners, not from a perspective that certain paradigms or models are superior or inferior" (p. 416).

Third, internationalization refers to the indigenization of the counseling profession in local settings and discovering the culture-specific elements that are central to practice in one's own region. Savickas (2007) identified indigenization as one of the main goals of the international counseling psychology community, suggesting that the profession should "formulate and implement strategies that facilitate development of indigenous psychological theory and research that are grounded in the specific cultural context where they are practiced" (p. 186). Indigenization stands in contrast to a "transfer of technology" approach, in which counseling is viewed as a system of theory, research, and practice that could be imported or transferred from one region to another (Leung, 2003; Pedersen, 2003).

Indeed, in regions around the world where counseling is starting to develop, it is all too easy for internationalization to follow the paths and leadership of regions where counseling is more developed (e.g., the United States) and to search for a universal system of theories, research, and standards of practice that could be applied worldwide. However, the "one-size-fits-all" approach will not meet the diverse mental health needs of individuals across cultures. It will also serve to disengage the counseling profession from the richness of cultural differences and diversities of those we serve. Referring to the limited cultural validity of U.S. psychology, Leong and Ponterotto (2003) pointed out that "with the increasing recognition for the need for cross-cultural and international research has come the realization that U.S. psychology is really an indigenous psychology" (p. 384). As such, internationalization should not be the "Americanization" or "Westernization" of counseling being wrapped around on the outside by a nice wrapping paper with an "international" label.

Contextualizing the Internationalization of the Counseling Profession

A number of trends and developments inside and outside the United States have facilitated the unintentional internationalization of the counseling profession from the United States to other parts of the world. Three distinguishable waves include (1) the need for counseling in post-World War and post-conflict regions, (2) international students completing degrees in U.S. counseling programs bringing their training back to their home countries, and (3) the growing international emphasis of counseling and psychology professional organizations in the United States.

First, the aftermath of U.S. engagement in two World Wars and subsequent regional interventions, such as in Korea, Vietnam, or the Balkans, led to the exportation of the idea and practice of counseling to affected regions. Furthermore, according to Yakushko (2005),

> The fall of the Soviet Union created a unique situation for people who have lived behind the Iron Curtain . . . The change in the political and economic systems of the newly formed independent states resulted in unprecedented changes in the lives of millions of people. (p. 161)

Yakushko (2007) also emphasized that political changes have profound effects on career development and vocational paths of citizens of these countries. For example, career counseling, established in the United States in the early 20th century, spread into post-war Europe, where rebuilding economies gave rise to a logical request for this knowledge and expertise.

In the wake of political and societal restructuring, such as in former Soviet bloc countries, the need for services in the helping fields was also paramount (Watts, 1997). Nations looked to other nations for new models to help their societies, and the United States was willing to send "experts." Because of their interests and connections, these experts often worked in foreign venues without connections to U.S. policy. For example, Szilagyi and Paredes (2010) discussed Romania as an example of a country relying on U.S. experts and using the U.S. model as a framework for developing its own system of counseling:

> A clearly defined scope of practice that integrates the tasks identified in various government policies will help Romanian counselors better articulate their professional role . . . with a professionalization strategy that borrows from the experiences of counseling practitioners in the United States . . . focused on the simultaneous development of a counseling association, counselor training standards, credentialing mechanism, and expansion of the knowledge base. (p. 26)

Szilagyi and Paredes (2010) commented that the development of counseling as a practice and a profession in post-Communist Romania has been expedited by drawing on the history of counseling in the United States. The formalization of the profession started in 1995 (Peteanu, 1997), and the progress made in under 15 years has been quite remarkable. It is not merely a strategically good time for the growth of counseling; there is also a clear need for counseling skills to assist Romania and its people in assuming their new identities and new roles in the world. Even though Romania has drawn from the successes and failures of the professional models developed in the United States to accelerate her own formalization process, the counseling profession in Romania is still distinctly Romanian and seeks to serve the needs of its citizens at this critical juncture in the nation's history.

Education is another aspect of the unintentional internationalization of the counseling profession. The concept of school counselors, an outgrowth of the career development movement, aroused strong international interest (e.g., Canales & Blanco-Beledo, 1993; Gysbers & Henderson, 2006). This concept is currently championed by UNESCO in all its 192 member nations. Most countries have some form of "guidance" in the schools. As a result of funding by the National Defense Education Act of 1958 (NDEA) many guidance and counseling institutes and master's degree programs were established in the United States. These educational programs became accessible to hundreds, and now thousands, of foreign students. International students who study in the United States have provided valuable knowledge to their American classmates and have no doubt enriched the quality of training. The international perspectives developed through cross-cultural interactions inside and outside the classroom can prepare all students to face the global world. At the same time, as discussed in Chapter 4 (this volume), international students educated in U.S. settings can face significant challenges in navigating or influencing the distinctly American and "U.S-centric" counselor training programs, particularly when, as is usually the case, they are the only or one of a very few international students in a particular program.

Most U.S.-educated international counseling professionals return to their home countries to teach, research, and/or practice, bringing their knowledge of the U.S. profession with them. Clearly, after four decades of training international master's and doctoral students in counseling and counseling psychology, the U.S. model of counselor training and education has had a significant impact on the development of the counseling profession in many countries. Indeed, with the U.S. model in mind, professionals in many countries have influenced their home country policy and practice. Yet, while there was probably no intent on "exporting" the profession for any sort of imperialistic purpose, the values and worldviews connected to dominant U.S. counseling paradigms often accompanied the "uncritical" exportation process (see Chapter 4, this volume, for further discussions). To date, we note a paucity of discussion in the literature during the early years regarding how to deal with the cultural relevancy issues connected to bringing a distinctly U.S. counseling paradigm into countries outside the West. Of course, as Gilbert Wrenn noted, the U.S. counseling profession was and still is also dealing with cultural encapsulation issues within its own U.S.-generated counseling theories, models, and practices (Wrenn, 1962). We agreed with Gerstein and Ægisdóttir (2007) that students and teachers of counseling, including international students, should be encouraged to critically evaluate the applicability of theories (e.g., education, counseling, psychological theories) that originated in the United States or other parts of the Western world to their own cultures.

Finally, in the past decade, professional organizations in the United States (e.g., American Counseling Association [ACA], American Psychological Association [APA]) have expressed a strong interest in developing international linkages and collaborations (e.g., Douce, 2004; Gerstein & Ægisdóttir, 2007). International students who have returned home following study in the United States have heard much about these professional organizations during their professional training, and many have attended ACA or APA conferences. Publications by these professional organizations are widely read and cited in the international literature, and the annual conventions of these organizations often attract sizable international attendees. The collaborative liaisons being created by these professional organizations and individuals have laid the necessary groundwork for current and future efforts to develop the counseling profession internationally.

From here, internationalization of the counseling profession needs to proceed in ways that are different from the process of economic globalization (see Chapter 1, this volume). Unlike trading and manufacturing, there is very limited room for international outsourcing, off-shoring, supply-chaining, or uploading of counseling or mental health services (Friedman, 2006). Counseling and mental health services usually require direct personal interactions with clients conducted by professionals with similar cultural and language backgrounds. Counseling services provided from someone at a distant site are unlikely to meet substantial local needs (Greenwald & Kahn, 2009). Furthermore, internationalization should not mirror the negatives of globalization, such as monopolizing of multinationals, importation/ imposition of values from dominant economies, elimination of local, indigenous enterprises, and perpetuation of a unitary, homogenous system of practice (Stiglitz, 2003). Internationalization of the counseling profession should be a process to develop and enhance the mental health capacities of nations and cultures in ways that are consistent with local cultures and settings. This capacity-development function of internationalization is best illustrated by the following excerpt by economists Greenwald and Kahn (2009) from their book titled *Globalization: The Irrational Fear That Someone in China Will Take Your Job*:

> The clear implication of this extensive diversity among nations is that individual countries and their governments must establish their own policies, even in a supposedly global world. They best understand the possibilities and constraints by local conditions, and they have to live with those consequences. The principle of vesting decisions in those most familiar with the relevant conditions is reinforced by the complementary principle that better decisions are made by those who are subject to the cost and benefits of their choices. (pp. 50–51)

In summary, internationalization in counseling is a continuous process of synthesizing knowledge generated through research, scholarship, and practice from different cultures and using this knowledge to solve problems in local and global communities. Internationalization involves collaborations and equal partnerships in which cultural sensitivity and respect are required for success. Most important, internationalization should be accompanied by continuous efforts to indigenize the counseling profession in different regions so that counseling theories, practice, and systems are developed and anchored in the local culture. Counseling must first become relevant to local communities before it can make a difference across national borders. Hence, *internationalization* is the preferred term for this chapter, compared with *globalization,* because internationalization conveys a clearer message of collaboration under the conditions of equal partnership and the preservation of cultural diversity. With that in mind, in the following section, we examine the broad meaning of indigenization based on the literature on indigenous and cultural psychology and discuss how indigenization could be carried out in the counseling profession.

Approaches to Indigenize the Counseling Profession

Sinha (1997) suggested that the term *indigenous* bears two basic features. First, it refers to something that is native and not transplanted from the outside. Second, it refers to something that is of and designed for the natives. Similarly, Blowers (1996) defined *indigenous* as "the study of grass-roots thinking, the everyday, the commonplace, as ingrained among inhabitants of a community and a culture" (p. 2). *Indigenous* reflects "the sociocultural reality" of a given society, which might be different or similar to realities in other societies or cultures (Sinha, 1997). Accordingly, indigenous psychology was referred to by Ho (1998) as "the study of human behavior and mental processes within a cultural context that relies on values, concepts, belief systems, methodologies, and other resources indigenous to the specific cultural groups under investigation" (p. 94). Indigenous psychology is a tradition in psychology that is grounded in the assumption that human behavior should best be interpreted and understood from indigenous frames of reference and culturally derived categories, rather than from the standpoint of imported categories and foreign theories (Ho, 1998; Kim, Yang, & Hwang, 2006; Kunkel, Hector, Coronado, & Vales, 1989; Sinha, 1997). Indigenous psychology takes the position that Western theories of psychology are essentially indigenous models and that "only by recognizing the nature of mainstream theories as indigenous, can we arrive at true (vs. illusory) universals" (Greenfield, 2000, p. 232).

Indigenization is a continuous, ongoing process rather than a finished product (Sinha, 1997). Enriquez (1993) distinguished between two broad routes to indigenize psychology, which were called "indigenous from within" and "indigenous from without." "Indigenous from without" was similar to what Sinha (1997) called "indigenization of the exogenous." It refers to a process of transforming and adapting imported psychological theories, concepts, and methods to make them appropriate to and correspond with the local cultural context. Researchers should not assume that a particular theory or approach is valid universally unless it is proved to be the case. In contrast, in the "indigenous from within" approach, researchers rely on a process of "internal indigenization" (Sinha, 1997) and develop theories, categories, and constructs from within a culture, using indigenous information or informants as primary sources of knowledge. The purpose is to generate indigenous theories and models that fully reflect local cultural characteristics.

The indigenization of the counseling profession should be approached from without and from within (Leung & Chen, 2009). "Indigenous from without" is most concerned with issues of contextual relevance and adaptability. Leung and Chen (2009) suggested that the cultural relevance of counseling theories could be enhanced by (a) adapting and enriching counseling theories and concepts based on the knowledge of local researchers and practitioners about local cultural and contextual characteristics, (b) testing the adapted counseling theories using local samples and diverse research methodologies in the natural contexts of local participants, and (c) generating alternative models and frameworks where both the indigenous and universal elements are addressed and integrated. The "indigenous from without" approach allows counseling scholars to achieve one of the major goals of internationalization and indigenous psychology, which is to discover psychological universals in social, cultural, and ecological contexts (Kim & Berry, 1993; Kim et al., 2006).

However, many cross-cultural scholars perceive "indigenous from without" as an accommodative approach in which "new and different perspectives are simply added on to an existing paradigm (Kim, Park, & Park, 2000, p. 65). As such, the outcomes do not challenge the basic scientific paradigms that characterize Western counseling and psychology. "Indigenization from within" is regarded as the more "authentic" approach to indigenizing psychology. Yet it is an approach that will require time, as well as concerted efforts and resources from those within the target culture.

Blowers (1996), incorporating both the "from within" and "from without" approaches, posited that the indigenization of psychology could proceed via three different levels. The first is the *local* level, which is the study of what is on the mind of the ordinary person in a particular culture, such as the processes that shape personality, motivation, and behavior (e.g., culture-specific views on mental health). The second level is *national,* which is the development of psychology as a formal and institutionalized discipline anchored to the needs and characteristics of the local culture (e.g., training programs, certification systems). The third level is *practice,* referring to the study of psychological intervention and practices that have been developed and used effectively within a cultural context (e.g., use of various culture-based alternative counseling treatments; see Moodley & West, 2005). The levels of indigenization introduced by Blowers (1996) offered a useful taxonomy for counseling scholars to indigenize counseling from within their own cultural settings (Leung & Chen, 2009) as well as to modify and adapt imported models and practices to indigenize from without.

Indigenization at the national or institutional level is extremely critical (Diaz-Loving, 2005; Sinha, 1997). First, a core group of counseling scholars (including practitioners) must articulate, define, and agree on an indigenous agenda relevant to the local context. Second, indigenous scholarship must be valued and supported by the institutions and organizations where they are conducted. Third, scholars have to develop a mechanism to disseminate indigenous theory and practice locally and internationally. Fourth, the institutionalized system has to maintain, renew, and expand its capabilities to deal with evolving national and cultural concerns. Indigenization in counseling can be viewed as a continual process of capacity development involving people, resources, and cultural insights.

A case of indigenization at the national level was described by Gabrenya, Kung, and Chen (2006), who studied the Taiwan Indigenous Psychology Movement (TIPM). Gabrenya et al. (2006) described the indigenization of psychology in Taiwan as "a social phenomenon occurring in a historical, political, and cultural context" (p. 598). The authors found that the TIPM has helped psychologists study issues that were more relevant to the concerns of Taiwan, to develop an indigenous intellectual identity, and to accumulate a volume of research in multiple domains within psychology that can inform practice.

"Indigenous from without" and "indigenous from within" are important pathways to indigenize the counseling profession in diverse cultural regions. The weaving together of cultural-universals and cultural-specifics will continue to be an important task for counselors and psychologists worldwide (Poortinga, 1999). Whereas sustainable, indigenous efforts generate rich and diverse local knowledge that is relevant and valid to local settings, the next important linkage to address is between indigenization and internationalization. That is, how can indigenous knowledge and experience accumulated in a culture be transformed and become useful internationally (Poortinga, 2005)? In the following section, we feature the work of the NBCC in the United States to illustrate the interface between internationalization and indigenization. NBCC's forthcoming examples underscore the point that internationalization and indigenization in counseling are parallel, complementary, and mutually enhancing processes.

Building Indigenous Counseling Capacity Through International Efforts: The Case of NBCC

Developing the counseling profession globally is a long and complex process requiring partnerships, mutual interactions, formulation, planning, and careful implementation. This section explores an intentional effort on the part of the NBCC to collaborate and support the development and indigenization of the counseling profession in local contexts. *Counseling* in this context is the profession (i.e., institutional-structural level), which, of course, includes the practice. The history, agenda, and strategies of the NBCC have always reflected domestic and international priorities and have operated from a mutually influencing global and national perspective. For example, Clawson (2001) noted that "the inevitability of the global economy, the strides in communication technology, and the surge of international distance education changed the discussions [concerning the possibility of promoting a counseling profession worldwide] from 'whether' to 'how' can a strategy be developed" (p. 1).

Both the nature and mission of counseling lend themselves to internationalizing. Counseling as a body of knowledge is a flexible, evolving discipline that can be shared, transformed, and refined for application in cultures and countries around the world (Clawson, 1999). In addition, the mission of the counseling profession is to help those with needs through individually and culturally sensitive counseling interventions; thus, it is a mission compatible with, and facilitated by, internationalization. A counseling profession in a global context increases the number of people who are served and helped by counseling while magnifying the visibility and influence of the profession and its values. The NBCC assumes that much of the counseling work can be done by local experts, practitioners, allied professionals, and policymakers with no influence from the NBCC or the U.S. counseling community. Yet the NBCC could serve as an alliance to facilitate the development of an infrastructure or professional system where local counseling activities would take place.

In its efforts to support the provision of urgently needed counseling services and the professionalization of counseling, the NBCC engaged in a number of strategies in 2001, including (a) gaining recognition as a nongovernmental organization (NGO) through world bodies, (b) developing close contacts with five existing counselor certification boards in other countries (Australia, Britain, Canada, Ireland, and New Zealand), and (c) offering technical assistance to countries who were considering or were in the process of developing counselor credentials. To provide financial support for the global projects, the NBCC in the United States offered an initial financial investment, supported by international funding from organizations with whom the NBCC has formed alliances.

U.S. professionals need to take precautions to avoid actions and attitudes that could be perceived as imperialist by the nations and cultures involved in internationalizing efforts. However, "certainly no profession has more experience and tools in cultural sensitivity than counseling" (Clawson, 2001, p. 2). The U.S. Multicultural Counseling Competencies (Sue et al., 1998) promote awareness regarding the need to guard against an ethnocentric, U.S.-dominant, culture-based approach. Also, given that counseling in the United States is a profession that is well aware of the need for identity and autonomy due to its developmental history (e.g., Heppner, Casas, Carter, & Stone, 2000), practitioners are in a unique position to deeply empathize with countries facing challenges and concerns about professional identity. With a healthy balance of cultural sensitivity, understanding of quality practice, and awareness of lessons we learned from our developmental journey as a profession, the NBCC felt that it could assist countries with their own emerging context-based professional counseling movements to define the basic tenets of their counseling professions, including counselor development, counselor education/training, supervised practice/experience, and ethical standards and guidelines (Clawson, 2001). The international efforts by the NBCC have been guided by what Gerstein and Ægisdóttir (2007) called an *anthropological model,* where the professional counseling movement is implemented with full involvement of the host community without disruption to its national integrity or identity.

Although some have been concerned that internationalization efforts may undermine domestic professional endeavors, the NBCC argued that the international development of the counseling profession benefits credentialed counselors and their clients in the United States, as stated by Clawson (2001):

> The point I think we've missed in the United States is that international recognition of counseling by world bodies and nations can only help the prestige of counseling here. Not only will recognition by organizations like the United Nations Educational, Scientific, and Cultural Organization (UNESCO) or the World Health Organization (WHO) enhance our stature at home, but it will give future generations of National Certified Counselors (NCCs) far greater possibilities for global practice—whether via Internet or emigration. (p. 2)

In 2003, the NBCC developed an international division, NBCC International (NBCC-I) and successfully pursued recognition and collaboration with the World Health Organization (WHO) and United Nations Educational, Scientific, and Cultural Organization (UNESCO). Currently, NBCC-I is engaged in major cooperative projects with WHO and is officially recognized by UNESCO as an NGO.

NBCC International and Mental Health Facilitator

In this section, we detail an example of an international effort taken up by the NBCC to internationalize and indigenize counseling to meet urgent local needs in various parts of the world: the Mental Health Facilitators (MHF) project. Over the past 8 years, the NBCC has established a process for helping interested countries develop local standards of practice and monitor quality practice through certification. The NBCC approach has been to support the development of indigenous mental health capacity while recognizing the problems with "uncritical exportation" of a mental health delivery system based on U.S. assumptions about human behavior (Gerstein & Ægisdóttir, 2007). The MHF project is intended to be a unique, intentional, indigenous mental health model that enriches and advances the theories and techniques that are effective with diverse populations. It invites people living in diverse cultures to share their expertise with each other (Clawson, 2001).

Although more than 450 million people worldwide are faced with unmet mental health needs, 1 in 4 people meets criteria for a diagnosable mental health disorder (WHO, 2001). Thus, a great need has emerged for available and effective global mental health care. One major obstacle is the scarcity of competent mental health care providers worldwide. Low-income countries rank highest in the critical shortage of mental health resources (WHO, 2001). The need to proactively address this gap has been identified by WHO and various other national and international organizations.

At a 2003 meeting of leaders of the NBCC and its affiliates and WHO Director of Department of Mental Health and Substance Dependence, Dr. Benedetto Saraceno, the idea to develop a system to address urgent international mental health needs was deliberated. To respond to the concerns of underserved and never served populations around the world, NBCC proposed that its international division, NBCC-I, help with the development of a specific program of intervention. NBCC-I, comprising an international board of directors, collaborated with WHO's Department of Mental Health and Substance Dependence to develop the MHF project. MHF is a certificate program aiming to strengthen trainees' competence to meet mental health needs in diverse local communities. The MHF program has the following unique features: (a) It is a flexible training program on mental health knowledge designed to be applied locally based on cultural context and needs, (b) it is aimed at recognizing and responding to people with mental health disorders who would otherwise remain unserved, and (c) it is exclusively designed to be delivered in a culturally specific way. Pedersen (2003) reminded us that in the internationalization and indigenization process, it is important to remember that countries and cultures rely on a range of "helpers and healers," many of whom are not professionals, in responding to local mental health needs. In accordance with this point, the MHF is not designed as a professional certification; thus, it does not imply mastery of the knowledge and skills at a level attained by mental health professionals. The MHF training program can be used to build capacity among service providers at various levels (e.g., Hinkle, Kutcher, & Chehil, 2006). For example, informal community care and services are offered by grassroots community members who have not received formal mental health education or training. This non-clinical level of mental health care emphasizes psychological support or advisement by community leaders, family groups, and local elders (including indigenous healers). At the primary health care level, general medical practitioners, nurses, and other health care personnel with higher health care skills can provide acute and long-term treatment to individuals with a variety of mental disorders. MHF training can be used to supplement the efforts of traditional health care providers. Furthermore, mental health facilitators can augment their knowledge and skills with advanced, specialized training, including a focus on functioning within a mental health care team to provide family support and education, follow-up monitoring, and targeted counseling.

The MHF training program has a number of strengths:

1. Since the MHF training is transdisciplinary, traditional professional helping disciplines are not reinforced, and competencies are linked to mental health needs of specific populations rather than to professional ideologies. Thus, individuals with MHF training can effectively respond to community mental health needs, without being constrained by issues of professional identification.

2. Mental health facilitation also provides equitable access to quality first-contact interventions (including mental health promotion; advocacy; monitoring; referral and treatment) that respect dignity and human rights, meet population needs, and are based on current global, regional, or local sociocultural, economic, and political realities.

3. Context-specific competencies are identified and included in MHF training programs by local stakeholders. As a consequence, consumers and policymakers can assume that MHF training provides culturally relevant services to the local population. The MHF training curriculum is a dynamic document that is revised at regular intervals based on input from institutions and individuals who provide MHF training.

4. Individuals seeking MHF training, which may differ by vocation and location, represent a broad cross section of society. The diversity of trainee backgrounds, augmented by context-specific training content, increases the possibility that services can fill various gaps in mental health care. It provides added human resources for governments and NGOs to position mental health interventions where they are most needed. For example, priorities may focus on the development of community-based mental health responses to natural disasters or the development and delivery of suicide risk mitigation strategies. Other priorities may include identification, initial intervention, and long-term monitoring of individuals with mental disorders in collaboration with existing health care providers. This flexibility can help policymakers, service providers, communities, and NGOs meet local mental health needs without costly investments in infrastructure. The introduction of MHF training can also be expected to facilitate the continual development and delivery of therapeutic community-based care consistent with the WHO recommendations for addressing global mental health needs.

The MHF training model provides culturally relevant training to local personnel, who can offer valuable services in low- and middle-income countries. The program equips local mental health service providers with skills and culturally specific strategies to serve in their communities, and to bridge the gap between mental health needs and service availability. We believe that if operated continuously, this model will bring substantial gains in well-being to individuals and communities where they reside.

MHF programs are implemented in a variety of ways. NBCC-I has funded training in Mexico, Malawi, and Malaysia. Training in China, Bhutan, Botswana, and Bulgaria are also seriously being considered. Future training will be made available via local government funding, via joint funding by foundations and local NGOs, and through university teams assisting with culture-centered curriculum development. More information on the MHF initiative, NBCC-I, and other NBCC projects can be found on the National Board for Certified Counselors website at http://www.nbcc.org.

Internationalization and Indigenization as Professional Attitudes and Visions

In this chapter, we have examined the meaning and nature of internationalization. We also discussed the importance of developing counseling in indigenous cultural contexts and identified categories and levels of indigenization that could be carried out by counseling professionals to advance the cultural relevance of counseling theory and practice. Internationalization and indigenization are parallel, compatible, and complementary processes that could enhance the substance and standing of the counseling profession in one's own country as well as internationally. We have used initiatives taken by the NBCC as examples of international efforts to strengthen indigenous mental health service delivery.

Internationalization and indigenization both involve professional behaviors and actions, yet we would like to emphasize the importance of viewing internationalization and indigenization as professional attitudes and visions. We want to identify three aspects of internationalization and indigenization as attitudes. First, internationalization and indigenization require counseling professionals to have a global mind-set, as well as awareness and understanding of the characteristics and needs of individuals in diverse cultural settings. Second, internationalization and indigenization require counseling professionals to respect counseling practice and scholarship developed around the world and to avoid an attitude of ethnocentrism, professional and cultural encapsulation, and/or cultural superiority (Heppner, 2006; Pedersen, 2003). Third, internationalization and indigenization require the counseling profession to value one's cultural practice and scholarship without underestimating or overestimating the potential contributions of these materials locally and internationally. Indigenization will not attain its desired outcomes if counseling professionals underestimate the value of their own indigenous content, as they will always look elsewhere to "import" theories and practice that might not be culturally relevant. Conversely, internationalization will become a unilateral process if counseling professionals in one region overestimate the universality of the indigenous content they have developed and seek to "export" it to other cultural regions.

Internationalization as a vision for the counseling profession, and the professional and scholarly benefits that could be derived from the process have been articulated by many leaders of the counseling profession in the past decade (e.g., Douce, 2004; Gerstein &Ægisdóttir, 2005; Heppner, 2006; Kwan & Gerstein, 2008; Leong & Blustein, 2000; Leong & Ponterotto, 2003; Savickas, 2007). Yet we would also like to emphasize the importance of seeing indigenization as a vision, particularly for counseling professionals in regions where counseling is developing. In some of these regions, there is a still strong tendency to regard the established counseling literature developed in the United States or Western countries as the dominant source of knowledge to inform research and practice (e.g., defining merit of academic publications in terms of whether they are published in venues in the Western world) and to see their professional systems as the blueprint to follow (e.g., Leung & Hoshmand, 2007). We hope that a vision of indigenization in counseling will slowly take root in these regions: (a) that counseling professionals will look more into their own cultural contexts, in research and practice, and value their own discovery; (b) that counseling professionals will nurture indigenous scholarship and publication venues, and influence their peers and institutions to give these venues the same level of respect that they have been given to scholarly venues in the Western world; (c) that counseling professionals will develop and appreciate their indigenous and international identities; and (d) that there will be a stronger synthesis of indigenous literature to inform global research and practice.

Conclusion

Internationalization and indigenization are shaped by our attitudes and visions, and they are ongoing processes that have to be carried on by generations of counseling professionals. We presented some rationales and conceptual directions in this chapter and provided examples of implementation. It is our hope that internationalization and indigenization can be synthesized into the everyday work of counseling professionals and that through concerted efforts, the profession can make a bigger difference locally and globally.

Chapter Questions

1. It has been pointed out that the internationalization of the counseling profession involves developing a global perspective in counseling scholarship, through our teaching, research, practice, and service. What are your views about this position? What are some of the ways that counseling professionals could nurture such a global perspective? What are the barriers?

2. What are some of the ways that you could learn more about the development of the counseling profession in different parts of the world? How could knowledge about the international counseling profession strengthen your practice and scholarship?

3. What are the advantages and disadvantages of taking a system of credentialing counselors from one country to other locations, as illustrated by the initiatives of the National Board for Certified Counselors Inc. & Affiliates (NBCC)? Discuss what needs to be done to ensure that such initiatives could meet local needs and be sustained.

4. Brainstorm examples of research studies that could be conducted to indigenize counseling in your geographic location. What steps could be taken to internationalize counseling scholarship (e.g., enrich the international content of counseling journals)?

References

Blowers, G. H. (1996). The prospects for a Chinese psychology. In M. H. Bond (Ed.), *Handbook of Chinese psychology* (pp. 1–14). Hong Kong: Oxford University Press.

Canales, L., & Blanco-Beledo, R. (1993). Professions and educational counseling in Mexico and Latin America. *Journal of Career Development, 20,* 51–55.

Clawson, T. W. (1999, October). *Expanding professions globally: Seeing the United States as a place to bring professional interests.* Speech presented at Center for Quality Assurance and International Education (CQAIE) Conference, Washington, DC.

Clawson, T. W. (2001, April). *Globalization: Not a foreign concept.* Speech presented at Center for Quality Assurance and International Education (CQAIE) Conference, Montreal, Quebec, Canada.

Diaz-Loving, R. (2005). Emergence and contributions of a Latin American indigenous psychology. *International Journal of Psychology, 40,* 213–227.

Douce, L. A. (2004). Society of counseling psychology, Division 17 of APA presidential address 2003: Globalization of counseling psychology. *The Counseling Psychologist, 32,* 142–152.

Enriquez, V. G. (1993). Developing a Filipino psychology. In U. Kim & J. W. Berry (Eds.), *Indigenous psychologies: Research and experience in cultural context* (pp. 152–169). Newbury Park, CA: Sage.

Friedman, T. L. (2006). *The world is flat: A brief history of the twenty-first century.* New York: Farrar, Straus & Giroux.

Gabrenya, W. K., Jr., Kung, M-C., & Chen, L-Y. (2006). Understanding the Taiwan Indigenous Psychology Movement: A sociology of science approach. *Journal of Cross-Cultural Psychology, 37,* 597–622.

Gerstein, L. H., & Ægisdóttir, S. (2005). A trip around the world: A counseling travelogue! *Journal of Mental Health Counseling, 27,* 95–103.

Gerstein, L. H., & Ægisdóttir, S. (2007). Training international social change agents: Transcending a U.S. counseling paradigm. *Counselor Education and Supervision, 47,* 123–139.

Greenfield, P. M. (2000). Three approaches to the psychology of culture: Where do they come from? Where can they go? *Asian Journal of Social Psychology, 3,* 223–240.

Greenwald, B. C., & Kahn, J. (2009). *Globalization: The irrational fear that someone in China will take your job.* Hoboken, NJ: Wiley.

Gysbers, N. C., & Henderson, P. (2006). *Developing and managing your school guidance program* (4th ed.). Alexandria, VA: American Counseling Association.

Heppner, P. P. (2006). The benefits and challenges of becoming cross-culturally competent counseling psychologists: Presidential address. *The Counseling Psychologist, 34,* 147–172.

Heppner, P. P., Casas, J. M., Carter, J., & Stone, G. L. (2000). The maturation of counseling psychology: Multifaceted perspectives, 1978–1998. In S. D. Brown & R. W. Lent (Eds.), *Handbook of counseling psychology* (3rd ed., pp. 3–49). New York: Wiley.

Hinkle, J. S., Kutcher, S. P., & Chehil, S. (2006, October). *Mental health facilitator: Curriculum development.* Paper presented at the NBCC Global Mental Health Conference: Focus on the Never Served, New Delhi, India.

Ho, D. Y. F. (1998). Indigenous psychologies: Asian perspectives. *Journal of Cross-Cultural Psychology, 29,* 88–103.

Kim, U., & Berry, J. W. (Eds.). (1993). *Indigenous psychologies: Research and experience in cultural context.* Newbury Park, CA: Sage.

Kim, U., Park, Y.-S., & Park, D. (2000). The challenge of cross-cultural psychology: The role of indigenous psychologies. *Journal of Cross-Cultural Psychology, 31,* 63–75.

Kim, U., Yang, K. S., & Hwang, K. K. (2006). *Indigenous and cultural psychology.* New York: Springer.

Kunkel, M. A., Hector, M. A., Coronado, E. G., & Vales, V. C. (1989). Expectations about counseling in Yucatán, Mexico: Toward a "Mexican psychology." *Journal of Counseling Psychology, 36,* 322–330.

Kwan, K.-L. K., & Gerstein, L. H. (2008). Envisioning a counseling psychology of the world: The mission of the international forum. *The Counseling Psychologist, 36,* 182–187.

Leong, F. T. L., & Blustein, D. L. (2000). Toward a global vision of counseling psychology. *The Counseling Psychologist, 28,* 5–9.

Leong, F. T. L., & Ponterotto, J. G. (2003). A proposal for internationalizing counseling psychology in the United States: Rationales, recommendations, and challenges. *The Counseling Psychologist, 31,* 381–395.

Leung, S. A. (2003). A journey worth traveling: Globalization of counseling psychology. *The Counseling Psychologist, 31,* 412–419.

Leung, S. A., & Chen, P.-W. (2009). Developing counseling psychology in Chinese communities in Asia: Indigenous, multicultural, and cross-cultural considerations. *The Counseling Psychologist, 37,* 944–966.

Leung, S. A., & Hoshmand, L. T. (2007). Internationalization and international publishing: Broadening the impact of scholarly work in counseling. *Asian Journal of Counselling, 14,* 141–154.

Marsella, A. J. (1998). Toward a "global-community psychology": Meeting the needs of a changing world. *American Psychologist, 53,* 1282–1291.

Marsella, A. J., & Pedersen, P. B. (2004). Internationalizing the counseling psychology curriculum: Toward new values, competencies, and directions. *Counseling Psychology Quarterly, 17,* 413–423.

Moodley, R., & West, W. (2005). *Integrating traditional healing practices into counseling and psychotherapy.* Thousand Oaks, CA: Sage.

Pedersen, P. B. (2003). Culturally biased assumptions in counseling psychology. *The Counseling Psychologist, 31,* 396–403.

Peteanu, M. (1997). Educational and vocational guidance in Romania: Short history. *Revista de Pedagogie, 1*(12), 314–324.

Poortinga, Y. H. (1999). Do cross-cultural differences in behavior imply a need for different psychologies. *Applied Psychology: An International Review, 48,* 419–432.

Poortinga, Y. H. (2005). The globalization of indigenous psychologies. *Asian Journal of Social Psychology, 8,* 65–74.

Savickas, M. L. (2007). Internationalization of counseling psychology: Constructing cross-national consensus and collaboration. *Applied Psychology: An International Review, 56,* 182–188.

Sinha, D. (1997). Indigenous psychology. In J. W. Berry, Y. H. Poortinga, & J. Pandey (Eds.), *Handbook of cross-cultural psychology* (Vol. 1, pp. 129–170). Needham Heights, MA: Allyn & Bacon.

Stiglitz, J. E. (2003). *Globalization and its discontents.* New York: W. W. Norton.

Sue, D. W., Carter, R. T., Casas, J. M., Fouad, N. A., Ivey, A. E., Jensen, M., et al. (1998). *Multicultural counseling competencies: Individual and organizational development.* Thousand Oaks, CA: Sage.

Szilagyi, A., & Paredes, D. M. (2010). Professional counseling in Romania: An introduction. *Journal of Counseling and Development, 88,* 23–27.

Watts, A. G. (1997). The role of career guidance in societies in transition. *Revista de Pedagogie, 1*(12), 417–428.

World Health Organization. (2001). *The world health report 2001: Mental health, new understanding, new hope.* Geneva, Switzerland: Author.

Wrenn, C. G. (1962). The culturally encapsulated counselor. *Harvard Educational Review, 32,* 444–449.

Yakushko, O. (2005). Mental health counseling in Ukraine. *Journal of Mental Health Counseling, 27,* 161–167.

Yakushko, O. (2007). Career development issues in the former USSR. *Journal of Career Development, 33*(4), 299–315.

Chapter Seven

Crossing Borders in Collaboration

Kathryn L. Norsworthy, Seung-Ming Alvin Leung,
P. Paul Heppner, and Li-fei Wang

The internationalization of counseling and counseling psychology encourages cross-national contact among professionals around the world (Heppner, 2008; Leung, 2003; Pedersen & Leong, 1997). These "border crossings" can involve travel across regions for the purposes of work, research, study, and teaching, and inevitably bring challenges, learning, and potential growth.

In the midst of our efforts to internationalize, we are recognizing the significant influence and impact of U.S. psychology in defining the field globally. Meaningful internationalization acknowledges the importance of reinventing counseling and counseling psychology as professions "in a global context" (Pedersen, 2003, p. 402) and of indigenizing the discipline by professionals from countries and cultures outside the United States (Kim, Yang, & Hwang, 2006; Marsella & Pedersen, 2004). Yet Arnett (2008) concluded that most psychological research is conducted with individuals from the United States, or less than 5% of the global population, and is most often assumed to be universally applicable. Given the vastly different worldviews, cultures, and contexts of the remaining 95%, current psychological knowledge and skill sets are grossly incomplete and unrepresentative of most of the human population on this planet. Thus, cultural competency and ongoing efforts to cultivate a respectful, power-sharing approach to international work is a prerequisite for Western counselors and psychologists engaged in international research and practice. Additionally, international students educated in Western institutions face challenges in navigating the U.S. education system and society as well as in translating or transforming Western-based models into culturally grounded, indigenous counseling and counseling psychologies appropriate for people in their home countries.

Recognizing the need to offer guidance in the internationalization process, in 2004, the American Psychological Association (APA) passed the "Resolution on Culture and Gender Awareness in International Psychology" (see Appendix, Chapter 4, this volume). This document noted the significant influence of U.S. psychology globally, challenged Western psychologists to become aware of ethnocentric attitudes and practices in our international work, and suggested adding an international focus in our training programs. The resolution reminds psychologists to engage in efforts at unlearning colonizing and hegemonic attitudes as well as practices we may have internalized in our training. Rice and Ballou (2002), leaders in the development of the resolution, emphasized five principles to be centralized in our international work: (1) understanding experiences in diverse cultures and contexts, (2) respect for pluralism based on differences, (3) awareness and analysis of power, (4) critical analysis of Western perspectives, and (5) international and interdisciplinary social-cultural perspectives. In Chapter 4 (this volume), Norsworthy, Heppner, Ægisdóttir, Gerstein, and Pedersen discuss this topic in greater detail and emphasize the importance of cultivating and employing "decolonizing" methodologies in our international activities. The five principles explicated by Rice and Ballou point in the directions of mutuality, power sharing, and building a field that is truly relevant for the diversity of human experience around the world. Reflections by professionals from various countries and regions engaging in cross-cultural and cross-national professional activities or study regarding how they collaborate, learn, and negotiate their relationships, work, and educational experiences can offer invaluable insights about the internationalization process.

With these points in mind, we will discuss three kinds of "border crossings" in counseling and counseling psychology. Based on more than 20 years of conducting research with colleagues in Taiwan and other parts of the world, Puncky Heppner (United States) weaves together current literature and his own experiences with cross-cultural and cross-national research teams, particularly focusing on the benefits, challenges, and personal qualities of the researchers. Then, using auto-ethnographic narratives, Alvin Leung (Hong Kong) and Kathryn Norsworthy (United States) describe what they have learned through their experiences of crossing borders. Alvin offers a first-person account of his own experiences in traveling to the United States for graduate school, then returning to his home country to work and "indigenize" the largely Western knowledge base accompanying him. Kathryn describes her 12-year process of collaborating in research, practice, and activism projects with Southeast Asian colleagues in grassroots, nongovernmental, and governmental venues, particularly highlighting the partnership with Thai colleague, Ouyporn Khuankaew. All three coauthors emphasize the importance of understanding the context of the country in which one works or studies and outline strategies for successful collaboration. We also review challenges to effective cross-cultural and cross-national partnerships and learning, offering suggestions about functioning effectively in these relationships and environments. Finally, we discuss critical events linked with our collaborative international relationships and the role of creating reciprocal and mutually beneficial relationships. Li-fei Wang (Taiwan) concludes the chapter by noting themes, observations, and recommendations for the ongoing internationalization of counseling and counseling psychology, with a particular focus on cross-national and cross-cultural partnerships as a valuable source of learning, growth, and influence on the professions of each partner's home country.

Crossing Boundaries: Cross-Cultural and Cross-National Research Collaboration
(PUNCKY HEPPNER)

Psychological research across all psychological specialties published in APA journals has focused "narrowly on Americans" and neglected the rest of the world's people (Arnett, 2008, p. 602). Consequently, the generalizability of the research conducted by most U.S.-based psychologists to populations outside the United States is not only questionable but also seriously restricts the utility or applicability of research by U.S. psychologists. Despite a growing internationalization of U.S. counseling and counseling psychology (Heppner, Leong, & Gerstein, 2008), the counseling profession in the United States is not an exception and is still an insular profession (see Cheung, 2000; Leung, 2003) with relatively little collaborative cross-national research.

Cross-cultural and cross-national research collaboration has been extremely rewarding in my career and has greatly affected me personally and professionally, in terms of my worldview as a research psychologist and the way I think about and conceptualize my research. In Chapter 8 (this volume), Li-fei Wang and I discuss our long-term personal and professional collaborative relationship within the context of our developmental cultural journey from a more personal and auto-ethnographic perspective. Based primarily on that relationship as well as other research with international graduate students, in this section I provide a brief overview of some of the benefits of crossing borders to establish cross-national and cross-cultural research collaboration.

In my view, research collaborations between U.S. counseling psychologists and colleagues in other countries, especially non-Western countries, have the potential to greatly enhance "the depth and richness of our knowledge bases and theoretical models" (Heppner, 2008, p. 814). I reached this conclusion after more than 20 years of conducting cross-cultural and cross-national collaborative research as well as analyzing the development of the coping and applied problem-solving research that I conducted in my career. I believe that my research maps very well onto the broader U.S. research bases on these topics (see Heppner, 2008). In essence, I believe that cross-national collaboration not only provides a much more complex and rich database in psychology but also substantially broadens our psychological theories and greatly expands the cultural competencies and the worldviews we bring to our professional work and our personal lives.

How Can Cross-National and Cross-Cultural Collaboration Strengthen Research in Counseling Psychology?

There is a wide array of benefits from conducting cross-cultural research. I will briefly discuss five benefits: (1) examining the external validity or generalizability of research findings across different cultures; (2) creating knowledge pertaining to how different cultural contexts affect psychological processes; (3) broadening one's perspective of particular psychological constructs; (4) enhancing the researchers' cultural awareness, knowledge, and skills, which in turn enhance their sensitivities in future cultural research; and (5) deepening personal and professional relationships among the investigators.

First, for some time scholars have maintained that cross-cultural research can be very useful to test the external validity of research findings in other cultures (Heine & Norenzayan, 2006; Quintana, Troyano, & Taylor, 2001; Ægisdóttir, Gerstein, & Çinarbaş, 2008). In short, there has been a tendency to assume that research findings, repeatedly yielded under tightly controlled experimental conditions, are universal and that they are applicable across cultures. Thus, over the years, scholars have issued cautions about the tendency to assume the universality of research findings, and they have specifically urged testing the generalizability of the findings in other cultures. This issue of external validity has been examined particularly with regard to the utilization of instruments developed in one cultural context (most often in the United States) and subsequently used in another culture. Previously, researchers had suggested that such inventories be carefully translated linguistically (in terms of form, meaning, and structure) to ensure equivalence or comparability across cultures (see Lonner, 1985). Lonner, however, also suggested other types of equivalence such as functional equivalence (referring to the function of the behavior being studied), conceptual equivalence (similarity in meaning), and metric equivalence (the manner in which constructs are quantified). In short, there are many measurement complexities in cross-cultural research. One basic purpose of cross-cultural research collaboration is to test the external validity or generalizability of research findings from one sample or culture to another culture.

Second, from my experience, cross-national collaboration among international colleagues can promote a greater understanding of psychological processes within different cultural contexts, particularly indigenous norms, values, and customs in cultures outside the United States. In so doing, we not only learn more about the nuances within particular phenomena, but such research also offers possibilities for deepening our understanding of new or different psychological processes in another culture. For me, it is most exciting to deepen my scientific understanding of a coping process in another cultural context and to find coping processes not explored in the U.S.-based literature that may very well apply to various U.S. populations or other cultural groups in other countries (see Heppner, 2008). In this way, the counseling profession can greatly expand our knowledge bases of psychological processes related to psychological and vocational adjustment as well as physical health within different cultural contexts across the globe. Such knowledge bases are particularly beneficial because far too often, the cultural context has been ignored in U.S. psychology (Arnett, 2008; Heine & Norenzayan, 2006; Heppner, 2008). For example, I have learned very clearly from my research that coping constructs based on the dominant U.S. culture do not come close to telling the whole story about coping across U.S. cultural groups or cultures around the world (see Heppner, 2008). In short, cross-national collaborative research can promote the development of knowledge bases by specifically explicating how cultural dynamics affect psychological processes. In so doing, we participate in developing psychological knowledge that reflects the diverse cultures of the world. To me, it is a wonderful feeling after conducting research for more than 30 years on applied problem solving and coping to still look forward to contributing to a more complex and inclusive knowledge base of how people handle stressful events in their lives across diverse cultures.

In the past, there has been an over reliance on Western-based theories, which not only marginalizes non-Western cultures (Heine & Norenzayan, 2006) but also served to greatly limit our own knowledge bases and psychological theories. However, by studying constructs in more than one cultural context, different variables or complexities can be identified that not only "paint an increasingly detailed picture" (Heine & Norenzayan, 2006, p. 254) and a "much more complex mosaic" (Heppner, 2008, p. 806) of our constructs but also greatly expand our conceptualization of cultural similarities and differences. In this way, cross-cultural research can enhance the sophistication of our research, expand the depth and richness of our psychological knowledge, promote the development of more complex theoretical models (Heine & Norenzayan, 2006; Heppner, 2008; Quintana et al., 2001), and increase the range and effectiveness of our counseling interventions across a broad range of populations (Heppner, 2008).

Third, cross-cultural and cross-national research teams in particular can provide many opportunities to broaden one's perspective of psychological phenomena and aid in understanding particular psychological constructs at a more complex level. For example, it is often difficult for scholars from very different cultures to learn from one another through professional publications that are in different languages or unfamiliar publications outlets. In essence, important knowledge bases are inaccessible across countries and continents. Cross-national partnerships can enhance the team members' cultural sensitivities as well as promote the flow of cultural information across countries and cultures. Thus, collaboration among international colleagues can expand our awareness of the nuances and complexities of psychological constructs that might not have been apparent from one's primary cultural perspective (Heine & Norenzayan, 2006; Heppner, 2006, 2008). One such example from my experience was the development of an East-Asian-based Collectivistic Coping Styles (CCS) inventory (Heppner et al., 2006), which was greatly influenced by the cultural worldviews of the Taiwanese and Korean members of our research team. Our research found that the CCS contained new coping factors not found in U.S.-based coping inventories (Heppner et al., 2006). These results have implications for coping not only in Taiwan and Korea but also quite likely for ethnic minority groups in the United States and for future theoretical development. In my view, we stand to learn tremendously by getting outside our ethnocentric worldviews and listening to others' perspectives based on cultures different from our own.

Fourth, cross-cultural and cross-national research collaboration can greatly enhance one's cultural awareness, knowledge, and skills (AKS; see multicultural guidelines by American Psychological Association, 2003; Sue, 2003). That is, my experience has been that both my international colleagues and I have greatly enhanced our cultural AKS not only from our research but also through talking and working as colleagues. The latter sometimes involves hours of discussion, cross-cultural observations, reflection, and even processing aspects of our relationship. Not surprisingly, the more we enhance our cultural AKS, the better or more sophisticated our research becomes.

Finally, successful cross-cultural and cross-national research collaboration has typically deepened our personal and professional relationships. For me, this has been a profoundly gratifying outcome or benefit. It is this spirit of not only collaborating but also reaching across cultural similarities and differences to connect both interpersonally as well as emotionally that helps achieve a research goal. And when it is all done, the relationships are most meaningful and celebratory, can last a lifetime, and also serve as the bases for additional cross-national collaborations, most often with increased cultural sensitivities.

A Few Factors That Can Enhance Cross-Cultural and Cross-National Research Collaboration

Depending on the magnitude of cultural differences among team members, it is generally insufficient for cross-national researchers to only have a wide array of research skills; successful cross-cultural and cross-national research collaboration often require cross-cultural competencies. In Chapter 8 (this volume), Li-fei and I discuss a number of factors that affected our cross-national collaborations. Based on our work, I will briefly highlight and elaborate on four factors that seem particularly relevant for research collaboration: (1) cross-cultural competencies, (2) reciprocal and mutually beneficial as well as respectful personal and professional relationships, (3) active problem solving, and (4) having common content-specific expertise. It is important to note that all four of these factors synergistically add exponentially to cross-cultural and cross-national collaboration.

Cross-national teams are unique in that members often bring very different cultural perspectives, not only about the research topic but also about many other aspects of the research project. Partners may have differing expectations of how each will behave with each other as colleagues, how they might express agreement or disagreement, and the manner of dividing research tasks. From our experiences, a critical component of cross-national collaboration pertains to the cross-cultural competence that the team members bring to the team. The cultural AKS competencies involve a wide range of skills (see analyses by Worthington, Soth-McNett, & Moreno, 2007). In addition, in this context it has been important for me to remain cognizant that I am a white American male and of the sociopolitical dynamics that sometimes accompany that part of my identity. Moreover, since the focus of our research has been on cultural dynamics different from my own, I make special efforts to remember that I am a cultural outsider who is most often unaware of the many cultural complexities we are investigating. That is, the greater the members' cross-cultural competencies, the more skills they have to effectively deal with the myriad research decisions as well as their working alliance. This also requires the ability to focus on the research tasks while remaining cognizant of the cultural context.

Another very important factor in cross-national research pertains to the reciprocal and mutually beneficial and respectful personal and professional relationships among collaborators (see Singer, 2008). In our view, the relationship can be best conceptualized as a working alliance. An open, egalitarian, respectful, deep, trusting, and caring relationship can go a long way in promoting a successful cross-national research project. This type of relationship is often characterized by the mutuality of goals, bonds that develop through honest and genuine interpersonal reactions and disclosures, power sharing, reciprocity, and a reflexive examination of the personal and professional relationship.

Even with the best communication, there will be many obstacles, misperceptions, and problems to resolve. Thus, it is also essential for cross-national collaborators to have good problem-solving skills to resolve a wide array of methodological issues, content-specific decisions, statistical questions, and data collection procedures. Moreover, many times problem solving revolves around cultural issues. From our experience, it is extremely important for the collaborators to be aware that when they come from outside the cultural context of investigation, they need to be mindful that their understanding is most likely limited and incomplete. Thus, it can be helpful to "listen more than talk," to focus on acquiring a deeper understanding of the cultural context, and to ask questions to seek information or clarify. Conversely, we have learned that sometimes the "outsider" is also in a good position to offer different perspectives or share observations that might stimulate additional thinking or brainstorming in the team.

It is helpful for each cross-national research team member to have content-specific knowledge to contribute to the collaboration. In our view, the most successful cross-national research teams do not consist of one member "helping" the other but rather recognizing that each member has strengths that he or she brings to the team, whereby the combined strengths within the team support high-quality research.

In sum, there are many benefits to cross-national research collaboration, all of which can strengthen the counseling profession. We strongly encourage scholars to cross not only national boundaries to engage in cross-national research but also cultural boundaries to immerse themselves in other cultures to learn more about the multifaceted influences of culture on human behavior. In so doing, we become better cross-cultural researchers. In the end, "conducting culturally sensitive research in many cultures will greatly expand the depth and richness of our knowledge bases and theoretical models . . . which will make us better psychologists, better scholars, teachers, mentors, therapists, consultants—and better people" (Heppner, 2008, p. 814).

This section has elucidated the benefits and challenges of cross-national research partnerships. The ideas presented are also quite relevant to cross-national education and practice. In the following sections, Leung and Norsworthy take a narrative turn, giving more personal accounts of their "border crossings" and what can be learned in each case.

Border Crossing to an Unfamiliar Home Turf: Counseling Professionals Returning Home
(SEUNG-MING ALVIN LEUNG)

As the counseling profession develops and becomes more visible in countries around the world, international students have increasingly chosen to undertake advanced study in fields related to counseling, psychology, and mental health in the United States and in other countries where established programs are available. Many of these students eventually assume leadership positions in counseling research, training, and practice in the United States or back in their home countries. Wherever they choose to advance their careers, international graduates of counseling training programs are valuable "ambassadors" of the profession, as they bring unique perspectives to the field of counseling that are local and global, indigenous and international.

In this section, I would like to elaborate on the experience of international graduates who choose to return to their home cultures after an extensive period of study and involvement in the field of counseling in the United States. I explore the process of adjustment and adaptation that they might have to go through and examine the personal and professional benefits that could be derived from this journey. This section is conceptualized in reference to my personal experience and is therefore written from a first-person perspective.

Adaptation and Adjustment

After residing in the United States first as an international student, then as a counseling psychology faculty member at two different universities, I decided to return to Hong Kong, a place where I was born and raised, to take up a faculty position. The decision was made after a long period of deliberation, reflection, and struggle. It was the beginning of a tedious process of preparing for and making the move. It also involved saying goodbye to the social and professional networks that I and my family had become attached to over the years as we grew and progressed in our life stages. Beneath feelings of excitement and anticipation over the opportunities ahead, there were a host of negative feelings, including confusion, fear, sense of loss, and sadness.

Indeed, the journey to reenter my home culture was not an easy one. I found that the process of cultural adaptation was more complex and longer than I had expected, more painful and lonely than I had anticipated, yet more rewarding and fruitful than I had imagined. I would like to elaborate on three aspects of culture-related challenges requiring adaptation and adjustment, which were (1) social and cultural identity, (2) cultural limitations of scholarship I learned in the United States, and (3) professional isolation. I would also like to discuss strategies that I employed to cope with these challenges.

The first challenge is cultural identity. After years of residing in the United States, I have integrated facets of U.S. culture into my identity. At the beginning stage of my entrance back to my home culture, I experienced significant distress and confusion because I was not sure where my "home" was. I felt "homesick" and I missed being around my "home" in the United States, even though I was physically residing in the place where I was born and raised. The struggle with social and cultural identity was expressed in many other forms, including language, food, social space, and interpersonal relationships. The cognitive and emotional nature of the experience could be conceptualized as a case of reverse culture shock (Leung, 2007; Pedersen, 1995). I came to realize that I had to actively engage in a process of re-acculturation and re-adaptation to a once familiar home turf. In retrospect, I have learned three important lessons from my experience in making transitions across borders back to my home culture. First, I found out that re-acculturation and re-adaptation are ongoing processes, and after more than 12 years of reentering my home culture, I am still re-acculturating and re-adapting. Second, crossing borders often involves synthesizing multiple social and cultural identities (e.g., synthesizing my U.S.-acquired identity with my evolving Chinese identity), and the more the layers of identities one has accumulated, the harder it is to re-acculturate and re-adapt because the home culture is unlikely to provide the multiplicities of experiences required of the multicultural identities. Third, finding individuals who have similar cross-cultural transition and/or re-transition experiences is instrumental in consolidating and sustaining the re-acculturation process. I have been able to find empathy, support, and encouragement from those with similar sojourning experiences as mine.

The second challenge is cultural limitation of scholarship I learned in the United States. International counseling psychologists often return home with a sense of mission, hoping to use and apply what they have learned in their own cultural context. They discover very soon that what they have learned has to be substantially adapted to be useful and meaningful in their home context. I would like to describe two experiences as illustrations. First, having been trained in the United States, I had become quite fluent in my English usage and my professional vocabulary was all in English. Initially, I had trouble teaching my classes in the Chinese language. Counseling is indeed a process based on the local language, and my lack of language fluency was a major barrier in teaching and in counseling supervision. I was quite embarrassed, as Chinese was supposed to be my first language. Fortunately, this was a problem that could be overcome through hard work. I started to develop detailed lecture notes and presentation outlines in Chinese, and through that I was able to conduct my classes more fluently. After several years of refining and upgrading my Chinese course materials, I was able to improve the impact of my teaching, and my student course evaluation ratings have also improved substantially. Second, with years of training and professional experience in counseling psychology, I was expected by students and professionals to be an "expert" in the field. I soon found out that my knowledge of counseling is actually knowledge of counseling in the United States and that I knew very little about the counseling system in Hong Kong. I had to learn and relearn my context to make my knowledge and expertise applicable. An important aspect of counseling in Hong Kong is its application in educational settings, and I had to teach many counseling related classes to teachers. To supplement my lack of knowledge about the local setting, I collaborated with experienced teachers, visited schools, and talked to my students who were teachers and used them as my "informants." In the span of a few years, I was able to contextualize my teaching and training materials substantially. I have used a similar process to contextualize other skills I learned in the United States, including setting up a counseling lab, editing a journal, and conducting career development workshops. Drawing from the above experiences, I think that it is important for counseling psychologists who crossed borders to return home to understand that a "transfer-of-technology" approach is not adequate (Pedersen, 2003). They should bear in mind that they need a significant period of time to refamiliarize with their home cultures and contexts and that much effort is needed to "indigenize" their teaching and scholarship.

The third challenge is professional isolation. There were few counseling psychologists in Hong Kong and fewer with the training experiences that I had. At times, I had to explain to others the nature of my training and professional credentials. There were times when I felt misunderstood, unappreciated, and disappointed. The first few years of my reentry to Hong Kong were actually characterized by a strong sense of loneliness and isolation. I felt that I was all by myself in my journey to be "the one who would make a difference in my profession." In my effort to escape from my despair, I came to the realization that I had to be humble and should not think of myself as superior to others because of my past experience in the United States. Through this new perspective, I was able to regain my professional and personal energies and to reorient myself toward the future. I was able to slowly establish a local professional support network and at the same time maintain my contacts with colleagues in the United States. I learned that to make a difference at home, I have to work with others and I have to abandon my sense of superiority/inferiority and think of myself as one of them, locally and internationally.

Maintaining and Broadening Impact

Slowly and surely, counseling professionals crossing borders to return home will adapt and adjust to the cultural and professional realities in their home turf. As they mature in their careers, their work will increasingly make an important impact to the counseling profession locally and internationally. Sustaining their impact, however, requires conscious efforts to take care of one's professional and physical well-being, as well as to locate the niche where they could make their best contribution.

First and foremost, counseling professionals who return to their home countries might find themselves overwhelmed by demands from all sides to share their expertise. As they become more established, as their scholarly work is adapted and grounded in local contexts, many opportunities would arise locally and internationally. Yet from my experience as a counseling psychologist who also specializes in career and life planning, I realize how important it is to prioritize my goals and activities and to avoid overstretching. To avoid going over my limits, I have learned to avoid "overestimating" my ability, to share opportunities, and to say "no" to requests and demands that are very tempting. Counseling psychologists who crossed borders are often driven by a sense of mission, yet to maintain their capacity to fulfill goals and objectives that are important, they need to be on guard against stress and burnout.

Second, to broaden their impact, counseling professionals returning to their home countries have to find ways to accommodate and balance between local and international professional objectives. Using myself as an example, I am fully aware of the need to indigenize, adapt, and document my scholarly work in Chinese so that I can share with professionals in my community. At the same time, there are also expectations from my institution to publish my scholarly work in leading journal venues in the Western world (often in English language) and to develop an international reputation in the field of counseling. The dual missions to make one's work relevant and known to people locally (e.g., indigenization) and to those in the international community are especially burdensome to counseling professionals who return to a home region where the counseling profession is at a beginning stage of development and where significant efforts are needed to adapt what they know about counseling to local people in local languages (Leung & Hoshmand, 2007). There is no magic solution to resolve this "dichotomy," yet I have the following experience to share.

First, one has to consider his or her personal mission. I have put significantly more time and efforts to "indigenize" because that was the major reason I returned to my home culture. Second, I have made significant efforts to be active in corresponding professional organizations at home and abroad. Through these professional activities, I was able to weave together indigenous and international professional goals and agendas. Third, I looked for opportunities to engage in scholarly projects that would facilitate indigenous and international objectives. For example, I have invited colleagues from various parts of the world to collaborate in seminars and workshops in Hong Kong and to serve as co-investigators in research projects, the results of which could be published in local as well as international journal venues.

Finally, to maintain and broaden one's impact, counseling professionals returning to their home countries should seek ways to mentor future generations of counseling professionals who can carry on the tasks of indigenization and internationalization. Mentoring should not be limited to training of postgraduate students; returning counseling professionals can share their indigenous and international missions and visions with fellow counselors and scholars at home and in international settings. Meanwhile, they also serve as "role models" to students and peers through their active involvement in the local and international communities of counselors and psychologists.

In summary, international graduates in counseling who return to their home cultures are unique assets to the counseling profession. Their multiple professional identities and affiliations are instrumental to cross-cultural and cross-national collaboration and the development of counseling internationally. Their understanding of multiple cultures and languages allows them to play the role as ambassadors of the counseling profession as well as to serve as "bridges" that connect cultures and nations so that counseling can become a truly international discipline.

Crossing Borders in Practice and Solidarity Work
(KATHRYN NORSWORTHY)

On the topic of internationalizing counseling psychology, Varenne (2003) remarked, "Recent scholars have also pointed out that once a dialogue has begun across what used to be boundaries, both sides will be involved in the constitution of a new field" (p. 397). This section chronicles some of the pivotal dialogues and experiences that have constituted my journey and contributed to my learning as a white, U.S. counseling psychologist working in South and Southeast Asia over the past 12 years. In the first section,

I offer a brief auto-ethnography of how I came to work in the region and some highlights of the friendship and professional relationship between my Thai colleague, Ouyporn Khuankaew, and me that explain the evolution of several of my most important discoveries in connection to practicing outside the United States. In the latter part of this section, I reflect on our experiences of working together and with groups throughout Southeast and South Asia and articulate key learnings that may be useful for Western psychologists "crossing borders" to practice and do solidarity work outside their home countries and regions as well as back in our countries of origin.

The Beginning

My first trip to Asia was in 1985, awakening me to the teachings of Buddhism while in Ladakh, the Tibetan Buddhist state of northern India. A rich and diverse society, India penetrated into me, showing me how people holding a range of religions, worldviews, and cultures struggle to live under one flag. Of course, I come from a country of diversity, yet often we understand our own cultures through the reflections of someone else's. While pursuing Buddhist studies, I began to explore Thailand, finding a different expression of the same religion within a cultural context unique to this Southeast Asian country. During the next decade, I returned to this region many times, traveling, studying yoga and meditation, and spending hours talking with locals in the tea shops, markets, trains, and buses. Though I was aware that my understanding of the cultures of countries such as India and Thailand was quite limited, I do not think that I fully grasped just how complex, nuanced, and layered these societies actually are. I had not yet formed any close relationships with people from either country or spent extended time living, studying, or working there.

In 1996, during a Buddhist studies course in Barre, Massachusetts, I stumbled on a newsletter devoted to issues of international Buddhist women. Noting that the editor was a Thai professor of religion, Dr. Chatsumarn Kabilsingh, I resolved to pay her a visit on my next trip to Bangkok. Later that year, I found myself at Thammasat University sitting across the desk from Dr. Chat, discussing the recent and extraordinary gathering of more than 35,000 women just outside Beijing at the NGO Forum on Women. In exploring this and other topics, Dr. Chat determined that it would be beneficial for her feminist activist colleague, Ouyporn Khuankaew, and I to meet due to our common interests and commitments. Using the mailing address Dr. Chat provided during that meeting, I wrote to "Ms. Khuankaew," sharing my interests in Buddhism, various social issues such as violence against women, HIV/AIDS, and feminist counseling. Much to my delight, Ouyporn replied expressing interest in meeting and working together. We made a plan to offer a workshop focusing on counseling women survivors of violence in December 1997. I would "teach" the workshop and Ouyporn would translate.

In December 1997, my partner, Deena, and I traveled to Thailand, where we met Ouyporn for the first time. We all made our way to Kanchaniburi, where Ouyporn and I would be facilitating the workshop with the staff of a local nongovernmental organization. As the workshop progressed, with me as the primary facilitator and Ouyporn translating, we increasingly began to turn to one another to discuss what to do next and to debrief the process. Ouyporn regularly and spontaneously added to my comments and very skillfully made the workshop more relevant and grounded in the Thai context. At the end of the 4 days, we shared with one another our experiences of working together on this project and quickly agreed that we were not satisfied with the arrangement of facilitator/ translator. Because we both recognized that we each brought crucial and unique contributions to the table, we made an explicit commitment to shift to a co-facilitation, power-sharing approach. Furthermore, we pledged to regularly reflect on "the process" of our collaboration, both with one another, as well as with our local partners in future projects, to ensure that we stayed true to these values. We recognized that the dynamics of our own partnership would influence participants with whom we would be working. If they saw a Thai facilitator and a white U.S. facilitator sharing power, mutually respecting one another, and valuing one another's input and perspectives, we knew that this would influence the participants' own feelings of empowerment and agency.

Thus began our journey together. For the past 12 years, Ouyporn and I have worked with groups from Thailand, Cambodia, the refugee communities of Burma, as well as Asia regional groups and international groups, including participants from nearly every continent. While continuing to work with local partners on issues such as violence against women, HIV/AIDS, women's leadership, and feminist counseling, we now also collaborate with groups focusing on peace building, anti-oppression, social justice education, and capacity building through training of trainer experiences.

Over the span of our work, Ouyporn and I have spent considerable time engaging between ourselves and with local partners in a reflexive process focused on inventing, articulating, and refining the methodology we are using in our projects. We have deliberately noted the contributions from postcolonial theory; radical, critical, global, and transnational feminist theories; liberation theory; and participant action research (see Norsworthy & Khuankaew, 2004, 2006, 2008, for a full discussion of this evolving methodological framework). In keeping with the participant action principle of "passing the torch," we have supported and mentored a significant number of second- and third-generation practitioners into this liberatory model and now are proud to facilitate with many of them on projects around the region.

The years have also brought a deepening of the relationship between Ouyporn and me. In facing challenging and confusing critical workshop incidents, experiencing the joys and satisfaction of effective collaboration, through difficult dialogues in which we worked through misunderstandings and conflicts, we agree that our trust, respect, and appreciation for one another has exponentially deepened and increased. We recognize the multiple dimensions of our relationship to one another as mentors, teachers, friends, colleagues, and "sisters."

Reflections: What Is to Be Learned From These Experiences?

As a white, U.S. counseling and peace psychologist working and conducting research in South and Southeast Asia for more than a decade, I have learned much from and with Ouyporn and my other local collaborators, partners, and project participants, as well as from the experience of doing the work in so many parts of the region. However, it is clear to me that spending considerable time in India, Thailand, and other parts of Asia, studying indigenous spiritual practices, and absorbing and acclimating to the cultures were extremely important preparation for working in these countries. In cultivating a degree of comfort and appreciation of the cultures and the people as well as some basic skills in functioning in cultural contexts very different from my own, particularly during times of ambiguity and uncertainty, a "bonding" process began to take place that would serve as an important foundation for the challenges ahead. Still, I was quite naive initially and had only a superficial understanding of the cultures and the people until I began to work in the region, developed personal relationships, studied the Thai language, and lived with people on a daily basis for more extended periods of time.

As is clear from my reflections about Ouyporn's and my initial experience with one another, consistent with my U.S. enculturation, I approached the situation as the "expert," assuming that Ouyporn would be the "support" person, and she did the same. Fortunately, for both of us, we each had strong feminist and social justice sensibilities that created dissonance about the initial power arrangements, and we were able to openly debrief and change the arrangements. Through Ouyporn's and my lived experiences and our respective educations, we were aware of the U.S. global dominance politically, economically, educationally, and militarily. We both knew that my country and disciplines, U.S. counseling and psychology, profoundly influence and affect the rest of the world, often through hegemonic systems defining "standards" by which others must or "should" operate (Leong &

Ponterotto, 2003; Varenne, 2003). Over the years of work and dialogue with my Asian colleagues, this "concept" was brought to life. I frequently heard them express concerns. For example, one colleague from Burma living in exile in Thailand reported,

> We had a Western "expert" come in to consult with us about HIV/AIDS. He was a link to funding that could have really helped us set up crisis counseling services and train local personnel. But he thought we had to have "professionals" with master's degrees and PhDs to provide the services and this is not available at this time inside the country or in the refugee communities here in Thailand. Most of the universities in Burma have been closed down by the dictatorship. We escaped from the regime and do not have access to such education right now nor do most of us have legal documents so that we can attend Thai schools. So, he got frustrated and left. He did not want to work with us to see if we could come up with a more workable solution. (Tan, pseudonym to protect security; personal communication, July 17, 2004)

What comes to mind here is the justification statement for the 2004 APA Resolution on Culture and Gender Awareness in International Psychology, which encourages psychologists "to become aware of and act differently from the historical processes of global imperialism and colonialism by educating themselves about cultural and gender issues and systems of power, privilege, and domination in international psychology" (Rice & Ballou, 2002, p. 1).

Both Ouyporn and I have come to realize that we are likely to encounter the effects of colonization and imperialism in ourselves and in others (ComasDiaz, 1994; Moane, 1994). My local partners, participants, and I were all enculturated into societies based on systems of hegemony, power, and oppression and, without awareness or conscientization, would likely enact internalizations of these dynamics. Thus, we were all challenged to "unlearn" these attitudes and behaviors and to develop a critical consciousness (Freire, 1972) in order to create collaborative partnerships among ourselves and with participants. As articulated in the multicultural competencies (Sue, Arredondo, & McDavis, 1992), this takes awareness, knowledge, and skills.

My local partners have also pointed out to me that their societies are hierarchical (Norsworthy & Khuankaew, 2006). If Westerners enter without an understanding of this, we run the risk of reinforcing already existing power dynamics that privilege particular groups and systematically exclude or silence other groups and their needs. This again points to the importance of getting to know the local context, including the social, political, cultural, and historical dimensions and, if possible, partnering with local colleagues who are committed to values of empowerment and justice, in preparation for doing research or practice projects.

Additionally, most work done outside the West is in English, so professionals traveling outside the West rarely have the opportunity to talk directly with people on the ground (unless the person speaks the language) (Norsworthy & Khuankaew, 2006). Therefore, it is important for Western counselors and psychologists to recognize the limits of their understanding of local psychologies, indigenous ways, contexts, issues, concerns, models of healing and "helping," and solutions. This makes a compelling case for arranging, when possible, to interact with local people holding a range of identities, social locations, levels of education, and diverse perspectives in preparation for and in the process of working, researching, and/or doing activism in countries outside our own.

Finally, theories, printed materials (e.g., books, tests, training manuals), research, and other professional literature that come from the West are constructed from a Western paradigm and worldview; thus, they may or may not be relevant, even with adaptation or redesign, for a context outside the West (Leung, 2003; Norsworthy & Khuankaew, 2006). This points to the importance of indigenization of counseling and psychology and suggests that the most useful role for the Western counselor or psychologist may be to offer to collaborate with local people in articulating and valuing their own knowledge, wisdom, and practices, then exploring in what ways (or not) Western perspectives can inform or map on in developing indigenous psychological and counseling paradigms, frameworks, and practices.

I have found that even when I have spent much time in a country or culture, learning the language, studying and reading, engaging in relationships and work, there is much I do not know. Acknowledging my outsider status (Lykes, 2001) and that I am always in learning mode allows me to be open to new information and feedback. Ouyporn and I count on one another to be truthful and frank in our reflections, and we encourage the same within our partnerships with local groups.

During the first few years, I found myself a bit immobilized by my efforts to be aware of the power arrangements and to "unlearn" the ways I had internalized Western privilege. Eventually, through ongoing reflection and conversation with Ouyporn and other local partners, I came to see that as an outsider (U.S. psychologist), I do have things to offer and can make valuable contributions to the work of the group precisely because of my "outsider" position.

For example, forging long-standing relationships with local partners is the key in developing the necessary mutual trust and honesty for engaging in authentic dialogue. These relationships, in combination with an explicit commitment to power sharing, lay the groundwork for ongoing, honest exchanges, where local partners and participants feel free to publicly accept or reject my ideas or input, and for me to publicly question or challenge their ideas. Ongoing reflection about the power dynamics also allows us to deepen our relationships by changing interactions that undermine mutuality and collaboration. Difficult dialogues, especially about power, can pave the way to effective and satisfying partnerships. Finally, when possible, engagement in similar reflexive processes between the groups with whom we work and ourselves can be very valuable in creating "decolonizing" processes, whereby group members take ownership for defining their own issues and concerns based on their cultural and community contexts and assert their ideas and perspectives in the process of developing solutions and action plans.

The learning and growth I have experienced through these border crossings also inform my work as a counselor educator and counseling psychologist back home in the United States. For example, in taking my practicum students to work in a local migrant community setting, we find that the issues for the migrant community greatly resemble those of the refugee community of Burma in Thailand. When students read Ouyporn's and my articles and chapters, they report that they feel more prepared to understand the challenges for people without legal documentation who are often on the receiving end of racism, xenophobia, and "psychological colonization," particularly in these social and political times in the United States. Furthermore, they comment on the importance of taking a power-sharing, collaborative stance, whereby they and their clients view one another as teachers and students in the therapeutic process, particularly since students and clients alike are in a conscientization process. As my colleague, Ouyporn Khuankaew, pointed out, "We all need to approach our cross-national work with a humble mind, acknowledging that we each stand to benefit and be most effective when we work in respectful, power sharing partnerships where everyone's input is valued and respected" (O. Khuankaew, personal communication, August 3, 2005).

Reflections and Conclusions

(LI-FEI WANG)

Through the reflections of these authors on their border-crossing experiences, the limitations and impact of defining the field globally solely from U.S. psychology's point of view were highlighted. Furthermore, the authors emphasized the importance of revisiting the "global" understanding of counseling and counseling psychology as professions extending to countries and cultures worldwide. Throughout the chapter, the value and meaning of internationalization of counseling and counseling psychology were revealed.

The three coauthors who shared their personal "border-crossing" experiences pointed out how important it is to explore and understand the contexts and cultures of the country while developing transnational collaboration.

Challenges, successful coping strategies, and suggestions for effective partnerships and collaboration were addressed. Critical factors and events demonstrating the value of creating reciprocal relationships based on mutuality and trust were described. Interestingly, all three authors reveal the ways in which their border-crossing experiences extended and enriched their own knowledge and practice of counseling psychology back in their home countries. Having local cultural informants with whom they had close relationships and regular communication, reflecting and redigesting their border-crossing experiences, and being open and flexible were major strategies for their learning, growth, and success.

In sum, the border-crossing adjustment and learning experience seems to be an ongoing spiral learning process that integrates "in-and-out" as well as "host-and-home" cultural learning processes. These experiences not only stimulate us to learn from the host country and culture but also propel us to redigest our home culture in a deeper way. Through self-reflection, communication, clarification, assimilation, and accommodation processes, we gradually develop our cross-cultural competencies and more deeply understand the importance of developing an interconnected international system of counseling and counseling psychology. Although there are more challenging, confusing, difficult, disappointing, lonely, and even misunderstanding experiences than we anticipate, our border-crossing experiences are more rewarding and fruitful than we could even imagine. We believe that learning from such border-crossing experiences not only increases our competencies in international collaboration but also enhances and deepens our understanding of our professions.

Chapter Questions

1. Construct a letter to a granting agency advocating for the importance of funding cross-national teams to study psychological constructs in a variety of cultural and country settings.

2. Imagine that you are going to engage in a "border-crossing" research or practice project for the first time, in a country to which you have never travelled. Discuss the preparations you would make in advance and the steps you would take during your work to ensure enactment of the Resolution on Culture and Gender Awareness.

3. Assume that you are a U.S. Native-born graduate student studying with international graduate students in a graduate program in counseling or counseling psychology. Discuss the ways in which you would, as a student, demonstrate cultural competency in relation to the presence and contributions of your international peers and so that their and your learning is enriched.

References

American Psychological Association. (2003). Multicultural guidelines: Education, research, and practice. *American Psychologist, 58,* 377–402.

American Psychological Association. (2004). *Resolution on culture and gender awareness in international psychology.* Retrieved January 11, 2003, from www .apa.org/international/resolutiongender.html

Arnett, J. J. (2008). The neglected 95%: Why American psychology needs to become less American. *American Psychologist, 63,* 602–614.

Cheung, F. M. (2000). Deconstructing counseling in a cultural context. *The Counseling Psychologist, 28,* 123–132.

Comas-Diaz, L. (1994). An integrative approach. In L. Comas-Diaz & B. Greene (Eds.), *Women of color: Integrating ethnic and gender identities in psychotherapy* (pp. 287–318). New York: Guilford Press.

Freire, P. (1972). *Pedagogy of the oppressed.* New York: Herder & Herder.

Heine, S. J., & Norenzayan, A. (2006). Toward a psychological science for a cultural species. *Perspectives in Psychological Science, 1,* 251–269.

Heppner, P. P. (2006). The benefits and challenges of becoming cross-culturally competent counseling psychologists. *The Counseling Psychologist, 34,* 147–172.

Heppner, P. P. (2008). Expanding the conceptualization and measurement of applied problem solving and coping: From stages to dimensions to the almost forgotten cultural context. *American Psychologist, 63,* 803–816.

Heppner, P. P., Heppner, M. J., Lee, D.-G., Wang, Y.-W., Park, H.-J., & Wang, L.-F. (2006). Development and validation of a collectivistic coping styles inventory. *Journal of Counseling Psychology, 53,* 107–125.

Heppner, P. P., Leong, F. T. L., & Gerstein, L. H. (2008). Counseling within a changing world: Meeting the psychological needs of societies and the world. In W. B. Walsh (Ed.), *Biennial review in counseling psychology* (pp. 231–258). Thousand Oaks, CA: Sage.

Kim, U., Yang, K. S., & Hwang, K. K. (2006). *Indigenous and cultural psychology.* New York: Springer.

Leong, F. T. L., & Ponterotto, J. G. (2003). A proposal for internationalizing counseling psychology in the United States: Rationale, recommendations, and challenges. *The Counseling Psychologist, 31,* 381–395.

Leung, S. A. (2003). A journey worth traveling: Globalization of counseling psychology. *The Counseling Psychologist, 31,* 412–419.

Leung, S. A. (2007). Returning home and issues related to "reverse culture shock." In H. D. Singaravelu & M. Pope (Eds.), *Handbook on counseling international students* (pp. 137–151). Alexandria, VA: American Counseling Association.

Leung, S. A., & Hoshmand, L. T. (2007). Internationalization and international publishing: Broadening the impact of scholarly work in counseling. *Asian Journal of Counselling, 14,* 141–154.

Lonner, W. J. (1985). Issues in testing and assessment in cross-cultural counseling. *The Counseling Psychologist, 13,* 599–614.

Lykes, M. B. (2001). Activist participatory research and the arts with rural Maya women: Interculturality and situated meaning making. In D. L. Tolman & M. Brydon-Miller (Eds.), *From subjects to subjectivities: A handbook of interpretive and participatory methods* (pp. 183–199). New York: New York University Press.

Marsella, A. J., & Pedersen, P. B. (2004). Internationalizing the counseling psychology curriculum: Toward new values, competencies, and directions. *Counseling Psychology Quarterly, 17*, 413–423.

Moane, G. (1994). A psychological analysis of colonialism in an Irish context. *Irish Journal of Psychology, 15*(2/3), 250–265.

Norsworthy, K. L., & Khuankaew, O. (2004). Women of Burma speak out: Workshops to deconstruct gender-based violence and build systems of peace and justice. *Journal for Specialists in Group Work, 29*(3), 259–283.

Norsworthy, K. L., & Khuankaew, O. (2006). Bringing social justice to international practices of counseling psychology. In R. I. Toporek, L. H. Gerstein, N. A. Fouad, G. Roysircar, & T. Israel (Eds.), *Handbook for social justice in counseling psychology* (pp. 421–441). Thousand Oaks, CA: Sage.

Norsworthy, K. L., & Khuankaew, O. (2008). A new view from women of Thailand on gender, sexuality, and HIV/AIDS. *Feminism and Psychology, 18*(4), 527–536.

Pedersen, P. (1995). *The five stages of culture shock: Critical incidents around the world.* Westport, CT: Greenwood Press.

Pedersen, P. (2003). Culturally biased assumptions in counseling psychology. *The Counseling Psychologist, 31*(4), 396–403.

Pedersen, P. B., & Leong, F. (1997). Counseling in an international context. *The Counseling Psychologist, 25*, 117–122.

Quintana, S. M., Troyano, N., & Taylor, G. (2001). Cultural validity and inherent challenges in quantitative methods for multicultural research. In J. Ponterotto, J. M. Casas, L. A. Suzuki, & C. M. Alexander (Eds.), *Handbook of multicultural counseling* (2nd ed., pp. 604–630). Thousand Oaks, CA: Sage.

Rice, J., & Ballou, M. (2002). *Cultural and gender awareness in international psychology.* Washington, DC: American Psychological Association.

Singer, J. A. (2008, December). The rich bounty of international collaboration. *Psychology International, 19*(5), 10–11.

Sue, D. W. (2003). *Overcoming our racism: The journey to liberation.* San Francisco: Jossey-Bass.

Sue, D. W., Arredondo, P., & McDavis, R. (1992). Multicultural counseling competencies and standards: A call to the profession. *Journal of Counseling and Development, 70*, 477–484.

Varenne, H. (2003). On internationalizing counseling psychology: A view from cultural anthropology. *The Counseling Psychologist, 31*(4), 396–403.

Worthington, R. L., Soth-McNett, A. M., & Moreno, M. V. (2007). Multicultural counseling competencies research: A 20-year content analysis. *Journal of Counseling Psychology, 54*, 351–361.

Ægisdóttir, S., Gerstein, L. H., & Çinarbaş, D. C. (2008). Methodological issues in cross-cultural counseling research: Equivalence, bias, and translation. *The Counseling Psychologist, 36*, 188–219.

Chapter Eight

Cross-Cultural Collaboration

Developing Cross-Cultural Competencies and Yuan-Fen

Li-fei Wang and P. Paul Heppner

It was perhaps a serendipitous event in 1989 that began our relationship; but over the last 20 years, both of us have invested a great deal of effort to achieve a productive, meaningful, and exciting cross-cultural collaborative relationship. In many ways, our relationship reflects the Chinese notion of *yuan-fen*, which means that the relationship has been influenced by good deeds from a previous life and continues to have significant meanings and influence today.

Our relationship began when Puncky was invited to Taiwan as a visiting scholar for 2 weeks to present several workshops and lectures. During that trip, we had two primary professional interactions as well as several social interactions; 1 year later Li-fei became a counseling psychology doctoral advisee of Puncky. Subsequently, we worked together for 5 years in the United States. After that, for the next 15 years, we communicated intermittently via snail mail, e-mail, and Skype, as well as visiting each other's home culture over 10 times collectively (from 2 weeks to 6 months). The frequency of communication has significantly increased over the years as the complexity of our collaboration and power sharing increased. We have collaborated across a full spectrum of professional and social activities, leading to outcomes such as (a) eight coauthored research publications; (b) numerous co-presentations, at the American Psychological Association (APA) and other international conferences; (c) the creation and implementation of a 2-week Bidirectional Cross-Cultural Immersion Program (BCCIP) for students/faculty in both our departments; (d) the establishment of a dual-degree master's program for both departments; (e) the development of departmental and university memoranda of agreement to promote cross-national research, faculty and student exchanges, and graduate student training; (f) the linking of our major professional organizations; and (g) most important, a deep, meaningful, and close friendship.

The purpose of this chapter is to promote the development of knowledge, awareness, and skills related to cross-cultural collaboration within the counseling profession. We have found that the development of each of our cross-cultural competencies has played a critical role in our cross-cultural collaboration as well as the growth of the mutuality and power-sharing within our relationship. Without all of these elements, we could not have produced the type of collaborative outcomes as mentioned earlier. Therefore, it is our hope that by sharing our personal and professional development and cultural journeys (joys and challenges), as well as our problem-solving strategies, we might stimulate awareness of critical incidents, personal attributes and values, and important learning experiences that not only figured prominently in our cross-cultural journeys and development, but also occurred subsequently in our cross-cultural collaboration. Moreover, we hope that our sharing will be useful for other sojourners as well as help normalize the developmental process and challenges inherent in international collaboration. Finally, we hope that our sharing might give others the courage to take personal and professional risks within their cross-cultural journeys to enhance their cross-cultural sensitivity and even, ultimately, promote international collaboration among our colleagues.

Through our own self-reflection and intensive discussion, we will discuss four critical incidents that affected the growth of our collaborative relationship within each of our individual cross-cultural journeys: (1) positive initial contacts, (2) repeated exposure and significant cross-cultural immersions, (3) integration of the two cultural contexts over time, and (4) actively promoting the acquisition of cross-cultural competencies in others for navigating the two cultural contexts. Each of us will discuss a little about our development, specifically our joys, personal challenges, problem-solving strategies, and cross-cultural discoveries and growth within these critical events and, most important, the ways in which our personal characteristics (e.g., personality attributes, values, coping styles) moderated those experiences. Perhaps the most important factor underlying our productivity has been the development of an evolving and ever-deepening personal and professional cross-cultural relationship throughout our 20-year friendship. Finally, in the last section of the chapter, we will draw some conclusions based on our experiences about developing meaningful and productive cross-cultural collaborative relationships.

In terms of my background, I (Li-fei Wang) am a Taiwanese middle-class, heterosexual, able-bodied woman from a cultural background with an intermix of Taiwanese, Hakanese, Chinese, Japanese, and native Taiwanese cultures. Obedience, filial piety, loyalty to family, hard work, emphasis on interpersonal harmony, and being calm and quiet are encouraged in my culture. In addition, education is highly valued in both my family and society, which gave me the courage to explore and a willingness to learn more about new cultures. Although I had traveled to 12 countries in my 20s, my understanding of other cultures was on a very surface and even "Taiwanese-ethnocentric" level.

In terms of my background, I (Puncky Heppner) am a white, heterosexual man of German-Russian descent with early socialization within a very predominantly American German and Scandinavian, low-income, rural cultural context in North Dakota and Minnesota. Common values within the intersection of these cultural perspectives included emotional restraint (especially in public), a strong work ethic (especially thoroughness, attention to detail, meeting responsibilities), a strong emphasis on education, love of land (and the family homestead), and a strong sense of fairness and social justice (see McGoldrick, Giordano, & Pearce, 1982). From a diversity perspective, my early life experiences led to a narrow worldview and very little exposure to other cultures; for example, as a high school senior, the only people I knew who had traveled abroad were my uncles who fought in World War II. However, beginning in the 1970s as a graduate student, and especially since the 1990s as a faculty member, many of my experiences within the U.S. multicultural movement led to the development of multicultural awareness, knowledge, and skills (see Sue & Sue, 2008); these multicultural competencies would later provide the foundation for the development of cross-cultural competencies, which further enhanced my multicultural competencies.

Positive Initial Contacts

Regardless of what we heard about the other's culture, our initial positive contacts based on real interactions (as opposed to our mostly stereotypical impressions) provided us with important knowledge as well as the will to explore more about the other's culture. In retrospect, if our initial contacts at such an early phase of our cross-cultural journeys had been negative, we may likely have experienced too much anxiety in this particular cross-cultural journey, and we might not have even pursued a personal and professional relationship. For example, although I (Li-fei) had traveled to 12 countries, in retrospect from a cross-cultural developmental perspective, I acted as a "tourist" and had very little knowledge about living in the United States and its people and cultures. For example, my first visit to the United States (1987) as a tourist provided me with very surface but important information. My first impression of Americans was that they were knowledgeable, friendly, respectful, and warmly welcoming of me. The various customs and rules seemed to be clear, simple, and easy to follow. My positive impression stimulated me to consider pursuing a PhD in the United States. When I met Puncky in Taiwan (1989), his kind, respectful, sincere attitudes and scholarly manner attracted me to pursue a PhD under his guidance. At this point, for me, the meaning of cross-cultural experiences was simply different, interesting, and curious.

Similarly, my (Puncky) strongest pre-contact association with Taiwan was a vague stereotypical sense of "Formosa" as an exotic, beautiful, tropical island. From a cross-cultural developmental perspective, I had lived and worked as a visiting professor in two European countries (Sweden and England) for about 8 months and had traveled as a tourist in another 7 to 8 European countries; these experiences had taught me some important things about the role of culture in affecting human behavior, and I mostly understood that cultural differences did not mean that one culture was inferior to another culture. I had witnessed several incidences of ethnocentric and arrogant American behavior in Europe (e.g., derogatory comments about cultural norms and customs) and felt very embarrassed by the cultural insensitivity. However, I had very few experiences outside of the United States and Europe.

My first real contact with Asian culture, and specifically Taiwanese culture, was a 2-week trip as a visiting scholar (1989), during which I had numerous memorable experiences with Taiwan's counseling professionals, food, customs, values, and numerous historic sites such as temples, monuments, and national parks; I experienced the Taiwanese people as friendly, kind, genuine, generous, inquisitive, respectful, and industrious. At the end of the 2 weeks, I remember feeling astonished with how much I had learned about Taiwan and its people. I felt that I had increased my cultural knowledge of Taiwan tremendously (e.g., 50-fold). In retrospect, starting with a base knowledge level near 0, a 50-fold increase still left me near the bottom of the "unaware" category, but I had no idea of how much of the Taiwanese cultural complexities I did not know, nor have much knowledge of the differences that existed across various Asian cultures.

In sum, both of us had positive initial impressions of the other's culture, and our first real contact in the other's culture was very positive; these positive experiences were major factors that not only encouraged but inspired us to learn more about the other's culture. In retrospect, our initial impressions were based mostly on surface-level knowledge and appreciation of the other's culture as well as the specific people we encountered. Our worldviews were very Eastern and Western, respectively. We were relatively early in our cross-cultural development journeys; our relative lack of accurate cultural information also led us to many incorrect assumptions and conclusions about the other's culture (e.g., assuming that collectivism meant that everyone worked together harmoniously solely for the common good; Americans are liberal and live in a gender-equal society). We were largely unaware of how additional cross-cultural experiences could affect both our personal and professional development.

Nonetheless, despite our relative lack of cultural and country knowledge, we both possessed some personal attributes and values that helped to propel us forward. We both embraced not just an interest and positive impression of the opposite culture but a strong sense of curiosity and willingness to learn about each other's culture; this powerful quest to discover and learn, coupled with our safe and enjoyable initial contacts, were important factors that led us to take additional steps and risks in our cross-cultural journey. We both were able to tolerate quite a bit of ambiguity or uncertainty within the other's culture and brought a sense of humility about being an outsider in the other's culture. We both displayed a functional sense of humor (e.g., making fun of our cultural challenges) that lowered our initial anxieties. We also approached our cultural encounters in terms of seeking mutually beneficial relationships, an egalitarian "give and take" attitude of mutuality as opposed to a one-down, one-up position. In addition, our relatively simple (undifferentiated) but respectful cross-cultural attitudes engendered positive responses from people in the other's culture that not only lowered our initial anxieties but also provided additional opportunities that deepened our understanding of the host culture as well as deepening our relationship. In essence, a number of personal attributes and values not only allowed us to approach the other's culture but also led to positive cultural experiences and to our acquiring more cultural knowledge so that we both wanted to pursue greater contact with the other and his/her culture.

Repeated Exposure and Significant Cross-Cultural Immersions

Immersion in another culture for a significant period of time provides a very different type of experience from the one typically obtained from a short personal or professional trip. I (Li-fei) was an international student in the United States for 5 years (1990–1995). I (Puncky) was a Fulbright Scholar in Taiwan for 6 months (2002). In addition, I had worked closely with and mentored a dozen or so East Asian graduate students across the previous 12 years, which provided additional opportunities to understand Asian cultures prior to the immersion experience. These intense educational and work experiences of varying lengths provided us with very powerful, cross-cultural immersion experiences that greatly increased our discoveries and knowledge of each other's culture as well as the process of developing meaningful and productive power-sharing, cross-cultural collaborative relationships. These outcomes contributed greatly to our cross-cultural development journeys, but in different ways for each of us. However, initially, we were mostly unaware that along with the many wonderful cross-cultural experiences would come innumerable daily problems in living and relationships; cultural and identity confusion; ineffective and inefficient problem solving; additional time demands, stress, anxiety, frustration, and so on, all of which would take an emotional toll on both of us. These types of experiences have also been depicted in United States racial-identity theories (e.g., Sue & Sue, 2008; Thompson & Carter, 1997) as well as in cultural transition/adaptation models (e.g., Berry & Sam, 1997; Pedersen, 1995). But most important, within the myriad problems and ambiguities, we began to learn not only to solve problems across our different levels of adjustment and cross-cultural knowledge but to do so with a growing cultural sensitivity that deepened the mutuality of our personal relationship, which allowed our power-sharing and professional collaboration to grow.

More specifically, I (Li-fei) was not only an international student in the United States but also the first international student in the counseling psychology program (in the Psychology Department) at the University of Missouri (MU). My pioneering role not only provided me with a unique and special status but also presented a challenging environment that was less sensitive to cross-national and cross-cultural differences. In my 5 years at MU, I experienced a broad array of exciting and challenging cross-cultural experiences, including both positive and negative emotions. Cultural differences caused many ambiguities around cultural norms and thus a great deal of confusion. There were numerous things that needed to be clarified and explained and hunches that needed to be tested. Moreover, my approach and tendency to withdraw created countless challenges. Not knowing how to resolve the challenges (e.g., by asking pointed questions), coupled with language restrictions, created many self-doubts and feelings of inferiority, all of which were in stark contrast to my previous exceptionally successful life as a teacher and counselor in Taiwan. In addition, my advisor (Puncky) and classmates also served as my cultural consultants and informants and significantly helped my understanding of American culture and subcultures. Over time, I acquired a deeper understanding of being a minority and a cross-cultural explorer. Although I cognitively believed in the benefits of new personal and professional explorations, the constant trial and error combined with language restrictions left me feeling overwhelmed, frustrated, and sometimes even like I was emotionally drowning. I gradually recognized that taking risks and not treating every obstacle as a personal fault was a useful strategy.

By sharing my own experiences and listening to people from different cultural backgrounds, I gradually recognized that there was not a superior or inferior culture, but just different cultures, which stimulated my worldview to become broader and more flexible. In addition, by frequently failing to overcome my language restrictions, I was able to more clearly understand the inner psychodynamics of being physically and psychologically challenged, as well as experiencing failure. Most important, from these experiences, I gained an understanding of developing cross-cultural relationships, cross-cultural empathy, and some ideas as to how to resolve cross-cultural challenges.

I (Puncky) had my first significant cultural immersion in Taiwan on my third trip to Taiwan, this time as a Fulbright Fellow. In terms of my cultural-development journey, I had now lived and worked as a psychologist in Ireland and South Africa for a total of 10 months. In these settings, I had learned a great deal about the many faces and lives of oppression, racism, privilege, greed, and different worldviews in both countries as well as the United States.

Living in Taiwan came at an intermediate point in my cross-cultural development. Subsequently, the experience brought many memorable and touching moments through (a) developing and deepening interpersonal relationships with faculty, students, and community members and (b) learning and experiencing Taiwanese and Chinese art, history, philosophy, architecture, religion, geography, food, medicine, and social customs. At the same time, I experienced, on an almost daily basis, ambiguity and confusion in this Asian culture. Understanding interpersonal dynamics within Taiwanese culture was perhaps the most significant challenge, in large part because of insufficient information about cultural values, norms, and customs and because of the critically important language barrier. Sometimes the language barrier would present major obstacles, for example, with some street vendors; but even when Taiwanese would speak English frequently, often there would be misunderstandings and belabored communication. My lack of knowledge, awareness, and skills inhibited the deepening of both my personal and professional relationships with acquaintances as well as others I interacted with frequently. At times, learning the many ways in which Asian values were operationalized in Taiwanese cultural customs seemed way too hard, and I would retreat physically and psychologically in confusion (e.g., reduce and/or avoid interactions with certain people). In addition, even though many Taiwanese spoke English, I encountered many challenges related to restrictions in my ability to communicate in Mandarin and Taiwanese. This limitation not only inhibited communication but also greatly slowed my discoveries and learning of the culture and interpersonal dynamics and was costly in terms of time and energy. Although these limitations were significant, I was determined to further my learning, and devoted time and energy to understand more of the cultural nuances. To cope with this challenge, I used strategies such as (a) acquiring essential language skills related to fiscal transactions, basic social interactions, and transportation; (b) asking questions of cultural informants; (c) regularly reading English sources of Taiwanese culture-related topics, including local newspapers; (d) regularly visiting local museums, talking to shop owners, and so on; and (e) allowing for additional time in my schedule.

Throughout the highs and lows, I became particularly appreciative of "cultural informants," people who taught me about the culture. Perhaps most important was developing problem-solving strategies such as (a) taking interpersonal risks to explore ambiguities and asking for clarification; (b) practicing cultural norms and customs; (c) being willing to follow Taiwanese interpersonal styles; (d) accepting and interacting within cultural norms rather than assuming Western customs, (e) disclosing my experiences; (f) being able to find humor within the many "trial and error" daily interactions; (g) reminding myself that this was a normal, time-consuming process in a new culture; (h) not taking myself too seriously; (i) being humble in the face of my lack of knowledge; and (j) feeling secure and even "normal" in my insecurity. All of these helped a great deal in helping me to deepen relationships in Taiwan and make meaningful, personal connections.

In sum, our repeated exposure and significant cultural immersions in the other's culture not only allowed us to acquire knowledge of the other's culture but also showed us how to engage in the host's cultural norms and practices. In essence, such knowledge allowed us to gain some cross-cultural competencies and enjoy the other's culture more, which we found deeply gratifying. It is important to highlight that to reach this point, it was very helpful that we both valued and appreciated what we were learning and thus were willing to spend the time and effort to enhance our relationship and process our cultural learning. For example, we engaged in a wide range of activities, such as participating in cultural and social festivals, cooking, spending time with each other's families in their homes, and so on. At the same time, acquiring skills to interact in the other's culture was often tiring and frustrating and sometimes painful. In retrospect, such challenges were more difficult at earlier points in our cross-cultural development. Most important, we each began to acquire more cultural awareness, knowledge, and skills along with enough self-efficacy to approach difficult cultural impasses (e.g., asking the other for specific cultural information, asking for interpersonal feedback, finding ways of supporting each other) and, in doing so, learned more about the other's cultural dynamics, deepened our personal and professional relationship, and acquired ways of successfully interacting in the other's culture. Throughout this part of our cultural journey, our awareness of cultural differences became clearer; we began to be sensitive to our worldview and to accept that what we understood from our cultural backgrounds did not mean that our "perceived reality" was accurate, best, or right. In essence, we were acquiring cross-cultural competencies, which greatly augmented both our relationship and cross-cultural collaboration.

In retrospect, some problem-solving strategies that seemed most helpful revolved around developing interpersonal competencies in each other's culture. Specifically, this included taking risks to disclose our confusion with cultural ambiguities as well as in our relationship, inquiring about ambiguities we experienced within the other's culture, asking for clarification of our feelings and understanding of the other's culture, and, most important, learning how and why cultural values were related to people's behaviors. For example, although the construct of collectivism seemed clear, the many ways it might be operationalized were ambiguous (e.g., there are different social rules for interacting with strangers, acquaintances, and family members). We also learned to attend more closely to the other's verbal (e.g., when a question was a suggestion; for example, sometimes a polite way of making a suggestion in Taiwan is done by asking a question such as, "Are you hungry?") and nonverbal behaviors (e.g., too much direct eye contact from a white American man can be misinterpreted as challenging by some Taiwanese men) and to learn to interpret them more accurately within the other's cultural context. All of these activities helped us to learn the cultural dynamics that initially were unknown and led to so much confusion. We also both gradually acquired a deeper sense of the joys and challenges of being a racial/ethnic minority in the other's culture after being part of the dominant culture in our home countries for so long. Specifically, we both experienced racial prejudice and discrimination. These experiences provided a range of feelings, such as frustration, hurt, anger, and betrayal, and they raised questions about our identity and even sometimes our desire to continue our cross-cultural journey.

Over time, we also became more comfortable in asking the other to serve as cultural informant, which increased our trust and appreciation of the other as well as the other's culture. Sometimes, in examining similarities and differences about our cultures, we also learned more about our own culture. Through our genuine and respectful interaction, we have learned to treat each other as "real" persons rather than just "authority figures"/ "advisors" and "students"/ "advisees." We value and also respect each other deeply. Moreover, the more we shared, the more cultural empathy we acquired, and the more culturally sensitive and appreciative we became. In essence, the more we shared, the more we learned from each other about sensitive topics such as race and privilege, national and international politics, as well as global power arrangements, and our personal and professional worlds. In addition, we also both grew and developed in becoming more sensitive hosts for each other, which deepened our relationship and trust of each other as well.

Integration of the Two Cultural Contexts Over Time

Both during and after the immersion experiences, we each began a deeper process of reflecting and synthesizing what we had learned from our cultural experiences, and seeing how that knowledge fit, or did not fit, the cultural context of our home culture. For example, I (Li-fei) quickly discovered that when I applied the West-based psychological knowledge I had learned in graduate school, I could not obtain the same outcome with Taiwanese clients and from my students. Similarly, the interpersonal interaction patterns and problem-solving skills I acquired in the United States did not result in the intended outcomes in Taiwan. Although I felt confident about my PhD training and was aware of many cross-cultural differences, the limited applicability to my home culture was disappointing. Subsequently, I began to re-immerse myself in my home culture and to explore my own cultural heritage in greater depth. The challenges I encountered in this transition back to my home culture surprised me and subsequently led me to new research and practice topics.

For example, through my research and practice in Taiwan, I recognized that the integration of Western and Eastern counseling experiences could enhance the effectiveness of counseling psychology. For instance, by contrast with emotional regulation theory in the United States, my research suggested that children in Taiwan attended less to emotional awareness and expression; rather, emotion management was much more important to meet cultural expectations around interpersonal harmony. I also started to recognize the importance and power of my cultural roots in psychological healing and the problem-solving process. I found that I learned a great many things about the counseling process in Taiwan from my Taiwanese clients and local practitioners, none of which was discussed in my Western PhD training. I found that I could perform more effective counseling when I was able to smoothly integrate Western counseling philosophies and techniques with the values and customs of my indigenous culture. For instance, education is highly valued in my country. I found that parents would have higher motivation to collaborate with me when I explained the concept of "receiving counseling" as a way to increase their child's learning and academic performance in school. It was also more acceptable to view "receiving counseling" when it was described as a way of "going to class" rather than receiving a "treatment." I also acquired a deeper understanding of diversity within my country, which I previously viewed as a uniform cultural society. I gradually recognized that I was raised in a diverse culture that included Taiwanese, Hakanese, Chinese, Japanese, and native Taiwanese cultures; moreover, through much cultural exploration and reflection, I not only became even more proud of my cultural heritage, but I also became more aware that the diversity of my cultural background is much more complex than I had previously thought. In short, through my research, practice, and personal reflections, I gradually recognized the powerful role that culture plays in human behaviors in Taiwan and the United States and especially in counseling and psychotherapy. This was not taught in my previous training.

A major reflection and integration activity for me (Puncky) spanned 5 to 6 years after the immersion stage (and still continues). An important part of my learning was to share my cross-cultural understanding with Taiwanese faculty and East Asian students in order to seek greater understanding of East Asian culture in general, and particularly Taiwanese culture. These discussions also included asking specific questions to clarify the cultural nuances and what might seem like contradictions within the culture (e.g., after a particular team meeting that did not seem very collectivist, I asked for clarification of the interpersonal dynamics). During this process, I was fortunate to be working closely with several international students from East Asia who were willing to share their cultural knowledge, which greatly augmented my understanding of various aspects of East Asia, specifically Taiwanese and Chinese cultures. In addition, I was also seeking greater understanding of my identity as a white, American, heterosexual, able-bodied man professor on a developmental cross-cultural journey with growing understanding of Taiwanese culture and to a lesser extent a few other cultures in East Asia (e.g., China). Although improving somewhat, my language restrictions still inhibited my interactions and learning about the cultural nuances.

In essence, my reflective cultural activities involved a clearer understanding of the assumptions and values in my culture and Taiwanese culture as well as being able to treasure various aspects of both cultures and even seemingly incompatible cultural customs. With reflection and greater cultural sensitivity and understanding also came greater understanding and empathy for people not only in my current but in past cross-cultural journeys in Taiwan along with my host and primary Asian confidant (Li-fei) as well.

In sum, reflection on our immersion experiences raised awareness of our own personal cultural heritage as well as our professional worldview as counseling psychologists, especially as we returned to work and live in our home cultures. Moreover, in our case, additional exposure and learning of the other's culture allowed us to not only broaden our worldview but also integrate our learning with a clearer understanding of the assumptions and values of each other's culture (and how others may perceive us in the other's culture) as well as our own. In essence, an important outcome was greater culture-specific knowledge, awareness, and skills in both cultures that then allowed us to be more culturally sensitive and empathetic in our personal and professional relationship with each other and to more successfully navigate across both cultures with different language and customs. The more we learned from our cross-cultural journey and our cross-cultural relationship, the more benefits we experienced and treasured (e.g., understanding the other more fully; deeper, more trusting, disclosing, mutual, power-sharing relationships; more direct and less stressful communications). We also realized that this was a very complicated but highly rewarding process and considerably more complicated than we had ever imagined before. In retrospect, a major outcome of our reflection and integration was the ability to not just establish a relationship but build a deeper and more complex relationship with knowledge about the cultural context of relationships in each culture. More important, our cross-cultural competencies increased within each of us at roughly the same time, which allowed us to deepen our personal relationship and working alliance.

Generativity: Promoting Others' Cross-Cultural Competencies

As we both engaged in the integration of Eastern and Western cultures, we began to feel a strong sense of generativity to promote cross-cultural awareness, knowledge, and skills in our students and the next generation. We also began to more clearly understand that our professional organizations could greatly benefit through international collaboration. In essence, we began to see beyond our relationship and our professional collaboration and to envision ways in which we could contribute to a larger cross-national movement to not simply promote cross-cultural collaboration, but, more important, to enhance cultural sensitivity and cross-cultural competencies as central and core elements in our profession. In essence, our growing cross-cultural competencies allowed us to see more possibilities to advance cross-national research, training, and practice.

Although we still collaborate on joint research projects and professional presentations, we have also focused on several systemic interventions to promote the development of each other's cross-cultural development, particularly that of the next generation in counseling and educational psychology. For example, in 2005, we created and implemented a 2-week, Bi-Directional Cross-Cultural Immersion Program (BCCIP) for students and faculty in each other's universities. This program provides a 2-week-long intensive opportunity for professional, cultural, and individual exploration for our graduate students and faculty in counseling and educational psychology. The first immersion was in 2005; 13 students and 1 faculty member from National Taiwan Normal University (NTNU) came to the University of Missouri (MU). In 2007, 11 students and 3 faculty members from MU went to NTNU for 2 weeks. In 2008, 19 students and 2 faculty members from NTNU came to MU for 2 weeks. Our evaluations revealed powerful cross-cultural learning for both the visiting and host students on both personal and professional outcomes, such as increasing awareness of self-identity and career exploration as well as cross-cultural competencies (Chiao, Allen, He, Kanagui, & Garriott, 2008; Chien et al., 2008; Huang, Chao, Chou, Chang, & Chu, 2008; Wang, 2008).

In the fall of 2007, we also began to implement a dual-degree master's program for both departments. This program allows master's students from one department to study at the other's department for 1 year and obtain master's degrees from both institutions in 3 years. Initial informal feedback from students suggests that this program also promotes greater cross-cultural understanding on both personal and professional levels. Likewise, other systemic interventions led to (a) the development of departmental and university memoranda of agreement to promote cross-national faculty research (b) a Summer Internship Program for doctoral students to practice psychotherapy in Taiwanese university counseling centers, (c) a coordinated bachelor's master's degree program, as well as (d) formal linkage of communication through the websites of our major professional organizations (i.e., Division 17 of APA and Taiwan Guidance and Counseling Association). The outcomes from these new programs have been deeply rewarding, and the process has also served to further deepen our personal and professional relationships.

It is important to note that these programs, which aimed at enhancing students' cross-cultural competencies, challenged us pedagogically. For example, we learned that our lectures on cross-cultural issues were well received by students but also fell short of our learning goals (e.g., students did not seem to be able to understand how specific cultural values affected culturally appropriate actions). Conversely, experiential teaching methods, especially those that facilitated even short immersion experiences between Taiwanese and U.S. students resulted in not only greater cross-cultural awareness but the initial development of cross-cultural relationships. We also learned that students' cross-cultural experiences seemed to be enhanced by having regular opportunities to process their experiences, either by journal writing or small group discussions and reflections. Our experiences led us to conceptualize cross-cultural learning within a developmental framework, and thus students with varying levels of cross-cultural experiences would need different types of pedagogical experiences to promote different students' cross-cultural development.

In addition, developing cross-cultural learning experiences across two countries necessitated not only program-development skills but also change agent and system-level skills within our respective training programs, departments, and universities: for example, developing relationships with administrators, identifying resources and allies, conceptualizing and writing formal binding agreements between our universities. Our experience has been that such system level changes involve more people (e.g., upper-level university administrators such as presidents, provosts, and deans as well as department chairs, faculty, and students). Consequently, these types of projects require sustained commitment to achieve satisfactory agreement among the various stakeholders. In addition, these cross-national programs required additional cross-cultural competencies, such as cross-cultural communication skills with university administrators from two cultures (culture-bridging skills). In addition, we have found it essential to be aware of our differential roles and power as we have interacted with others in each university and country; for example, sometimes the guest can say delicate things to upper-level administrators in a way that the host can not say (e.g., ask very direct questions about delicate topics such as the university's priorities and commitments).

Other cross-cultural competencies pertain to a broad range of cross-cultural problem-solving skills (as specified earlier in this chapter) as a multicultural team to resolve conflicts or impasses. Sometimes successful efforts in these activities are best characterized by a great deal of personal and professional trust, the type of trust that comes only after many experiences of being on the same team together. It involves not only knowing the other person's skills but also their reliability to follow through and trusting their value of and commitment for cross-cultural collaboration. It also involves a mutual "give and take," professionally and personally. All of these dynamics within a cross-cultural context underscores the importance of direct communication between us (Li-fei and Puncky), within us, mutual comfort and trust with each other, deep levels of sharing, and knowing each other's personality well enough to be able to support each other when we encounter difficult problems. In essence, these problem-solving activities are reflected in our communication patterns, and as with any team, the communication within the team directly affects our ability to reach our goals.

Conclusion

When we reflect on the many steps in our 20 years of cross-cultural collaboration, we are surprised about how many wonderful memories and outcomes have changed our personal and professional lives. We are also struck with how many challenges we went through and how lucky that we could be a team to resolve these challenges. In essence, it seems so long ago since we first met. There have been many twists and turns in the development both of our personal and professional relationship and cross-cultural competencies in general. We end this chapter with some observations and conclusions about cross-cultural collaboration that we have drawn from our many experiences over the last 20 years that might be helpful to others who choose to pursue similar goals.

1. *Positive Initial Contacts.* Our initial positive contacts with the other's culture were critically important in not only lowering our anxieties but also enhancing our desire to learn more about the other's culture, both of which positively influenced us to continue a deeper exploration of the other's culture. Several personal attributes (e.g., openness, respect) and positive cultural experiences (e.g., being well received in the host culture) also played major roles to propel us forward in our cross-cultural journey. We found that a willingness to respect and learn about the host culture is a crucial attitude that promotes positive initial contacts. Because we also had inaccurate information about the other's culture, our initial attitudes also played an important role to examine and challenge various stereotypes that we held. Developing a positive relationship in one's first contact can create possibilities for future learning and collaboration.

2. *Building a Trusting, Mutually Beneficial, and Appreciative Relationship (with good yuan-fen).* Perhaps the most important factor underlying our relationship and productivity is our trust in each other and our relationship, which has been an evolving and ever deepening, power-sharing personal and professional cross-cultural relationship. It is important to note that our relationship and subsequent collaboration would most likely have been different if we only had a professional or personal relationship. That is, having both a personal and professional relationship was cumulative and provided a stronger and more holistic working alliance in our cross-cultural collaboration. In essence, the multilayered relationship resulted in a broader array of interactions that deepened our relationship and promoted more effective interactions as well as enhanced the longevity of collaboration. Without the stability and support of both a strong

personal and a strong professional relationship, we doubt whether we would have been able to develop our existing levels of cross-cultural competence or be as successful in our professional pursuits. Because cross-cultural collaboration is built on a team of two or more people, a very important element is identifying and finding a partner with whom you can develop a good cross-cultural relationship, both on a personal and on a professional level. It is not possible for us to identify ideal characteristics to look for in a partner; as in developing personal or professional relationships in one's own culture, the ideal partner characteristics will differ across individuals. Moreover, we found the mutual respect, appreciation, power-sharing, and investment in a long-term relationship (known as good yuan-fen in Chinese culture) to be an important interpersonal factor that contributed to the development of the relationship. More specifically, within Chinese culture, relationships with good yuan-fen are those that by luck contain a special bonding characteristic, kinship, or chemistry that promotes the development of a good relationship. In essence, we not only respect each other but also appreciate the gifts that each of us brings to the relationship and feel lucky to be a part of this relationship.

We want to emphasize that a personal and professional relationship in one's own culture will most likely be different from a personal and professional relationship across two cultures because of the inherent cultural differences in establishing and maintaining personal and professional relationships. In our relationship, we found that it was essential to trust and even treasure the other's cultural perspective. We have experienced three different types of trust: (a) trust that you can be a good partner, (b) trust that your partner can be relied on, and (c) trust that you can collaborate in a mutually beneficial relationship and resolve challenges as a team. It is important to recognize that trust is not a given but is built over time and across many different experiences. When problems arise, sharing your thoughts, feelings, and concerns can be risky but also very helpful in developing a functional collaborative relationship.

3. *Increasing Both of Our Cultural Competencies.* Our process of cross-cultural collaboration has been greatly influenced by our level of multicultural and cross-cultural competence (knowledge, awareness, and skills), specifically, our culture-specific competence within the other's culture and our ability to resolve a myriad of challenges as a team of equal partners. We found that increasing our cross-cultural competencies was a bidirectional process. For us, it was important to not only increase levels of cultural competence in the other's culture, but also in our own culture. The more we learned about the other's culture, we then often redigested and reexplored our own cultural heritage (which seems to us as establishing a deeper cultural identity), which also resulted in a deeper understanding of both cultures. We also found that the more we appreciated and accepted our own culture, the more comfortable and accepting we became with ourselves, and subsequently, the more we became open to experience and value the host's culture. More important,

these experiences have later been part of important research topics in our cross-cultural collaboration.

4. *Learning by Experiencing.* In essence, acquiring cross-cultural competencies necessitates a proactive, planful approach, as well as an active, reflective, and integrative process. From our experience, significant and repeated exposure and immersions into the host culture for a significant period of time are necessary in acquiring cross-cultural competencies (as well as deepening multicultural competencies). Although traveling as a tourist was a useful learning process, we learned much more about the other's culture when we studied or worked in that cultural context. The normal tasks of living were excellent learning opportunities, as were the daily interactions with students and colleagues. However, just living in another culture in and of itself is not sufficient to enhance cross-cultural competence. We found that it was essential to reflect on the cultural context (e.g., values, norms) and continually seek to learn more of the complexities and nuances of the host culture. Being tolerant and open-minded instead of being judgmental and ethnocentric seem to be useful attitudes. In addition, we found that it was important to actively seek multiple-experiential cross-cultural experiences to learn and develop cross-cultural competencies. More experiential cultural experiences provided more learning opportunities to acquire cross-cultural competencies.

More important, we found that immersing in the host culture for a significant period of time was often very challenging and at times an overwhelming process. We would like to highlight that what may feel like an "up and down" process is a normal developmental process. There are so many things to learn about another culture, and it is typical and normal to make mistakes. It is similar to learning other complex tasks; there is always trial and error. Although such a process may be normative, it does not mean that it does not hurt to "fall down and scrape one's knees" during the learning process. Trust us, it does!

In short, it seems to us that acquiring cross-cultural competencies is a learning process that involves many ambiguities and many joyous moments as well as challenges and frustrations. Although this process is normal, it is sometimes not easy. Over time, we have found it most helpful to accept and learn from all aspects of this part of our cultural journey.

5. *Problem-Solving Attitudes and Approach.* A critical process that greatly affected our learning was how we coped with the ambiguities, stress, and challenges we encountered in our cross-cultural relationship and in the host's culture. Most important, we found that being willing to approach and clarify the ambiguities and challenges has been very important in our learning, but it also requires courage, risk taking, and energy. We found that it was helpful to consult with the other to more clearly understand the cultural context and nuances, as well as treating difficulties as problems that need to be discussed and hopefully resolved. Conversely, we found that a common reaction was

to withdraw or to be critical of either the host's or one's own culture; these reactions did not help us much in our cross-cultural development over time. Similarly, we found that blaming ourselves for the difficulties—as if they were caused by a personal fault—did not help. Although withdrawal and self- and/or other-blame are all normal reactions, we encourage others to be gentle with themselves and acknowledge the trial-and-error process as well as the positive things that they are doing.

6. *Multiple Benefits in Preparing the Next Generation.* From our experiences when we began to teach our students about cross-cultural competencies in the preparatory seminar as well as the BCCIP immersion itself, we ourselves also acquired additional cross-cultural competencies. For example, our experiences led us to conceptualize the process of cross-cultural learning more clearly within a developmental and cultural context, and thus we could then develop learning strategies based on students' developmental levels and cultural knowledge. In doing so, we became more clearly aware of the specific knowledge, awareness, and skills needed to navigate these two specific cultures, such as emphasizing the consequences of the cultural context in human behavior in that culture, the complexities within oneself and the other in cross-cultural communication, and knowledge about the cross-cultural journey process.

7. *Serving a Bridging Role as a Change Agent.* It has been necessary to serve as a bridge as we tried to contribute to a larger cross-national collaborative movement. Similarly, as we began to work with our colleagues in our universities and professional organizations, we also were challenged to extend our cross-cultural competencies related to being change agents in a broader system. In essence, we began to understand our roles as change agents in terms of bridging two cultures, not only negotiating differences between two universities situated in two cultures but also implementing the cultural context within our home institutions to facilitate the development of appropriate cross-cultural actions in developing our partnerships.

8. *Institutional Support.* Without institutional support, we could not provide various cross-cultural collaborative training programs (e.g., BCCIP, dual-degree master's programs) for our students. We have learned that institutional vision, support, and encouragement have been essential to pursue and continue our cross-cultural journey. From our experience, working closely with university leaders with international experience and vision has been essential and foundational in creating systemic changes that we as faculty could not have done alone without their guidance and support. In addition, we have recognized that our differential roles (e.g., guest) can be incredibly powerful to obtain institution support as we have interacted with others in each university and country. Thus, we found that our collaboration is an integration of Western and Eastern cultures into one effective and efficacious working team.

In conclusion, there have been many benefits from our cross-cultural collaboration, from scholarly products (publications and presentations), the development of international educational programs for students and faculty, and the development of cross-cultural competencies (awareness, knowledge, and skills). Moreover, our personal and professional lives have been greatly enriched by our cross-cultural journey and cross-cultural collaboration. That is, our cross-cultural journey and collaboration have changed our worldview, specifically how we view ourselves, the other, and what our profession might become to prepare the next generation to work and live in a global society. Our cross-cultural journey has resulted in a much deeper understanding of the multifaceted role of culture. We also found that such experiences were relevant for the development of a broader, global counseling psychology. Thus, we have worked together to build a conducive cross-cultural learning environment for the next generation of counseling psychologists.

At the heart of our journey have been our personal and professional relationship and the way our relationship has evolved and deepened in the context of our cultural dances in both countries, often being uncertain of everything going on around us, what the next steps might or would be, and where we might end up. The cultural dances have also involved a give-and-take, a mutual and reciprocal process of developing an equalitarian relationship across different cultures, one where we are on equal ground with mutual respect and appreciation for each other's culture and intuition. Perhaps it was a serendipitous event, or perhaps it was a good yuan-fen, the good luck by which people with the right chemistry are brought together for some reason. We hope that others will find something meaningful or educational in learning about our cross-cultural journey and collaboration. And we hope that good yuan-fen will be with others on their cross-cultural journey and collaboration and change both their personal and professional lives along the way.

Authors' Note: An earlier version of this chapter was presented in Wang, L. & Heppner, P. P. (2007, August), Reciprocity in Developing Productive and Meaningful Cross-Cultural Relationships. In S. A. Leung & P. Chen (Co-chairs), *International Counseling Psychology: Collaboration in a Flat World.* Symposium conducted at the 2007 Annual Meeting of the American Psychological Association, San Francisco, CA. We sincerely thank Yi-Jiun Lin and Catherine Hsieh for their helpful comments on an earlier version of this chapter.

Chapter Questions

1. What are the most important take-away messages you learned about developing cross-cultural collaboration?

2. What personal challenges would you expect to meet in developing cross-cultural competencies? What do you expect will be the biggest obstacle for you?

3. In what ways do you expect your personality might be a strength, as well as a weakness when developing cross-cultural competencies?

4. For the next 5 to 10 years, in what ways do you want to enhance and build your cross-cultural competencies? What steps can you take over the next few years to get relevant cross-cultural learning experiences?

References

Berry, J. W., & Sam, D. (1997). Acculturation and adaptation. In J. W. Berry, M. H. Segall, & C. Kagitçibasi (Eds.), *Handbook of cross-cultural psychology: Vol. 3. Social behavior and applications* (pp. 291–326). Boston: Allyn & Bacon.

Chiao, H., Allen, G. E. K., He, Y., Kanagui, M., & Garriott, P. O. (2008, August). Benefits of the BCCIP to host students. In P. P. Heppner & L.-F. Wang (Chairs), *Multiple benefits of a bidirectional cross-cultural immersion program*. Symposium conducted at the 2008 annual American Psychological Association Convention, Boston.

Chien, W., Chou, L., Lai, P., Lee, Y., Chen, C., Ting, S., et al. (2008, August). The benefits and challenges of being the BCCIP's visitors. In P. P. Heppner & L. Wang (Chair), *The multiple benefits of a bidirectional cross-cultural immersion program*. Symposium conducted at the 2008 meeting of the American Psychological Association, Boston, MA.

Huang, P., Chao, J., Chou, Y., Chang, Y., & Chu, S. (2008, August). The cross-cultural experience and competent development of the BCCIP. In P. P. Heppner & L. Wang (Chair), *The multiple benefits of a bidirectional cross-cultural immersion program*. Symposium conducted at the 2008 meeting of the American Psychological Association, Boston, MA.

McGoldrick, M., Giordano, J., & Pearce, J. K. (Eds.). (1982). *Ethnicity and family therapy*. New York: Guilford Press.

Pedersen, P. (1995). *The five stages of cultural shock: Critical incidents around the world*. Westport, CT: Greenwood Press.

Sue, D. W., & Sue, D. (2008). *Counseling the culturally diverse: Theory and practice* (5th ed.). Hoboken, NJ: Wiley.

Thompson, C. E., & Carter, R. T. (1997). *Racial identity theory: Applications to individual, group, and organizational interventions*. Mahwah, NJ: Lawrence Erlbaum.

Wang, L. (2008, March). The benefit and challenge of a Bidirectional Cross-Cultural Immersion Program: A Taiwan-USA example. In C. Duan & C. Juntunen, *Training implication of the internationalization movement in counseling psychology*. Symposium conducted at the 2008 International Counseling Psychology Conference, Chicago.

Chapter Nine

A Global Vision for the Future of Cross-Cultural Counseling

Theory, Collaboration, Research, and Training

*Lawrence H. Gerstein, P. Paul Heppner, Stefanía Ægisdóttir,
Seung-Ming Alvin Leung, and Kathryn L. Norsworthy*

The chapters in this book have offered an in-depth discussion on the conceptual, philosophical, methodological, and applied issues connected to engaging in cross-national, cross-cultural, and indigenous pursuits relevant to counseling. The dangers and potential benefits of relying exclusively on emic and/or etic counseling paradigms were highlighted, as were the consequences of promoting an ethnocentric, Eurocentric, or U.S.-centric model of counseling. Concrete suggestions for addressing these issues and their consequent dangers, challenges, and benefits were introduced as well.

In this concluding chapter, we identify common themes found throughout the book, discuss general implications for counseling and psychology in the United States and elsewhere, and raise ethical issues connected to international counseling activities. Additionally, we mention some of the strengths, challenges, and opportunities associated with cross-national collaboration and make recommendations about how to integrate and infuse international issues into counseling training programs and potential content to include in such programs, including essential cross-cultural and cross-national counseling competencies. Finally, we introduce many suggestions for the further development of theory, research, and practice linked with international counseling activities.

As Pedersen (2003) observed, counseling practices and functions have existed for thousands of years, performed by members of cultural communities holding varied roles, including local healers, spiritual leaders, physicians, teachers, and elders. The formal professions of counseling and counseling psychology, in contrast, are relatively new. For the most part, they have emerged within a Western and primarily U.S. context and from particular social, political, and economic structures that are informed by and reinforce a set of values and worldviews (i.e., individualism, autonomy, competition, logical positivism). As the professionalization process subsumes the functions and practices of counseling, indigenous wisdom and helping can become marginalized and devalued. This is especially the case when Western counseling and counseling psychology professionals use their power and influence (often unconsciously) to define the standards of practice internationally and when Western models and approaches are uncritically transported to other parts of the world.

This book clearly reveals the presence of an international movement to resist the globalization of Western counseling models and the attendant pressures toward homogenization and the discrediting of local healers, helpers, and wisdom. Some contributors to this book observed that Western counseling professionals infrequently publish in or read other countries' scholarly journals, nor do they attend or present at their conferences. Conversely, there is an increased trend toward international "border crossings" whereby counseling professionals from different parts of the world partner and collaborate in research and practice projects or engage in advanced training as international students. Several of our authors shared their experiences with cross-national and cross-cultural professional relationships, emphasizing the importance of power sharing, reciprocity, and mutual respect as a foundation for growth and learning. A key to cultural competence and successful collaborative projects across cultures involves the development of a critical consciousness about the current global power arrangements in relation to the counseling profession, a humble mind, and devoting considerable time and energy to understanding the local culture and contexts.

International students attending U.S. counselor education and counseling psychology training programs are also increasingly participating in cross-cultural and cross-national partnerships. They bring to light the importance of internationalizing the curriculum and breaking through the cultural encapsulation that characterizes much of the counseling and psychology training in the United States. Yet, while U.S. counseling and psychology have historically been more inwardly focused than internationally focused, the diversity, multicultural, and social justice movements (and the associated awareness, knowledge, and skills) within the professions are probably one of the most potentially important contributions of U.S. counseling to the larger global profession.

This book is a venue for addressing one of the major challenges associated with inventing a counseling profession that reflects and responds effectively to the wide range of human experience globally—that is, the need for the exchange of knowledge and skills across countries and cultures. Since, as we have pointed out earlier in this book, diversity is the key to surviving and thriving, we all need one another to cultivate a connected, interactive, international system of counseling professionals through which we can draw on our collective wisdom and experiences to respond to the complexities of life in the 21st-century global village. Thus, we need to develop and nurture cross-national and cross-cultural research and practice partnerships and information exchanges vis-à-vis literature, conferences, and professional exchange/immersion programs. Furthermore, attention and resources devoted to expanding cross-cultural research methods, focusing on the emic and etic constructs as part of a unified whole and using qualitative and quantitative research approaches, are essential in shedding light on the important questions related to culture, identity, and context in the counseling process.

We strongly echo previous scholars who have observed that counselors and counseling psychologists potentially have the awareness, knowledge, skills, and motivation to participate in addressing many serious challenges faced by people around the world, ranging from trauma resolution to reconciliation and peace building (e.g., Gerstein, 2006; Heppner, 1997; Leong & Blustein, 2000; Norsworthy & Gerstein, 2003). The more we understand one another beyond our own personal and national borders and the more we as counseling professionals share the locally and cross-culturally generated knowledge and skills needed to fulfill our important roles locally and globally, the greater our ability to create a peaceful planet that will sustain life for future generations.

Cross-National Collaboration: Strengths, Challenges, and Opportunities

Currently, national and geographic boundaries have been reduced by advances in communication technologies (e.g., e-mail, Internet information technologies, and Skype). Increased access to a variety of workflow technologies (e.g., word-processing and statistical software) allow individuals from different corners of the world to collaborate without leaving their offices and homes (see Chapters 7 and 8). This book, an example of international collaboration involving scholars from a number of countries involved a substantial amount of communication cross-nationally, yet almost all these cross-national efforts were performed within our homes, offices, or communities.

International collaboration is facilitated by the awareness that we are all members of a global village and that despite our differences there is much to learn from each other and much we could do to help one another grow. Through the process of working on the *International Handbook of Cross-Cultural Counseling: Cultural Assumptions and Practices Worldwide* (Gerstein, Heppner, Ægisdóttir, Leung, & Norsworthy, 2009), we discovered several consistent themes related to international collaboration: (a) counseling professionals from around the world perceive that such collaboration can strengthen the development of counseling in their own region; (b) international collaboration has and will continue to facilitate the development or adaptation of theories, practices, research, and tools for use in local cultures and contexts; and (c) international collaboration will become increasingly important in an age in which many local concerns could have an international impact (e.g., HIV prevention, terror incidents, and the 2009 financial tsunami). Counselors and counseling psychologists can encourage collaboration among professionals by offering their expertise and working conjointly across national borders. Additionally, cross-national teams of counseling scholars can conduct research and publish important cross-cultural studies, capitalizing on the various strengths that diverse counseling professionals offer. This consensus on the importance of international cooperation is a valuable strength that will foster greater collaboration on into the future (Heppner, 2006).

International collaboration also brings challenges. Perhaps one of the most important challenges is how counseling professionals can collaborate as equals. Historically, counseling professionals from the United States have dominated in developing and disseminating counseling theories, practice, training, and research. Counseling professionals in other parts of the world, on the other hand, have adapted to varying degree the materials from the United States while their own indigenous models and methods of healing and helping typically have not been included in Western counseling literature. As pointed out in this book, the new paradigm of international collaboration needs to be bilateral and multilateral in the sense that counseling professionals are co-leaders and co-followers (Leung, 2003) and also are equal in terms of the distribution of formal and informal power (Horne & Mathews, 2006; Norsworthy, 2006). The counseling profession would become more relevant locally and globally if counseling theories and practices were developed to be consistent with the local context (see Chapter 6).

A second challenge of international collaboration is language and communication (see Horne & Mathews, 2006). Ideally, counseling professionals engaged in international collaboration should be multilingual or, at the very least, conversant in the language used by the parties connected to the collaborative activity. This would enhance comprehending the cultural context, increase knowledge about the content connected to the project, and greatly improve communication between all involved parties.

Counseling professionals outside the United States, however, can use their multilingual, cross-cultural, and cross-national knowledge and skills to make scholarly contributions through summarizing and reviewing literature from non–English language sources. In this regard, international collaboration also requires documentation of what has been done locally and within different cultures so that members of the profession can use, adapt, and refine those strategies and outcomes. Making indigenous materials developed in different cultures and countries available worldwide will continue to be a challenge to international collaboration, but we hope that bilingual professionals could serve as the bridge to having these "treasures" be known and used in the international counseling community.

The magnitude and size of the problems that the global village is experiencing (e.g., natural and human-created disasters, global warming and weather changes, wars and conflicts, and the financial tsunami) have posed many challenges to the human race, and as much as we do not want these problems to surface and threaten the fabric of our societies, these are also opportunities for counseling professionals to make a difference. Counseling professionals around the world are in a unique position to collaborate and provide community-developed solutions for regional and global problems. Such efforts require the concerted and sustained collaboration of multiple professionals. The global financial tsunami is a case in point: Counseling professionals could use their knowledge and skills in mental health and career development to assist individuals experiencing financial and employment uncertainties. There are many ways that counseling professionals could share their experience and resources to promote mental health and well-being at such a challenging time.

Moreover, we suspect that future international collaboration will have the potential to change the face of counseling and counseling psychology forever. For example, as Heppner (2006) predicted, "In the future . . . the parameters of counseling psychology will cross many countries and many cultures" (p. 170). Furthermore, the cumulative knowledge base of the counseling profession will be grounded in information obtained from all corners of the world, putting "the puzzle together as an extraordinary picture of a worldwide psychology" (Heppner, Leong, & Chiao, 2008, p. 82). International collaboration has a great deal of potential to strengthen our research and practice, enhance our knowledge of the cultural context (see Heppner, 2008), and further our understanding of how culture shapes and influences ethical professional behavior.

Ethical Issues Connected to International Counseling Activities

The codes of ethics of various mental health professions, such as those developed by the American Psychological Association (APA) and the American Counseling Association (ACA) are designed to provide guiding principles as well as standards for professional conduct. Ethics are not simply proper etiquette (Heppner, Wampold, & Kivlighan, 2008), but rather they are expressions of our values and a guide to achieving them (Diener & Crandall, 1978). Not surprisingly, ethical codes in psychology date back over 50 years (see Golann, 1970). Although the codes are relatively easy to read, their application to specific situations is often complicated by intersecting and competing principles. In essence, complex ethical problems require decisions and actions that often cannot be prescribed by particular principles.

Moreover, ethical codes are intertwined within a context, specifically a cultural context. For example, Pedersen (1995, 1997) asserted that the ACA and APA ethical codes of the late 1990s were based on the dominant U.S. cultural perspective and minimized or ignored the impact of cultural context in ethical issues. Subsequently, U.S. scholars provided ethical decision-making models that included cultural assumptions, relevant cultural data, and cultural conflicts (Ridley, Liddle, Hill, & Li, 2001). In short, the cultural context is critical in any professional counseling or psychological code of ethics, and more recently, the ethical codes of the ACA and APA have attempted to address context (Pack-Brown & Williams, 2003).

Additionally, some books have been published on various ethical challenges and strategies for psychologists conducting research with diverse ethno-cultural populations and communities (e.g., Trimble & Fisher, 2006). Furthermore, other books advise counseling professionals to consider cultural issues when engaged in ethical decision making (Houser, Wilczenski, & Ham, 2006). In fact, Houser et al. (2006) discussed Western (i.e., Native American), Eastern (i.e., Confucius, Taoist, Hindu, and Buddhist), Middle Eastern (i.e., Jewish and Islamic), and southern-hemisphere (i.e., Hispanic/Latino and Pan-African) theories of ethics in relation to counselor decision making. These chapters are quite revealing and informative, and they offer counseling professionals the opportunity to develop an appreciation and respect for how different philosophical and religious worldviews can influence and guide ethical decision-making.

Given the richness of the philosophical and religious worldviews just mentioned, it is not surprising that many countries have developed ethical codes and guidelines to regulate the practice of psychology. For example, Leach (2008) has compiled a listing of 44 ethical codes (mostly in English) of national psychology associations from around the world. As of this writing, Leach is in the process of adding most of the ethics codes of South American national associations of psychology as well. Leach and Oakland (2007) have also compared the ethical standards influencing test development and use across 31 ethical codes, affecting practice in 35 countries.

The General Assembly of the International Union of Psychological Science (IUPsyS), the International Association of Applied Psychology (IAAP), and the International Association for Cross-Cultural Psychology have developed a "universal declaration of ethical principles for psychologists" to address "the common moral framework that guides and inspires psychologists worldwide toward the highest ethical ideals in their profession and scientific work" (Ad Hoc Joint Committee, 2005, p. 2). This is a generic set of moral principles based on shared human values around the world, and it avoids prescribing specific behaviors because such conduct is considered relative to the local cultural customs, beliefs, and laws. More specifically, the principles emphasize values, such as respect for the dignity of all human beings; respect for diversity among human beings; working to maximize benefits and minimize harm to individuals, families, and communities; striving for honest, open, and accurate communication; and being responsible to society. In essence, the universal declaration provides a shared moral framework for the work of psychologists within a larger social context.

There is a need for greater attention to ethics in national associations in counseling professions throughout the world. Some have suggested a very basic universal declaration of ethical principles in counseling (see Chapter 3). Such delineation could be very useful to underscore our common values and to establish a shared moral framework. In addition, there are currently a range of broad cross-national professional activities (e.g., consultation, training, research, and practice) involving participation across at least two countries that potentially raise an array of ethical issues related to cross-cultural competence, exploration, and the benefits to the larger society. That is, these cross-national issues can be conducted with varying degrees of cultural sensitivity. Aware of some of these issues, the APA adopted a "Resolution on Culture and Gender Awareness in International Psychology" (APA, 2004, Appendix 4; see Appendix, Chapter 4, this volume) that addresses some of these important challenges. However, much more attention is needed to deal with the many complexities related to cross-national collaboration within the counseling profession as well as in psychology in general (Heppner, Leong, & Chiao, 2008; Leong & Lee, 2006). In short, in this closing chapter, we want to remind readers of the many ethical complexities in crossing national borders, and that, as responsible members of the counseling profession, we must carefully attend to these complexities and be knowledgeable about the work being done in this arena.

Internationalizing Training of Counseling Professionals: Challenges, Opportunities, and Competencies

Challenges Associated With Training

At the heart of the internationalization process is the preparation of professionals who are truly global citizens and who have the awareness, knowledge, skills, and ethics relevant for work across cultures, national boundaries, identities, worldviews, and contexts. Culturally sensitive counseling professionals are also truly motivated to question their own assumptions and biases and increase their knowledge and skills to more effectively work with others outside their own cultures and comfort zones (Ægisdóttir & Gerstein, 2010). As previously discussed in this book, the counseling field has been tremendously influenced by Western, and particularly U.S., paradigms, research and professional literature, and models of practice, much of which tends to be ethnocentric and culturally encapsulated. With this in mind, Marsella and Pedersen (2004) warned that internationalizing the training of U.S. counselors might be challenging, specifically due to the existing cultural biases in the U.S. professional literature (e.g., Arnett, 2008); because of the unwillingness to acknowledge the need to be more cross-culturally, cross-nationally, and internationally competent; and as a result of the lack of interest among many Western and U.S. academics to internationalize the curriculum. Marsella and Pedersen (2004) argued that to internationalize,

> Our training will need to be more multicultural, multisectoral, multinational, and multidisciplinary. We will need constantly to be aware of the importance of developing new Western psychologies, indigenous psychologies, and syncretic psychologies that resist the hegemonic imposition or privileged positioning of any psychology because of its powerful economic, political, or cultural context. (p. 415)

Our colleagues and students outside the United States are often most likely to recognize the need to invent a 21st-century counseling profession that takes into account local context, worldviews, and practices of healing and helping (e.g., Cheung, 2000; Leung, 2003; Yang, Hwang, Pedersen, & Daibo, 2003). This recognition often occurs during their Western or U.S.-based training process, either at home or in a Western or a U.S. university. On returning to their home countries, they are challenged to find ways to indigenize the Western or U.S.-based counseling models.

Throughout this book, we pointed out logical directions and steps for infusing international perspectives into the training of counselors and counseling psychologists. The following discussion is an effort to further the conversation within our professional organizations, university training programs, and classrooms, recognizing that the internationalization process is ongoing and evolving with ever-changing local and global contexts.

Opportunities Associated With Training

Counseling and counseling psychology training programs can broaden the curriculum to include information about counseling and other forms of psychological helping from various countries and regions of the world, particularly emphasizing the need to understand the social, political, and cultural contexts from which different models arise (Ægisdóttir & Gerstein, 2010). As Gerstein et al (2009) argued, in many cultures and countries people in distress, needing guidance and advice, or having significant psychological concerns often seek the assistance of indigenous healers, religious leaders, elders, or other respected members of the community before turning to counselors or psychologists (if these professions even exist locally). Thus, providing training opportunities aimed at exploring the broad array of healing and helping approaches as well as collaborating with such indigenous healing and support systems will enhance culturally sensitive practices (e.g., Atkinson, Thompson, & Grant, 1993). Counseling training programs must take steps to reduce the stigma of the use of indigenous healing systems. Instead, training programs need to focus on ways to investigate and research the effectiveness of such systems on people's well-being as stand-alone treatment options or in combination with more traditional counseling services. Students should also be taught some basic concepts and strategies connected to indigenous forms of healing. Furthermore, a focused discussion in classrooms on cultural constructions of psychological "disorders" would offer trainees ways to understand client diversity and provide more effective psychological and counseling services.

We believe that focusing on and valuing indigenous healing systems and the cultural contexts of psychological difficulties supports and fosters the development of indigenous psychologies and counseling approaches. Privileging indigenous psychologies and counseling approaches requires training that integrates traditional Western models with indigenous knowledge and skills and details on how counseling is being indigenized in cultures and countries in which the profession is developing. Therefore, we urge educators of counselors and counseling psychologists to offer this type of training by providing examples of such efforts. Many chapters in the *International Handbook of Cross-Cultural Counseling: Cultural Assumptions and Practices Worldwide* (Gerstein et al., 2009) present models of counseling that integrated Western paradigms and indigenous forms of healing (e.g., Ecuador, Turkey, Pakistan, Malaysia, Singapore, Taiwan, and Japan). Additionally, there are a number of other books that discuss traditional forms of healing, the integration of these approaches with Western strategies of counseling, and the challenges of employing these models in professional practice (e.g., Adler & Mukherji, 1995; Gielen, Fish, & Draguns, 2004; Hoshmand, 2006; Moodley & West, 2005; Santee, 2007).

The training curriculum must also incorporate a greater emphasis on issues of cross-cultural research competence by introducing students to concepts such as equivalence and bias (see Chapter 5). Counseling professionals can potentially enhance the indigenization of counseling and psychology in different countries and cultures by developing a richer knowledge about the intricacies of conducting cross-culturally valid research.

A primary objective for publishing this book was to advocate and provide resource material for internationalizing the training curriculum in counseling and counseling psychology. Counseling professionals need to realize that they may have very limited and culturally encapsulated information about the models and tools linked with their field. This is especially true of U.S. counseling professionals given the limited information available on international topics and the minimal inclusion of international topics and cross-cultural research in the U.S. counseling and psychology literatures (e.g., Arnett, 2008; Gerstein & Ægisdóttir, 2007; Ægisdóttir, Gerstein, & Çinarbaş, 2008). Moreover, as Draguns (2001) noted, "The development of a truly international psychology is obstructed at this point by the massive disregard of contributions that are published in languages other than English" (p. 1019). Thus, incorporating readings from sources such as this book and the *International Handbook of Cross-Cultural Counseling: Cultural Assumptions and Practices Worldwide* (Gerstein et al., 2009) and encouraging students to search for journal articles and book chapters providing diverse perspectives and populations relevant to their course topics, might help in this regard. Furthermore, it is important for faculty members in counseling and psychology programs around the world to collaborate and explore the use of web-based conferencing and other available technologies to discuss among themselves and with students course-related issues and how they may be affected by culture.

Another important step toward internationalizing the training of counseling students and professionals is implementing structures and policies that empower international students studying in Western and U.S. universities (e.g., Gerstein & Ægisdóttir, 2007; Heppner, 2006). These students should be strongly encouraged to share their cultures, worldviews, and indigenous knowledge and practices in the classroom and on research teams within contexts that affirm and value their contributions. They should also be encouraged to critically examine the validity and applicability of theories and methodologies to their home culture and to discuss their ideas with their classmates and their professors (Gerstein & Ægisdóttir, 2007; Ægisdóttir & Gerstein, 2010). International students who feel empowered in their programs to critically evaluate Western theories, counseling approaches, and methodologies in relation to their home cultures and countries will not only benefit more from their training, they will enrich their training programs and contribute substantially to the internationalization and domestic diversity efforts of university programs. Such critical examination and the discussion of theories, approaches, and methodologies could also be accomplished by using web-based conferencing technologies to network classrooms of students meeting in different corners of the world.

In research classes in the counseling curriculum, it is critical to encourage the use of emic (within culture) and etic (cross-cultural) constructs and approaches (see Chapter 5). This can help trainees appreciate the fact that these are not separate constructs but instead parts of a larger unified whole. In so doing, students' knowledge about the intersections of culture, identity, and psychological functioning is broadened and deepened. Including a cross-cultural component in every research methods class or offering a cross-cultural research methods class would greatly enhance students' cultural competence in research.

Important Cross-Cultural and Cross-National Competencies

In addition to the previous suggestions concerning how to train counseling professionals to be effective cross-nationally and in an international context, it is critical to identify a set of essential competencies for engaging in such activities. In this section, we discuss some of these competencies. A multicultural and cross-cultural perspective plays a complementary role in promoting culturally competent and sensitive research, interventions, and training in counseling and counseling psychology in the United States and internationally (see Heppner, Leong, & Chiao, 2008; Chapter 2, this volume). Based on existing literature articulating multicultural (Arredondo et al., 1996; Atkinson et al., 1993; Sue, Arredondo, & McDavis, 1992) and cross-cultural (Heppner, Leong, & Gerstein, 2008; Ægisdóttir & Gerstein, 2010) counseling competencies, we want to focus on four main dimensions of cross-cultural competence: motivation, awareness, knowledge, and skills (C-C MAKS) (Ægisdóttir & Gerstein, 2010). A description of these dimensions follows with suggestions about how to acquire such competencies.

Motivation is the driving force behind the effective incorporation of culture and context into the science and practice of counseling and psychology. Many counseling professionals continue to minimize the interdependence of people and nations despite the fact that direct and indirect contact between cultures is increasingly more apparent and subject to both positive and negative consequences. This interrelatedness among cultures confirms the importance of developing an understanding and appreciation for international issues and populations. Given the fact that current psychological knowledge in the United States is only based on a small proportion of the world population (Arnett, 2008) and that this knowledge is widely and, at times, uncritically exported worldwide, cross-cultural knowledge, challenges, and issues faced by people and societies throughout the world should be incorporated into current counseling training paradigms. Further, scholars need to pursue international research and topics to advance science and practices of counseling that are globally and culturally relevant. As others have suggested (e.g., Gerstein & Ægisdóttir, 2007; Marsella & Pedersen, 2004; Ægisdóttir & Gerstein, 2010), we concur that, to enhance motivation to learn about and pursue international issues and topics, we call on counseling faculty members and students to create informal (e.g., roundtable discussions) and formal (e.g., poster and paper sessions, symposiums, and courses) mechanisms in their departments and at conferences to introduce individuals to international work and research and to provide opportunities for rich discussion about such content. Additionally, to increase the motivation of individuals to engage in international activities, university administrators should be encouraged to offer internal grants to increase faculty and student travel to international conferences and to pursue collaborative research and applied projects in other countries. Professional organizations around the world must be urged to provide support as well. Furthermore, networking between students and departments throughout the world may enhance individuals' motivation to pursue international work and explore the role of culture and context in issues relevant to counseling.

The second dimension of C-C MAKS is awareness. This dimension refers to counseling professionals' awareness of their own and their clients' worldviews, cultural values and biases, and how one's cultural background and experiences influence help-seeking behavior and beliefs about psychological processes (e.g., Arredondo et al., 1996). To increase awareness, counselors must have an ecological-systems perspective to help understand the influences of culture on attitudes, values, and behavior (Bronfenbrenner,

1979; Heppner, Leong, & Gerstein, 2008; Neville & Mobley, 2001). According to Bronfenbrenner, contextual influences are rooted in five different systems and the interactions between them: microsystem, mesosystem, exosystem, macrosystem, and chronosystem. These systems range from structures in which the individual is directly connected (microsystem; e.g., family, church, neighborhood, and healers) through societal and political structures, norms, and cultural belief systems, to the transitions and environmental events influencing individuals over time (chronosystem). Counseling professionals providing services and performing research internationally need to think of themselves and others in the contexts of these systems and their influence on individuals' thoughts, feelings, and behavior. Such awareness, therefore, involves being cautious about generalizing findings and constructs across cultures (Pedersen & Leong, 1997; Varenne, 2003; Ægisdóttir et al., 2008), learning from scholars around the world (Heppner, 1997; Leong & Blustein, 2000), and separating observations from interpretations, as interpretations of one's surroundings are heavily influenced by one's values, biases, and experiences (Ægisdóttir & Gerstein, 2010).

The third dimension, knowledge, refers to having information about another person's cultural heritage, worldviews, and customs and how such information affects definitions of normal and abnormal behavior and the process of counseling. Obviously, knowledge is an important component of cross-cultural counseling competencies. Knowledgeable counseling professionals understand that culture affects a wide array of behaviors, such as personality formation, career choices, signs and expressions of disorders, help-seeking behavior, and the validity, suitability, and appropriateness of counseling approaches (Arredondo et al., 1996). As stated previously in this book, in the United States knowledge about psychology and counseling outside the United States is lacking. Gerstein and Ægisdóttir (2007) found that only 6% of articles published in 4 counseling journals over 5 years focused on an international topic. Also, Arnett (2008) found that in six premier APA journals over a 5-year span, 68% of the samples studied were in the United States, 14% were in other English-speaking countries, and 13% were in Europe. Only 3% of the samples were from Asia, 1% from Latin America, and less than 1% from Africa and the Middle East. To change this trend, we need more articles focusing on international issues in English-language journals (Heppner, 1997).

Additionally, learning more about cultures worldwide may involve students and professionals reading publications in other fields (e.g., cultural anthropology, political science, linguistics, or sociology) (e.g., Ægisdóttir & Gerstein, 2010), in languages besides English (Sexton & Misiak, 1984), and from a variety of countries. If students are proficient in multiple languages, they should be urged to read publications from original sources (Sexton & Misiak, 1984). Where multiple-language proficiency is lacking, it might be valuable for bilingual and international students and faculty members in mental health programs worldwide to explore the literature in psychology and anthropology written in languages other than English and share their findings with others in their program (Gerstein & Ægisdóttir, 2007). Faculty members are also encouraged to conduct more cross-cultural and international research, develop interdisciplinary teaching teams (Ibrahim, 1985), mentor students in conducting international research projects, and obtain training experiences relevant to the international arena (Heppner, 2006; Heppner, Leong, & Chiao, 2008; Heppner, Leong, & Gerstein, 2008). Mentoring students is critical to the acquisition of knowledge and competencies connected to working internationally (Ægisdóttir & Gerstein, 2010). Leong and Ponterotto (2003) also suggested that a modern-language competency, once again, be encouraged in U.S. counseling programs and that international publications be included in the curriculum. Additionally, counseling professionals must carefully evaluate the cross-cultural validity of psychological concepts, methods, and strategies found in the profession (e.g., Ægisdóttir et al., 2008; Chapter 5, this volume).

Finally, requiring or strongly encouraging students (and counseling professionals, for that matter) to complete international internships, immersion experiences, or home-country practicum placements in community settings serving marginalized and minority communities (under the direction of a culturally competent supervisor) can bring classroom and textbook learning to life (see also Ægisdóttir & Gerstein, 2010). Some authors have predicted that there will be a rise in international internships in the near future (Leach, 2005; Leong & Leach, 2007). These training opportunities are definitely needed in the counseling profession. In fact, according to Leong and Leach (2007), the APA has started a process to explore setting up a group to manage accrediting international internships. Former APA Division 17 president, Louise Douce (2004) also encouraged establishing international internships and externships. She reported that the APA Society of Counseling Psychology along with the Counseling Psychology Division of the IAAP had plans to pursue such placements. To date, however, this plan has not progressed.

Through community and international "engagement," students interact with and humanize those who may have been previously "othered" or completely unknown. They also learn firsthand how to work in partnership and enact power sharing rather than paternalism in transnational and cross-cultural relationships. Well implemented cultural immersion experiences, even of a limited nature, can be very powerful learning opportunities (Heppner, Leong, & Chiao, 2008; Chapter 2, this volume). Traveling to different countries, however, is not always possible. Instead, training programs can modify their courses to integrate material from cultures around the world using existing publications and information found on websites and by watching movies. Furthermore, web-based conferencing between counseling training program faculty and students around the world may be used to discuss a host of issues relevant to the cultural context of counseling and psychology. Online forums, web-based bulletin boards, and chat rooms could also be launched to discuss pertinent issues, to post individual professional interests and projects, and to announce opportunities for collaboration and networking.

The fourth dimension of C-C MAKS is skills. Skilled counseling professionals pursue educational, consultation, and training opportunities to become more competent in multicultural and international work (e.g., Arredondo et al., 1996; Ægisdóttir & Gerstein, 2010). They also understand the limits of their knowledge about other cultures and collaborate with local nationals when working in international settings, ever aware that hierarchies of power and access exist in all countries and need to be considered when deciding on entry points and, thus, whose interests are being served when engaging in cross-national partnerships (Norsworthy, 2006). Counseling professionals must be skilled in engaging within diverse "cross-cultural contexts with people who hold differing world views" (Heppner, 1997, p. 7) and who hold varying levels of power and privilege in their home countries (see Chapter 7).

As stated earlier, cultural-immersion experiences are effective ways to enhance one's skills to work and function in an international setting (e.g., Leong & Ponterotto, 2003; see Chapter 8, this volume). Furthermore, it is important to enhance counseling professionals' skills in the development of indigenous psychology outside the United States. Many of the recommendations mentioned earlier in this chapter and in this book can help accomplish this. We particularly encourage cross-national collaborations involving scholars, practitioners, and students.

While developing skills will contribute to cross-cultural competency, these skills must be combined with a rich philosophical framework. As such, counseling students must be trained to become aware of their own philosophy of life, their own capabilities, "and a recognition of different structures of reasoning and how all these variables affect one's communication and helping style" (Ibrahim, 1985, p. 636).

Based on the Atkinson et al. (1993) model and the work of Ægisdóttir and Gerstein (2010), we also suggest that more emphasis should be placed on counseling and psychology students developing skills in interacting with individuals while holding roles other than counselor or psychotherapist. In many cultures, the helping role needs to be adjusted to take into account local worldviews and conceptualizations of healing and helping, the locus of problem etiology, and whether the intervention needs to be preventive or remedial. Given this observation, counseling professionals must be trained and feel comfortable in the roles of adviser, advocate, facilitator of indigenous support or healing systems, consultant, or change agent. In this respect, it is critical that the current schism between scientific psychology or counseling and traditional folk healing be resolved. Achieving an effective resolution may enhance the development of indigenous psychologies and counseling systems worldwide. As part of this resolution, it is important for counseling professionals working internationally to consider how well their interventions and projects fit with cultural values and worldviews and adapt them accordingly.

Obviously, there is much more work to be performed to internationalize graduate training programs in counseling inside and outside the United States. We have provided some recommendations to accomplish this objective. Some writers have suggested, however, that such training should begin at the undergraduate level "with direct exposure to, and contact with, psychology abroad" (Sexton & Misiak, 1984, p. 1028). We agree with this suggestion and also strongly agree with Marsella and Pedersen (2004), who appealed to counseling psychology professionals:

> We call upon counseling psychologists throughout the world to dialogue, to exchange views and actual positions, to learn the challenges facing our world, and in the process, to create a new professional and global consciousness that can advance our field, resolve problems, and restore dignity. (p. 422)

Conclusion

The counseling profession around the world is growing rapidly and in unique ways to respond to the specific needs of diverse nations, cultures, people, and situations. Rich conceptual, research, and intervention paradigms have been developed, modified, and employed to address and meet these needs. Counseling professionals worldwide are actively engaged in a reflective and evaluative process to determine the validity, suitability, and applicability of various forms of counseling for their local constituents, cultures, and environment. In many parts of the world, this process has led to both considering and embracing an integration of emic (indigenous) and etic (universal) models of traditional healing and counseling as part of a unified whole. Cross-national collaboration among counseling professionals has contributed to the evolution of this exciting development, as has the growing recognition of the importance of designing and implementing paradigms of counseling that honor and respect indigenous cultural values and behaviors. It is hoped that with further cross-national interactions, counseling professionals will provide even greater support for the science and practice of the indigenization of counseling and psychology in all corners of the world. In this regard, it is relevant to heed the words of Gardner Murphy (1969):

> The study of the human predicament can come from a human race familiar with the method of science, but a human race speaking many tongues, regarding many values, and holding different convictions about the meaning of life sooner or later will have to consult all that is human. (p. 528)

Consistent with Murphy's (1969) decree, counseling professionals can take full advantage of the numerous available technologies that can facilitate intimate and immediate communication. Also, it is essential that more frequent international conferences be scheduled by professional counseling associations to offer opportunities for face-to-face interactions that allow for more in-depth sharing of scientific findings, innovative interventions, training paradigms, and challenges, as well as the potential for networking individuals from various locations around the world. Attending such conferences can greatly increase the possibilities for fostering collaborative activities (e.g., research projects, consulting projects, exchange programs, or jointly sponsored training programs) among counseling professionals living in different countries.

To enhance understanding about counseling in different parts of the world, a web-based clearinghouse of information easily accessible to all interested individuals would be highly beneficial. This multilingual clearinghouse should contain, for instance, a current listing of all professional counseling and psychology associations, relevant scholarly journals, credentialing bodies, ethical guidelines, and training programs. It should also feature bulletin boards, chat rooms, and networking forums where persons can post interests and dialogue about issues, challenges, and concerns. While there are a couple of web-based sites that include some of this information, most of the sites are outdated and not comprehensive. Of course, to design, implement, and manage the proposed clearinghouse would be quite difficult; it would require a major investment of time and resources (financial and human) and the ability of professionals to closely and effectively collaborate on a very intricate and complex task. Perhaps professional associations worldwide could select representatives to serve on a steering committee to begin discussing the value, practicality, and usefulness of such a clearinghouse.

As was reported time and again in this book, to increase understanding about counseling in different parts of the world there is also a need to make scholarly journals more accessible to a wider readership. Perhaps editors of counseling and psychology journals worldwide could agree to publish one article in each issue in a language other than the one featured in their own periodical. To accomplish this, editors could establish "article exchange" relationships between their own periodical and one published in a different country. A much simpler task would be for editors to publish at least one abstract per issue of an article from another country's journal. Another option would be to develop a new international counseling journal, and for each issue, have editors from around the world submit one article in their country's primary language. A similar recommendation was offered by Beier (1952). To date, however, we are unaware of any such publication!

Although we could not locate any journals structured in a fashion outlined in the previous paragraph, there are journals that feature content in multiple languages. For instance, *Applied Psychology: An International Review* publishes articles in English and abstracts in English and French. The *International Journal for the Advancement of Counselling* includes articles and abstracts in English and, if the author so desires, an abstract in an additional language. Furthermore, the *Interamerican Journal of Psychology* publishes articles in Spanish and abstracts in both English and Spanish. Last, the *International Journal of Psychology* features articles in English and abstracts in English, French, and Spanish, while the *International Journal of Psychology and Psychological Therapy* publishes articles in English and abstracts in English and Spanish.

One other initiative has the potential to increase understanding about counseling in various countries throughout the world. The definitions and functions of *counseling, counseling psychology, counselor,* and *counseling psychologist* vary from country to country, if the terms exist at all. Similarly, the credentialing and accreditation systems for counseling also widely differ. What might be helpful, then, is to establish forums or working groups wherein leaders of mental health professional associations from a host of countries could discuss the advantages and disadvantages of developing and implementing, for example, international standards for practice, credentialing, and accreditation. Another strategy to pursue standardized accreditation was recommended by Nixon (1990) who suggested that the IUPsyS and the IAAP might collaborate to assist national professional associations in establishing and accrediting training programs. Currently, the U.S.-based National Board of Certified Counselors—International (NBCC-I) has begun such an international project specifically focused on the counseling profession and this could serve as a model in this area. Given the complexity of developing and implementing international standards in the counseling profession and the diversity of the unique challenges to accomplish this task, specific tangible outcomes would be difficult to achieve in a short period of time. Regardless, the process of dialoguing about this task would result in greater understanding and, hopefully, deeper respect for the unique characteristics of the counseling profession in different countries. Furthermore, such a process could generate other types of achievable, collaborative projects between national professional counseling associations and professionals to address shared and unique needs and concerns.

In conclusion, it is rather evident that we are in the midst of a renaissance period in the counseling profession worldwide. Without a doubt, this period of reflection, evaluation, innovation, and cross-national collaboration will continue and evolve for decades into the future. It is difficult to predict how the field of counseling might change, how psychological services may be delivered, and how the texture and content of our collaborative professional relationships might develop and blossom. In the years ahead, however, we are absolutely convinced that new, refined, and creative approaches to counseling grounded in diverse cultural contexts and incorporating traditional forms of healing will continue to emerge and thrive. These approaches will revolutionize how helping professionals around the world conceptualize and offer assistance to individuals, groups, organizations, and nations. They will also dramatically alter how we think about science, philosophy, research, and the human experience. Ultimately, through such discoveries, helping professionals worldwide will be better equipped to effectively assist their clientele, and at the same time, these discoveries can reinforce and promote the indigenous cultures that enrich our lives and also preserve the unique humanity of our species.

Chapter Questions

1. Considering the code of ethics linked with the professional association you identify with, assess the code's strengths and weaknesses with regard to the inclusion of standards and guidelines connected with cross-cultural and cross-national activities (e.g., practice, research, training).

2. A number of competencies were identified as being important to be an effective counseling professional in diverse cultural and international settings. How can these competencies be integrated into different mental health training programs, and at the same time, be respectful and congruent with various cultural norms, beliefs, and behaviors in different countries? In your response, provide examples of two distinct countries.

3. In the next 25 years, how common and well respected will indigenous healers be in relation to mental health professionals in different regions of the world? Support your argument and provide examples.

References

Ad Hoc Joint Committee for the Development of a Universal Declaration of Ethical Principles for Psychologists. (2005). *Interim report: Developing a universal declaration of ethical principles for psychologists.* Retrieved April 29, 2009, from http://www.am.org/iupsys/resources/ethics/index.html

Adler, L. L., & Mukherji, B. R. (Eds.). (1995). *Spirit versus scalpel: Traditional healing and modern psychotherapy.* Westport, CT: Bergin & Garvey.

American Psychological Association. (2004). *Resolution on culture and gender awareness in international psychology.* Washington, DC: Author.

Arnett, J. J. (2008). The neglected 95%: Why American psychology needs to become less American. *American Psychologist, 63,* 602–614.

Arredondo, P., Toporek, R., Brown, S. P., Jones, J., Locke, D. C., Sanchez, J., et al. (1996). Operationalization of the multicultural counseling competencies. *Journal of Multicultural Counseling and Development, 24,* 42–78.

Atkinson, D. R., Thompson, C. E., & Grant, S. K. (1993). A three dimensional model for counseling racial/ethnic minorities. *The Counseling Psychologist, 21,* 257–277.

Beier, E. G. (1952). A problem in international communication. *American Psychologist, 7,* 592.

Bronfenbrenner, U. (1979). *The ecology of human development: Experiments by nature and design.* Cambridge, MA: Harvard University Press.

Cheung, F. M. (2000). Deconstructing counseling in a cultural context. *The Counseling Psychologist, 28,* 123–132.

Diener, E., & Crandall, R. (1978). *Ethics in social and behavioral research.* Chicago: University of Chicago Press.

Douce, L. A. (2004). Globalization of counseling psychology. *The Counseling Psychologist, 32,* 142–152.

Draguns, J. G. (2001). Toward a truly international psychology: Beyond English only. *American Psychologist, 56,* 1019–1030.

Gerstein, L. H. (2006). Counseling psychologists as international social architects. In R. L. Toporek, L. H. Gerstein, N. A. Fouad, G. Roysircar-Sodowsky, & T. Israel (Eds.), *Handbook for social justice in counseling psychology: Leadership, vision, and action* (pp. 377–387). Thousand Oaks, CA: Sage.

Gerstein, L. H., Heppner, P. P., Ægisdóttir, S., Leung, S. A., & Norsworthy, K. L. (2009). *International Handbook of Cross-Cultural Counseling: Cultural Assumptions and Practices Worldwide.* Thousand Oaks, CA: Sage Publications.

Gerstein, L. H., & Ægisdóttir, S. (2007). Training international social change agents: Transcending a U.S. counseling paradigm. *Counselor Education and Supervision, 47,* 123–139.

Gielen, U. P., Fish, J. M., & Draguns, J. D. (Eds.). (2004). *Handbook of culture, therapy, and healing.* Mahwah, NJ: Lawrence Erlbaum.

Golann, S. E. (1970). Ethical standards for psychology: Development and revision, 1938–1968. *Annals of the New York Academy of Sciences, 169,* 398–405.

Heppner, P. P. (1997). Building on strengths as we move into the next millennium. *The Counseling Psychologist, 25,* 5–14.

Heppner, P. P. (2006). The benefits and challenges of becoming cross-culturally competent counseling psychologists. *The Counseling Psychologist, 34,* 147–172.

Heppner, P. P. (2008). Expanding the conceptualization and measurement of applied problem solving and coping: From stages to dimensions in the almost forgotten cultural context. *American Psychologist, 63,* 805–816.

Heppner, P. P., Leong, F. T. L., & Chiao, H. (2008). The growing internationalization of counseling psychology. In S. D. Brown & R. W. Lent (Eds.), *Handbook of counseling psychology* (4th ed., pp. 68–85). New York: Wiley.

Heppner, P. P., Leong, F. T. L., & Gerstein, L. H. (2008). Counseling within a changing world. In W. B. Walsh (Ed.), *Biennial review of counseling psychology* (Vol. 1, pp. 231–258). New York: Routledge, Taylor & Francis.

Heppner, P. P., Wampold, B. E., & Kivlighan, D. M. (2008). *Research design in counseling* (3rd ed.). Belmont, CA: Thompson Brooks/Cole.

Horne, S. G., & Mathews, S. S. (2006). A social justice approach to international collaborative consultation. In R. L. Toporek, L. H. Gerstein, N. A. Fouad, G. Roysircar-Sodowsky, & T. Israel (Eds.), *Handbook for social justice in counseling psychology: Leadership, vision, and action* (pp. 388–405). Thousand Oaks, CA: Sage.

Hoshmand, L. T. (Ed.). (2006). *Culture, psychotherapy, and counseling: Critical and integrative perspectives.* Thousand Oaks, CA: Sage.

Houser, R., Wilczenski, F. L., & Ham, M. A. (2006). *Culturally relevant ethical decision-making in counseling.* Thousand Oaks, CA: Sage.

Ibrahim, F. A. (1985). Effective cross-cultural counseling and psychotherapy: A framework. *The Counseling Psychologist, 13,* 625–638.

Leach, M. M. (2005). Internationalization and applied psychology internships. *International Psychology Reporter, 9*(3), 22–23.

Leach, M. M. (2008). *Compendium: Codes of ethics of national psychology associations around the world. International Union of Psychological Sciences.* Retrieved April 29, 2009, from http://www.am.org/iupsys/resources/ethics/index.html

Leach, M. M., & Oakland, T. (2007). Ethics standards impacting test development and use: A review of 31 ethics codes impacting practices in 35 countries. *International Journal of Testing, 7,* 71–88.

Leong, F. T. L., & Blustein, D. L. (2000). Toward a global vision of counseling psychology. *The Counseling Psychologist, 28,* 5–9.

Leong, F. T. L., & Leach, M. M. (2007). Internalizing counseling psychology in the United States: A SWOT analysis. *Applied Psychology: An International Review, 56,* 165–181.

Leong, F. T. L., & Lee, S. H. (2006). A cultural accommodation model of psychotherapy: Illustrated with the case of Asian Americans. *Psychotherapy: Theory, Research, Practice, and Training, 43,* 410–423.

Leong, F. T. L., & Ponterotto, J. G. (2003). A proposal for internationalizing counseling psychology in the United States: Rationale, recommendations, and challenges. *The Counseling Psychologist, 31,* 381–395.

Leung, S. A. (2003). A journey worth traveling: Globalization of counseling psychology. *The Counseling Psychologist, 31,* 412–419.

Marsella, A. J., & Pedersen, P. (2004). Internationalizing the counseling psychology curriculum: Toward new values, competencies, and directions. *Counseling Psychology Quarterly, 17*(4), 413–423.

Moodley, R., & West, W. (Eds.). (2005). *Integrating traditional healing practices into counseling and psychotherapy.* Thousand Oaks, CA: Sage.

Murphy, G. (1969). Psychology in the year 2000. *American Psychologist, 24,* 523–530.

Neville, H. A., & Mobley, M. (2001). Social identities in contexts: An ecological model of multicultural counseling psychology processes. *The Counseling Psychologist, 29,* 471–486.

Nixon, M. (1990). Professional training in psychology: Quest for international standards. *American Psychologist, 45,* 1257–1262.

Norsworthy, K. L. (2006). Bringing social justice to international practices of counseling psychology. In R. L. Toporek, L. H. Gerstein, N. A. Fouad, G. Roysircar-Sodowsky, & T. Israel (Eds.), *Handbook for social justice in counseling psychology: Leadership, vision, and action* (pp. 421–441). Thousand Oaks, CA: Sage.

Norsworthy, K. L., & Gerstein, L. (2003). Counseling and building communities of peace: The interconnections. *International Journal for the Advancement of Counseling, 25*(4), 197–203.

Pack-Brown, S. P., & Williams, C. B. (2003). *Ethics in a multicultural context.* Thousand Oaks, CA: Sage.

Pedersen, P. B. (1995). Culture centered ethical guidelines for counselors. In J. G. Ponterotto, J. M. Casas, L. A. Suzuki, & C. M. Alexander (Eds.), *Handbook of multicultural counseling* (1st ed., pp. 34–49). Thousand Oaks, CA: Sage.

Pedersen, P. B. (1997). The cultural context of American Counseling Association Code of Ethics. *Journal of Counseling and Development, 76,* 23–28.

Pedersen, P. B. (2003). Culturally biased assumptions in counseling psychology. *The Counseling Psychologist, 31,* 396–403.

Pedersen, P. B., & Leong, F. (1997). Counseling in an international context. *The Counseling Psychologist, 25,* 117–122.

Ridley, C. R., Liddle, M. C., Hill, C. L., & Li, L. C. (2001). Ethical decision making in multicultural counseling. In J. G. Ponterotto, J. M. Casas, L. A. Suzuki, & C. M. Alexander (Eds.), *Handbook of multicultural counseling* (2nd ed., pp. 165–188). Thousand Oaks, CA: Sage.

Santee, R. G. (2007). *An integrative approach to counseling: Bridging Chinese thought, evolutionary theory, and stress management.* Thousand Oaks, CA: Sage.

Sexton, V. S., & Misiak, H. (1984). American psychologists and psychology abroad. *American Psychologist, 39,* 1026–1031.

Sue, D. W., Arredondo, P., & McDavis, R. J. (1992). Multicultural counseling competencies and standards: A call to the profession. *Journal of Counseling and Development, 70,* 477–486.

Trimble, J. E., & Fisher, C. B. (2006). *The handbook of ethical research with ethno-cultural populations and communities.* Thousand Oaks, CA: Sage.

Varenne, H. (2003). On internationalizing counseling psychology: A view from cultural anthropology. *The Counseling Psychologist, 31,* 404–411.

Yang, K. S., Hwang, K. K., Pedersen, P. B., & Daibo, I. (Eds.). (2003). *Progress in Asian social psychology: Conceptual and empirical contributions.* Westport, CT: Praeger.

Ægisdóttir, S., & Gerstein, L. H. (2010). International counseling competencies: A new frontier in multi-cultural training. In J. C. Ponterotto, J. M. Casas, L. A. Suzuki, & C. A. Alexander (Eds.), *Handook of multicultural counseling* (3rd ed., pp. 175–188). Thousand Oaks, CA: Sage.

Ægisdóttir, S., Gerstein, L. H., & Çinarbaş, D. C. (2008). Methodological issues in cross-cultural counseling research: Equivalence, bias, and translations. *The Counseling Psychologist, 36,* 188–219.

Index

About the Editors

Lawrence H. Gerstein is a George and Frances Ball Distinguished Professor of Psychology-Counseling, director of the doctoral program in counseling psychology, and director of the Center for Peace and Conflict Studies at Ball State University in Muncie, Indiana. He is co-editor of the *International Handbook of Cross-Cultural Counseling: Cultural Assumptions and Practices Worldwide* and the *Handbook for Social Justice in Counseling Psychology: Leadership, Vision, and Action*. He managed the Tibetan and Chinese translations of the book, *Buddha's Warriors*. He is a fellow of the American Psychological Association (Counseling Psychology, International Psychology, Peace Psychology), co-editor of *The Counseling Psychologist* International Forum, president of the International Tibet Independence Movement, and a past co-chair of the International Section of the Society of Counseling Psychology–American Psychological Association. He has published extensively on international and social justice issues as well as on loneliness, self-monitoring, and employee assistance programs. He received his Ph.D. in counseling and social psychology from the University of Georgia in 1983. Since his teenage years, he has traveled extensively throughout the world. He has been fortunate to collaborate with individuals in numerous countries.

P. Paul Heppner is currently a Curators' Professor of the Department of Educational, School, and Counseling Psychology at the University of Missouri. He is co-founder of and since 1998 has been co-director of the Center for Multicultural Research, Training and Consultation, and he was the inaugural co-chair of the International Section of the Society of Counseling Psychology. He has published more than 180 articles or book chapters and nine books, including serving as a co-editor of the *International Handbook of Cross-Cultural Counseling: Cultural Assumptions and Practices Worldwide*. He has made hundreds of presentations at national conferences and delivered more than 95 invited presentations across 14 countries. In addition, he has served on several national and international editorial boards and as editor of *The Counseling Psychologist*. He is a fellow of the American Psychological Association (Divisions 17 and 52) and the American Psychological Society. In 2005–2006, he served as president of the Society of Counseling Psychology. He has been honored to receive a named professorship, and to be the recipient of several awards (including the Leona Tyler Award and MU Curators' Professorship) for his leadership, research, teaching, mentoring, international work, and activities promoting diversity and social justice issues; he has been the recipient of three Fulbright awards. He received his doctorate in 1979 from the University of Nebraska–Lincoln.

Stefanía Ægisdóttir is a native of Iceland and an associate professor in the Department of Counseling Psychology and Guidance Services at Ball State University, Indiana. She is a former Fulbright scholarship recipient for pursuing doctoral studies in the United States and recently completed a 3-year grant from the Iceland Research Fund to study psychological help-seeking patterns of Icelanders. Her primary teaching interests are research methodology, assessment, program development and evaluation, and clinical training. She has written about cross-cultural research methods, attitudes and expectations about counseling, clinical judgment, and international and cross-cultural issues and competencies in counseling research and training. She is a co-editor of the *International Handbook of Cross-Cultural Counseling: Cultural Assumptions and Practices Worldwide*. She received her doctorate in counseling psychology in 2000 from Ball State University.

Seung-Ming Alvin Leung is Dean of Faculty of Education and professor in the Department of Educational Psychology, The Chinese University of Hong Kong. He previously held faculty positions at the University of Nebraska–Lincoln and the University of Houston. His major areas of scholarly interest include career development and assessment; cross-cultural, multicultural, and international issues in counseling; and counseling in educational settings. He is a co-editor of the *International Handbook of Cross-Cultural Counseling: Cultural Assumptions and Practices Worldwide*. He is currently the editor of *Asian Journal of Counselling*. He is the first counseling psychologist from outside the United States to serve as associate editor of *The Counseling Psychologist* (1999–2002). He is a fellow of the American Psychological Association (APA) and the Hong Kong Professional Counselling Association. He received the "Distinguished Contributions to the International Advancement of the Counseling Profession" Award at the 2008 International Counseling Psychology Conference in Chicago and the 2009 *"Distinguished Alumni Award"* from his alma mater, the University of Illinois at Urbana–Champaign. He is one of the three co-chairs of the International Section of the Division of Counseling Psychology of the APA (2008–2010).

Kathryn L. Norsworthy is a professor in Graduate Studies in Counseling, Rollins College, Winter Park, Florida and licensed psychologist. She is a fellow of the American Psychological Association (Division 17) and currently serves as chair of the international committee of the APA Division of Trauma Psychology. She is a co-editor of the *International Handbook of Cross-Cultural Counseling: Cultural Assumptions and Practices Worldwide.* Nationally, she received the 2003 American Counseling Association Kitty Cole Human Rights Award, the 2007 Outstanding International Psychologist and the 2009 Denmark-Reuder Award for Outstanding International Contributions to the Psychology of Women and Gender from the International Division of the APA, the 2008 Many Faces of Counseling Psychology Award and the 2009 Social Justice Award from the APA's Division of Counseling Psychology. Since 1997, she has been engaged in activist research and practice projects focusing on trauma, feminist counseling, social justice education, women's leadership, cross-national collaboration, mindfulness, and peace building in Thailand, Cambodia, and northern India, with refugee and internally displaced communities of Burma, and with international groups. Author and coauthor of numerous articles and book chapters on her international social justice work and cross-national partnerships, she was featured in the December 2007 issue of the *APA Monitor on Psychology* as a "Humanitarian Hero." She received her doctorate from the University of Minnesota.

About the Contributors

Thomas Clawson, EdD, NCC, is President and CEO of the National Board for Certified Counselors and Affiliates (NBCC). He is regarded as a preeminent counseling leader. He is a member of several international and national boards. Over the past three decades, he has been involved in initiatives to promote the advancement and strengthening of professional counseling and counseling services across the globe. He has numerous publications and awards in the area of counseling, standards of professional practice, and credentialing. He holds three advanced degrees, including a doctorate in counseling from the College of William and Mary, Williamsburg, Virginia.

Changming Duan is an associate professor of counseling psychology at the University of Missouri Kansas City. She is interested in multicultural and international issues in counseling. She has experience in teaching multicultural counseling classes as well as teaching counseling outside the United States.

Janet E. Helms, PhD, is the Augustus Long Professor in the Department of Counseling, Developmental, and Educational Psychology and Director of the Institute for the Study and Promotion of Race and Culture at Boston College. She is president of the American Psychological Association (APA) Society of Counseling Psychology (Division 17) and a fellow of this Division and Division 45 (Ethnic Diversity). She has written more than 60 articles and 4 books on racial identity and cultural influences on assessment and counseling practice. She received Division 45's 1999 Distinguished Career Contributions to Research Award, Division 17's 2002 Leona Tyler Award, APA's 2006 Award for Distinguished Contributions to Education and Training, the 2007 Association of Black Psychologists' Distinguished Psychologist Award, and the 2008 Award for Distinguished Contributions to Research in Public Policy.

Kwong-Liem Karl Kwan is a Hong Kong Chinese who in 2008 joined the Department of Counseling faculty at San Francisco State University. He is the coeditor of the International Forum for *The Counseling Psychologist*

(United States) and was the guest editor for a special issue titled Ethical Practice of Counseling in Asia for *Asian Journal of Counseling* (Hong Kong). He is an editorial board member of *Educational Psychology Bulletin* (Taiwan), *Journal of Counseling Psychology* (United States), and *Psychological Assessment* (United States). He received his doctorate in counseling psychology from the University of Nebraska–Lincoln.

Frederick T. L. Leong, PhD, is a professor of psychology at Michigan State University in the industrial/organizational and clinical psychology programs and serves as the director of the Center for Multicultural Psychology Research. He has authored or coauthored more than 120 articles in various psychology journals, 80 book chapters, and edited or coedited 10 books. He is a fellow of the American Psychological Association and American Psychological Society. His major clinical research interests center around culture and mental health and cross-cultural psychotherapy (especially with Asians and Asian Americans), whereas his industrial/organizational research is focused on cultural and personality factors related to career choice, work adjustment, and occupational stress.

Walter J. Lonner is the founding and special issues editor of the *Journal of Cross-Cultural Psychology* (*JCCP*). A charter member of the International Association for Cross-Cultural Psychology (IACCP), he has been involved with numerous books in the field, including *Counseling Across Cultures* (2007; P. B. Pedersen, J. G. Draguns, W. J. Lonner, and J. E. Trimble, editors, 6th edition, Sage) and *Discovering Cultural Psychology: A Profile and Selected Readings of Ernest E. Boesch* (2007; with S. A. Hayes). A former Fulbright scholar (Germany, 1984–1985), he is Professor Emeritus of Psychology at Western Washington University, where he cofounded the Center for Cross-Cultural Research in 1969.

Paul B. Pedersen is a visiting professor in the Department of Psychology at the University of Hawaii. He has taught at the University of Minnesota, Syracuse University, the University of Alabama at Birmingham, and, for 6 years, at universities in Taiwan, Malaysia, and Indonesia. He was also on the Summer School Faculty at Harvard University (1984–1988) and took part in the University of Pittsburgh—Semester at Sea voyage around the world (Spring, 1992). He has authored, coauthored, or edited 45 books, 100 articles, 82 chapters, and 22 monographs on aspects of multicultural counseling and international communication. He is a fellow of Divisions 9, 17, 45, and 52 of the American Psychological Association. He is a Senior Fulbright Scholar (National Taiwan University, 1999–2000); and has been a member of the Committee for International Relations in Psychology (CIRP) of the American Psychological Association (2001–2003) and a senior fellow of the East West Center (1975–1976 and 1978–1981).

Jennifer Rogers is currently a University Fellow at Syracuse University, where she is working toward her doctorate in counselor education and supervision. Her interests include the integration of mental health services within health care settings, clinical counseling instruction, and the globalization of the counseling profession. She received her MA in counseling from Wake Forest University.

Rex Stockton is Chancellor's Professor at Indiana University. He has received several major awards for his research in group dynamics and other counseling related topics. His career efforts have been honored by a special issue (September 2005) of the *Journal of the Association for Specialists in Group Work*. He has been active in international counseling for many years and currently directs a project implementing culturally appropriate counseling research and training programs for human service workers specializing in HIV/AIDS counseling in Africa. A fellow of the American Counseling Association and the American Psychological Association, he has held numerous offices and committee assignments, including the presidency of their group work divisions.

Andreea Szilagyi is an associate professor at Petroleum-Gas University of Ploiesti and one of the first counselor-educators in Romania. Her expertise is strongly oriented toward the practice of career counseling, particularly with Eastern Europeans (in educational and business organizations). She is at the forefront of research on counselor education in Romania, on the role of large-scale professional contracts in the development of the profession, and on certification across borders. She was Global Career Development Facilitator of United States in 2003, National Certified Counselor of United States in 2005, and Mental Health Facilitator in 2007. She was also Director of the National Board for Certified Counselors (NBCC)–Romania and Associate Vice President NBCC International–Europe. She received a master's degree in education from the University of Bucharest in 1995 and a doctorate from Alexandru Ioan Cuza University of Iasi (with the first counseling theme in Romania).

Antonio Tena, PhD, is the current chair in the psychology department at Universidad Iberoamericana in Mexico City, Mexico. His clinical interests include psychotherapy with eating disorders, adolescents and adults, and international issues in counseling. From 1998 to 1999, he was a visiting professor in the Department of Counseling and Human Services at the University of Scranton, Pennsylvania. He is one of the original collaborators in the ongoing partnership between the two institutions. He is a codirector of the Universidad Iberoamericana/University of Scranton grant, funded by the TIES/ENLACES program. He is a National Board for Certified Counselors International Member, Board of Directors.

Li-fei Wang is a professor of counseling psychology at National Taiwan Normal University, Taiwan, Republic of China. Besides her academic and teaching specialty in group counseling and psychotherapy, she served as the president of the Division of Counseling Psychology and general secretary of the Taiwan Guidance and Counseling Association (TGCA). She is not only passionate about bringing the world to Taiwan but has also extended her inspirations and collaborated with her former advisor Dr. Puncky Heppner to create several exchange programs benefiting both National Taiwan Normal University and the University of Missouri-Columbia students in expanding their worldviews and building stronger connections between her professional homes. She received her PhD in counseling psychology from the University of Missouri–Columbia in 1995.

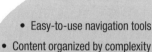